Considerations on the Fundamental Principles of Pure Political Economy

Considerations on the Fundamental Principles of Pure Political Economy (*Considerazioni sui principi fondamentali dell'economia pura*) was originally published as a series of five articles in the *Giornale degli Economisti* between May 1892 and October 1893. They were the first systematic representation of Vilfredo Pareto's contribution to pure economics and their publication in this volume in English closes a serious gap in the knowledge of the work of one of the founders of modern economic science.

In the book, Pareto deals with an impressively wide range of subjects including the nature and the limits of the new theories of marginalist economics, the use of mathematics in economics, the problem of method and the hedonistic hypothesis, the concept of *homo œconomicus* and, last but not least, the concept of final degree of utility.

These reflections make the *Considerations* an assessment of the state of the new economic theories expounded in a mathematical form at the beginning of the 1890s. These papers have exerted a great deal of influence in the subsequent development of economic theory. As such, the volume can be considered required reading for all serious economists across the world.

Roberto Marchionatti is Professor of Economics at the University of Torino, Italy. He has been a Visiting Scholar in Economics at New York University and at the University of Cambridge, UK.

Fiorenzo Mornati is Assistant Professor of Economics at the University of Torino, Italy. He has been Assistant de Recherche at the University of Lausanne (Centre Walras-Pareto), Switzerland.

Routledge Studies in the History of Economics

1 **Economics as Literature**
Willie Henderson

2 **Socialism and Marginalism in Economics 1870–1930**
Edited by Ian Steedman

3 **Hayek's Political Economy**
The socio-economics of order
Steve Fleetwood

4 **On the Origins of Classical Economics**
Distribution and value from William Petty to Adam Smith
Tony Aspromourgos

5 **The Economics of Joan Robinson**
Edited by Maria Cristina Marcuzzo, Luigi Pasinetti and Alesandro Roncaglia

6 **The Evolutionist Economics of Léon Walras**
Albert Jolink

7 **Keynes and the 'Classics'**
A study in language, epistemology and mistaken identities
Michel Verdon

8 **The History of Game Theory, Vol. 1**
From the beginnings to 1945
Robert W. Dimand and Mary Ann Dimand

9 **The Economics of W. S. Jevons**
Sandra Peart

10 **Gandhi's Economic Thought**
Ajit K. Dasgupta

11 **Equilibrium and Economic Theory**
Edited by Giovanni Caravale

12 **Austrian Economics in Debate**
Edited by Willem Keizer, Bert Tieben and Rudy van Zijp

13 **Ancient Economic Thought**
Edited by B. B. Price

14 **The Political Economy of Social Credit and Guild Socialism**
Frances Hutchinson and Brian Burkitt

15 **Economic Careers**
Economics and economists in Britain 1930–1970
Keith Tribe

16 **Understanding 'Classical' Economics**
Studies in the long-period theory
Heinz Kurz and Neri Salvadori

17 **History of Environmental Economic Thought**
E. Kula

18 **Economic Thought in Communist and Post-Communist Europe**
Edited by Hans-Jürgen Wagener

19 **Studies in the History of French Political Economy**
From Bodin to Walras
Edited by Gilbert Faccarello

20 **The Economics of John Rae**
Edited by O. F. Hamouda, C. Lee and D. Mair

21 **Keynes and the Neoclassical Synthesis**
Einsteinian versus Newtonian macroeconomics
Teodoro Dario Togati

22 Historical Perspectives on Macroeconomics
Sixty years after the 'General Theory'
Edited by Philippe Fontaine and Albert Jolink

23 The Founding of Institutional Economics
The leisure class and sovereignty
Edited by Warren J. Samuels

24 Evolution of Austrian Economics
From Menger to Lachmann
Sandye Gloria

25 Marx's Concept of Money
The god of commodities
Anitra Nelson

26 The Economics of James Steuart
Edited by Ramón Tortajada

27 The Development of Economics in Europe since 1945
Edited by A. W. Bob Coats

28 The Canon in the History of Economics
Critical essays
Edited by Michalis Psalidopoulos

29 Money and Growth
Selected papers of Allyn Abbott Young
Edited by Perry G. Mehrling and Roger J. Sandilands

30 The Social Economics of Jean-Baptiste Say
Markets and virtue
Evelyn L. Forget

31 The Foundations of Laissez-Faire
The economics of Pierre de Boisguilbert
Gilbert Faccarello

32 John Ruskin's Political Economy
Willie Henderson

33 Contributions to the History of Economic Thought
Essays in honour of R. D. C. Black
Edited by Antoin E. Murphy and Renee Prendergast

34 Towards an Unknown Marx
A commentary on the manuscripts of 1861–63
Enrique Dussel

35 Economics and Interdisciplinary Exchange
Edited by Guido Erreygers

36 Economics as the Art of Thought
Essays in memory of G. L. S. Shackle
Edited by Stephen F. Frowen and Peter Earl

37 The Decline of Ricardian Economics
Politics and economics in post-Ricardian theory
Susan Pashkoff

38 Piero Sraffa
His life, thought and cultural heritage
Alessandro Roncaglia

39 Equilibrium and Disequilibrium in Economic Theory
The Marshall-Walras divide
Michel de Vroey

40 The German Historical School
The historical and ethical approach to economics
Edited by Yuichi Shionoya

41 Reflections on the Classical Canon in Economics
Essays in honour of Samuel Hollander
Edited by Sandra Peart and Evelyn Forget

42 Piero Sraffa's Political Economy
A centenary estimate
Edited by Terenzio Cozzi and Roberto Marchionatti

43 The Contribution of Joseph Schumpeter to Economics
Economic development and institutional change
Richard Arena and Cecile Dangel

44 On the Development of Long-run Neo-Classical Theory
Tom Kompas

45 F. A. Hayek as a Political Economist
Economic analysis and values
Edited by Jack Birner, Pierre Garrouste and Thierry Aimar

46 Pareto, Economics and Society
The mechanical analogy
Michael McLure

47 The Cambridge Controversies in Capital Theory
A study in the logic of theory development
Jack Birner

48 Economics Broadly Considered
Essays in honour of Warren J. Samuels
Edited by Steven G. Medema, Jeff Biddle and John B. Davis

49 Physicians and Political Economy
Six studies of the work of doctor-economists
Edited by Peter Groenewegen

50 The Spread of Political Economy and the Professionalisation of Economists
Economic societies in Europe, America and Japan in the nineteenth century
Massimo Augello and Marco Guidi

51 Historians of Economics and Economic Thought
The construction of disciplinary memory
Steven G. Medema and Warren J. Samuels

52 Competing Economic Theories
Essays in memory of Giovanni Caravale
Sergio Nisticò and Domenico Tosato

53 Economic Thought and Policy in Less Developed Europe
The nineteenth century
Edited by Michalis Psalidopoulos and Maria-Eugenia Almedia Mata

54 Family Fictions and Family Facts
Harriet Martineau, Adolphe Quetelet and the population question in England 1798–1859
Brian Cooper

55 Eighteeth-Century Economics
Peter Groenewegen

56 The Rise of Political Economy in the Scottish Enlightenment
Edited by Tatsuya Sakamoto and Hideo Tanaka

57 Classics and Moderns in Economics, Vol. 1
Essays on nineteenth and twentieth century economic thought
Peter Groenewegen

58 Classics and Moderns in Economics, Vol. 2
Essays on nineteenth and twentieth century economic thought
Peter Groenewegen

59 Marshall's Evolutionary Economics
Tiziano Raffaelli

60 Money, Time and Rationality in Max Weber
Austrian connections
Stephen D. Parsons

61 Classical Macroeconomics
Some modern variations and distortions
James C. W. Ahiakpor

62 **The Historical School of Economics in England and Japan**
Tamotsu Nishizawa

63 **Classical Economics and Modern Theory**
Studies in long-period analysis
Heinz D. Kurz and Neri Salvadori

64 **A Bibliography of Female Economic Thought to 1940**
Kirsten K. Madden, Janet A. Sietz and Michele Pujol

65 **Economics, Economists and Expectations**
From microfoundations to macroeconomics
Warren Young, Robert Leeson and William Darity Jnr.

66 **The Political Economy of Public Finance in Britain, 1767–1873**
Takuo Dome

67 **Essays in the History of Economics**
Warren J. Samuels, Willie Henderson, Kirk D. Johnson and Marianne Johnson

68 **History and Political Economy**
Essays in honour of P. D. Groenewegen
Edited by Tony Aspromourgos and John Lodewijks

69 **The Tradition of Free Trade**
Lars Magnusson

70 **Evolution of the Market Process**
Austrian and Swedish economics
Edited by Michel Bellet, Sandye Gloria-Palermo and Abdallah Zouache

71 **Consumption as an Investment**
The fear of goods from Hesiod to Adam Smith
Cosimo Perrotta

72 **Jean-Baptiste Say and the Classical Canon in Economics**
The British connection in French classicism
Samuel Hollander

73 **Knut Wicksell on Poverty**
No place is too exalted
Knut Wicksell

74 **Economists in Cambridge**
A study through their correspondence 1907–1946
Edited by M. C. Marcuzzo and A. Rosselli

75 **The Experiment in the History of Economics**
Edited by Philippe Fontaine and Robert Leonard

76 **At the Origins of Mathematical Economics**
The economics of A. N. Isnard (1748–1803)
Richard van den Berg

77 **Money and Exchange**
Folktales and reality
Sasan Fayazmanesh

78 **Economic Development and Social Change**
Historical roots and modern perspectives
George Stathakis and Gianni Vaggi

79 **Ethical Codes and Income Distribution**
A study of John Bates Clark and Thorstein Veblen
Guglielmo Forges Davanzati

80 **Evaluating Adam Smith**
Creating the wealth of nations
Willie Henderson

81 **Civil Happiness**
Economics and human flourishing in historical perspective
Luigino Bruni

82 **New Voices on Adam Smith**
Edited by Leonidas Montes and Eric Schliesser

83 **Making Chicago Price Theory**
Milton Friedman–George Stigler correspondence, 1945–1957
Edited by J. Daniel Hammond and Claire H. Hammond

84 **William Stanley Jevons and the Cutting Edge of Economics**
Bert Mosselmans

85 **A History of Econometrics in France**
From nature to models
Philippe Le Gall

86 **Money and Markets**
A doctrinal approach
Edited by Alberto Giacomin and Maria Cristina Marcuzzo

87 **Considerations on the Fundamental Principles of Pure Political Economy**
Vilfredo Pareto (Edited by Roberto Marchionatti and Fiorenzo Mornati)

Considerations on the Fundamental Principles of Pure Political Economy

Vilfredo Pareto

Edited by Roberto Marchionatti and Fiorenzo Mornati

Routledge
Taylor & Francis Group
LONDON AND NEW YORK

First published 2007
by Routledge
2 Park Square, Milton Park, Abingdon, Oxon OX14 4RN

Simultaneously published in the USA and Canada
by Routledge
270 Madison Ave, New York, NY 10016

Routledge is an imprint of the Taylor & Francis Group, an informa business

Typeset in Times by RefineCatch Limited, Bungay, Suffolk
Printed and bound in Great Britain by TJI Digital, Padstow, Cornwall

British Library Cataloguing in Publication Data
A catalogue record for this book is available from the British Library

Library of Congress Cataloging in Publication Data
A catalog record for this book has been requested

ISBN10: 0–415–39919–X
ISBN13: 978–0–415–39919–7

Contents

Introduction

Roberto Marchionatti and Fiorenzo Mornati

Premise

Vilfredo Pareto is considered to be among the great economists in the history of economic thought and one of the founders of modern economic science, but economists still have very limited acquaintance with his thought. This lack certainly stems also from the fact that none of his major works in economics were available in English until the 1971 translation of the *Manuel d'économie politique* (1909). Thus only economists proficient in French or Italian could gain firsthand knowledge of his works. Before 1971, only a few of Pareto's papers had been translated in English: 'Sul fenomeno economico. Lettera a Benedetto Croce' (1900) and 'Economie mathématique' (1911) were published in the *International Economic Papers* in 1953 and 1955, respectively, in addition to 'The new theories of economics', 'a brief exposé' of his theory, published in the *Journal of Political Economy* in 1897. The *Cours d'économie politique* (1896–1897) was never translated into English, and neither was the 'Considerazioni sui principi fondamentali dell'economia pura', a series of articles published in the Italian *Giornale degli Economisti* between May 1892 and October 1893. They are translated here for the first time.

The set of articles making up the 'Considerazioni' are the first systematic representation of Pareto's contribution to pure economics. Above all, they are a methodological and theoretical reflection on the concepts of utility and marginal utility considered as the basic theoretical category of the new marginalist economics. The articles discuss and thoroughly examine a wide range of topics, including: the nature and the limits of the hypotheses on which the new theories of marginalist economics were based; the use of mathematics in economics; the problem of method; the hedonistic hypothesis and the concept of *homo oeconomicus*; the concept of final degree of utility; the conditions of maximization of collective utility (preliminary considerations); the analytical determination of the marginal utility of money; the law of demand. These reflections make the 'Considerazioni' a fundamental assessment of the state of the 'new economic theories' expounded in a mathematical form at the beginning of the 1890s. Later, these papers influenced the development of consumer theory and laid the groundwork for Eugen Slutsky's introduction of income and substitution effects in 1915.

The 'Considerazioni' have been increasingly recognized as crucial in the development of the Pareto's thought.[1] Nevertheless, they remain a much-quoted but little-read and studied work. This translation aims to close this gap. The following introduction reconstructs the genesis and development of the 'Considerazioni' in the contest of late nineteenth-century economic theory.

The new mathematical theories of economics at the time of the 'Considerazioni'

The new approach to economics characterized by the adoption of the mathematical method of reasoning came to life in the 1870s. The decade 1871–1881 witnessed the emergence of the mathematical revolution in economics in the works of William Stanley Jevons, Léon Walras, Alfred Marshall and Francis Ysidro Edgeworth. The 1880s saw the mathematical method in economics spread throughout Europe. The 1890s, particularly 1892–1897, produce an intense work in mathematical economics, which established itself as an important, although small, school in economics (see Marchionatti 2004).

The importance of Pareto's work in this context can be appreciated in the light of the theoretical situation in the years straddling the end of the 1880s and the beginning of 1890s. In those years major contributions in the field were published: the second edition of Walras's *Eléments d'économie politique pure* in 1889, the first (1890) and second (1891) editions of Marshall's *Principles of Economics*, and *Untersuchungen über die Theorie des Preises* by the Austrian economists Rudolf Auspitz and Richard Lieben in 1889. The late 1880s were also the years when the early controversies within mathematical economics emerged: Edgeworth, Walras, Bortkievicz, and Auspitz and Lieben were directly involved in two disputes that illustrate different conceptions of the role mathematics should play in economics (Edgeworth 1889a, 1889b and 1891; Walras 1890; Bortkievicz 1890; Auspitz and Lieben 1890; see also Walras 1965).

According to the pioneers of this new approach, mathematics – the 'sovereign science' as Edgeworth defined it – guaranteed scientific rigour because it permitted researchers to adopt rigorously deductive reasoning. The mechanical analogy of the classical physics made mathematical language the natural expression of an economic reasoning that seemed clearer and more precise than Ricardo's or Stuart Mill's language. Mathematical calculus was considered the most powerful tool for describing and understanding the general quantitative relations between the fundamental variables on which the theory was based. One fundamental feature of the new mathematical economics was the so-called hedonistic hypothesis, which holds that when individuals act they are motivated by their desire to obtain the greatest satisfaction of needs through the lowest individual effort. Such an hypothesis seemed tailor-made for the mathematics of differential calculus. In this vein, Edgeworth (1881) maintained that the principal inquiries in pure economics could all be seen as problems of the determination of a maximum, starting from quantitative relations of the form 'x is greater or less than y; and increases or decreases with the increase of z'. Edgeworth was actually the economist who gave the most complete formulation of the hedonistic hypothesis, building on Jevonian foundations. For him, economic calculus was the study of the equilibrium of a system of hedonistic forces that tend to maximize individual utility. On the analytical level, the main achievements of the new approach were in the field of the theory of consumer behaviour and on the theory of exchange. These theories started out from a limited number of abstract premises and ended up exhibiting a high level of generality and simplicity.

A central issue in the new economics was the role and the extent of mathematics in economics. Walras had a boundless admiration for the solid edifice of classical mechanics, which he regarded as the model for scientific knowledge. His book, based on the principle of general economic equilibrium, was inspired by his aim to build a science of political economy that was the same as the Newtonian science of mechanics. Walras's aim was to create a theory of economics with the same formal properties that characterized celestial mechanics, as Jaffé (1977) outlined. Walras considered economics a physical-mathematical science like mechanics. Hence mathematical method and language were the natural expression of reasoning in political economy.

Marshall thought differently. He conceived economics as a human science and emphasized the instrumental and limited use of mathematics in economics. Although Walras and Marshall concurred that mathematics was necessary for deductive reasoning, Marshall carefully limited the function and extent of abstract mathematical reasoning in economics. In Appendix D of his *Principles*, 'Uses of abstracting reasoning in economics', Marshall wrote that it is illusory to think that there is room for long trains of deductive reasoning in economics since economic material is often inadequate to bear the strains of the mathematician's machinery. Edgeworth (1889a) adopted a Marshallian line of thinking about the role of mathematics in economics. He emphasized that 'our little branch of learning is of quite rudimentary form' and that 'the solid structure and regular ramifications of the more developed mathematical sciences are wanting' (Edgeworth 1889a: 551).

The different conception of the nature of the economic science that separated Walras and Marshall (and Edgeworth) can explain not only the differing extent of their use of mathematics in economics but also their differing attitudes towards abstractions. Marshall and Edgeworth used greater realism in the hypotheses and models and thus thought that Walras's theories were ruined by an excess of abstraction. The contrast between Edgeworth and Marshall, on the one side, and Walras on the other, became an issue of public debate after Edgeworth reviewed the second edition of Walras's *Eléments* in *Nature* (September 1889) and after he delivered his Presidential Address 'On the Application of Mathematics to Political Economy' to section F of the British Association for the Advancement of Science Address a few days later. This began a controversy over Walras's theory of exchange that also involved Ladislaus Bortkievicz, at that time a young follower of Walras.[2] Edgeworth criticized three points that Walras considered fundamental to his theoretical work. First, he criticized the theorem on the maximum utility of new capital goods. Second, he criticized the theory of the entrepreneur who in equilibrium makes neither a profit nor a loss. Third, he criticized the theory of *tâtonnement* – i.e. the method Walras used to represent the determination of the equilibrium prices in a competitive market system. Edgeworth agreed with Walras 'in his plea for the use of mathematical reasoning in economics', but added that Walras prejudiced 'the case by his advocacy', because of his excessive use of mathematical symbols. Throughout his criticism Edgeworth's main point is that there is an excessive elaboration of mathematical reasoning in the *Eléments*, 'in such a manner as to justify the particular prejudice against it' (Edgeworth 1889b: 435). Bortkievicz (1890) took up the case for Walras in the *Revue d'économie politique*, maintaining that Walras's theory was logically correct and that Edgeworth's short article contained obscurities. In his reply Edgeworth (1891) conceded that his criticism of Walras was too succinct, but reaffirmed his view that Walras conceived the nature of industrial competition in a too-limited and narrow a way. In essence, the controversy between Edgeworth and Walras reveals the clash of two different methodological requirements. On the one hand, is Walras's requirement of rigour and simplicity that is brought on by the reduction of economics to mathematical treatment. According to Walras, his own simple model of free competition was the general case. Therefore, he thought, Edgeworth took the wrong approach because he subordinated the general case to particular cases. On the other hand, Edgeworth required a more realistic model. Thus he implicitly maintained that the Walrasian level of abstraction could not represent the general case. Edgeworth could only accept the Walrasian case as an extreme simplification.

The controversy between Walras and the English economists is echoed in another important controversy – the one between Walras and the pair Auspitz and Lieben after the publication of their book, *Untersuchungen*. Auspitz and Lieben had used partial analysis and had assumed the constancy of the marginal utility of money in a Marshallian-type theoretical context of partial equilibrium. The book widely uses an apparatus of curves like those used by Marshall in his 1879 essays. Walras (1890) attacks Auspitz's and Lieben's partial analysis of supply and demand. However, his real target was Marshall, whom Walras erroneously thought had inspired them (see Walras's letter to Pantaleoni of 5 January 1890, in Walras 1965, vol. II: 384–387). Ironically enough, Auspitz and Lieben had never known about Marshall's work when they were writing the book. Two points stand out in Walras's critique. First, Auspitz and Lieben had introduced money into the theory of exchange because they were aiming to integrate the theories of value and money from the beginning of their argumentation. Walras considered this methodologically unscientific. Second, Auspitz and Lieben's demand and supply curves represented quantity demanded or supplied as a function of the price of a commodity alone. Walras countered that this was not exact, because the demand and supply curves had been plotted under the *ceteris paribus* hypothesis – i.e. under the assumption that the prices of the other commodities and productive services had not been affected. Walras pointed out that when the price of a commodity changes, this change disturbs the whole of the existing equilibrium, whose every element must be readjusted in turn.

Auspitz and Lieben (1890) replied to Walras. They tried to make it clear that they had assumed the value of money constant for each individual because this seemed a better procedure than Walras's totally abstracting from money in his theory of exchange, something that they considered too drastic. In addition they rebutted Walras's critique of the *ceteris paribus* hypothesis. They pointed out that they were aware of the fact that the quantity demanded for a commodity is a function of all the prices, as they had written in Appendix IV of their book. Nevertheless, they had found that the *ceteris paribus* assumption was the best way to deal with a wide range of issues. Auspitz and Lieben further criticized Walras's conception of the cost function. Walras had assumed constant costs for all the producers in equilibrium. On the contrary, Auspitz and Lieben assumed increasing costs and, on this basis, they developed a theory of producer surplus. In addition, they examined Walras's position that free trade led to a consumer gain but not producer gain. This would imply, according to Auspitz and Lieben, that a producer had no motivation to develop his entrepreneurial activity. Furthermore, they rejected Walras's position that the equality of the cost of production and the price was the same thing as the equality of demand and supply. For them, everyday experience reveals that there are always differences between prices and costs even though the market always works to balance supply and demand. For them, Walras's idea that entrepreneurs make neither gain nor loss in a perfect competition market was equivalent to eliminating the entrepreneur.

Walras did not reply. He had first hoped that Bortkievicz would fill in for him, as he had against Edgeworth, but Bortkievicz chose to remove himself from the dispute. Then Walras wrote to him:

> It is not probable that I will decide to intervene. I am very tired and I think that the time has arrived for me to make way for somebody other. If it is necessary, I will wait to find people who know that the secret of the science is to put the general case up front and to relegate the particular cases and exceptions to the second level. This is the core of my controversy with Edgeworth.
>
> (Letter to Bortkievicz of 27 February 1891, in Walras 1965, vol. II: 434–435)

The crucial issues of the role and extension of the use of mathematics in economics and the partial equilibrium will appear again in the work of Vilfredo Pareto, the leading figure in the new economics between the 1890s and the First World War.

Pareto at the beginning of the 1890s

Pareto retired from his position in industry in May 1890, at the age of 42. He was to spend the next 30 years or so studying and carrying out his project to write a treatise on 'rational political economy' in the manner of treatises on rational mechanics. Born in 1848, he studied mathematics and engineering. He was awarded a degree in mathematics in 1867 and one in engineering in 1870 at the University of Turin. Around 1870 he started working as an engineer at the Railway Company of Florence (*Strade Ferrate Romane*). For the next 20 years Pareto worked as deputy manager and then general director of *Ferriere Italiane*, an iron works company at San Giovanni in Valdarno, near Florence. In 1890 he left the company and retired to Fiesole.[3]

At that time he was motivated in his theoretical work by his support of free trade, a policy championed by the Radical Party, a small opposition party that he had been sympathizing with from the mid-1880s. In the previous ten years he had been active in the ranks of the Conservative Liberal Party led by Ubaldino Peruzzi, a former Italian minister of the Interior and major of Florence. The commercial war between Italy and France that broke out in 1887 induced Pareto to think about the economic basis of economic liberalism. At first he borrowed ideas from Gustave de Molinari, the editor of the *Journal of Economistes*, and leader of the French liberalism (Mornati 2000). Both of them thought that it was necessary to describe the damage that protectionism brings. Pareto added two crucial points to de Molinari's arguments: he emphasized the need to find political and social allies for the free-trade policy and to give a new scientific and rigorous foundation to free trade. The development of Pareto's interest in the application of mathematics to political economy is connected with this second objective.

Pareto had admired the books and articles of Maffeo Pantaleoni and was to become a close friend of him.[4] Pantaleoni advised him to study the work of Léon Walras. Pareto had already started to read the 1877 edition of Walras's *Eléments d'économie politique pure* (letter to Walras, 12 September 1891), but he had broken off because he had no taste for its metaphysical components. Pantaleoni assured Pareto that there was something other than metaphysics in Walras's work (see the letter to Pantaleoni of 27 July 1892). Actually, Pareto was decisively inspired to undertake his political–scientific project through his reading of Pantaleoni's *Principi di economia pura* and of the second edition of Walras's *Eléments* as well as through his ensuing intellectual relationship with Walras.

Pareto was in no way an amateur, some retired engineer who was just tacking some new interest in economic theory onto his old passion for mathematics. On the contrary, he took on his project with all the attributes of a scholar who had a critical conception of scientific activities. He was an advocate of the prevailing standards of natural sciences as a practice strongly associated with experimental proof. For this reason, his attitude was strongly anti-metaphysical (see the letter to Walras of 15 March 1892). In fact, he began his *Cours* emphasizing that 'economics is a natural science, founded exclusively on facts' (Pareto 1896–1897, vol. 1, §1). This concept was also clearly expressed in the 'Considerazioni'. It implies that the method of economics is the experimental method – i.e. that of the natural sciences. Pareto brought John Stuart Mill into his discussion of method in economics. He had read his magnum opus, *A System of Logic*, in 1874 in the French translation (1866) of the sixth (penultimate) edition. Here Mill maintained that economics must use the 'concrete-deductive method' (the logico-experimental method in Pareto's terminology). This method follows these steps: an initial induction from observed phenomena, a theoretical deduction from them, a comparison between the deductions and the real facts, a subsequent modification and addition in order to obtain new ideal schemes of the observed facts, and so on indefinitely. However, Pareto did not accept everything in Mill. He disagreed over the role and importance of mathematics, holding that Mill underestimated the value of mathematics. In fact, mathematics is a sort of logic that helps researchers avoid formal errors of reasoning. Epistemological statements like these are incorporated and extensively discussed in the first part of the 'Considerazioni'.

The genesis of the 'Considerazioni'

Pareto's reflection on the issues discussed in the 'Considerazioni' started in mid-year 1891, partially in response to his reading of Maffeo Pantaleoni's *Principi di economia pura* (1889).[5] At that time Pareto had some knowledge of economic works by Cournot, Walras and Jevons, which he probably read in the Italian translation in the series of the *Biblioteca dell'Economista* edited by Gerolamo Boccardo. These readings aroused some misgivings in Pareto about the at times inappropriate or erroneous use of the mathematical method in economics and about the hedonistic theory, which was at the basis of the new economic theories. He expressed his doubts as well as his long-standing mistrust of political economy in several letters to Maffeo Pantaleoni in July and October 1891, and to Walras (letter of 21 September 1891). Pareto's doubts mainly focused on Cournot's attempts to demonstrate the advantages of the economic protection: 'I considered a method leading to such conclusions to be *hazardous*' (letter to Pantaleoni of 8 July, 1891, in Pareto 1984, vol. I: 45). His doubts were somewhat mitigated by his reading of Pantaleoni's *Principi* and Walras's *Eléments*. He called *Eléments* 'an important work' (letter to Pantaleoni of 7 October 1891, in Pareto 1984, vol. I: 77) that opened the scientific path to political economy (letter to Walras of 15 September 1891). Pareto's critique of the new theories touched many crucial issues: the shape of utility curves was based on limited empirical – i.e. experimental – evidence; the concept of *homo oeconomicus* was a notion of someone 'who does not exist in nature'; the hypothesis of intentionality – i.e. perfect rationality – of *homo oeconomicus*'s action contradicted the fact that 'men act on the basis of habits more than reason'; the hypothesis that in the exchange men compare the degree of utility of the various exchanged goods was far-fetched. Pareto wrote, 'I think that most people do not know how to do this'. The definition of the final degree of utility was highly imprecise, something that Pareto considered 'the crux of the matter' (letter to Pantaleoni of 3 October 1891, in Pareto 1984, vol. I: 67). On the other hand, he thought that there was a general agreement on the need to use mathematics in political economy:

> I think that as far as mathematics is concerned, we all agree. I do not deny that there are problems which are too complex to be treated other than mathematically. I admit that the graphical method is often the most elegant and simplest way to expound the solution of some problems. Far be it from me to be opposed to the mathematical political economy, I think that sooner or later it is going to be the basis of the economic science. . . . We also perfectly agree that the issue of the usefulness of mathematics in political economy is different from the issue on the validity of the theory of the final degree of utility.
>
> (Letter to Pantaleoni of 3 October 1891, in Pareto 1984, vol. I: 65)

Early in October 1891, when his ideas on these issues 'little by little become clear and assume a more precise form', Pareto started to write a paper on the final degree of utility (letter to Pantaleoni of 7 October 1891, in Pareto 1984, vol. I: 72–73). At the beginning of December he sent Pantaleoni the first part of his paper, commenting that it was getting longer and asking him for some comments. In the meantime he wrote a short paper on Cournot that was published in January 1892 in the *Giornale degli Economisti*, edited by Pantaleoni himself. Pareto's topic was Cournot's misuse of mathematics, but his critique was meant to be extended to all those economists who thought that the simple mathematical expression of a line of reasoning was a guarantee of its truth. In a letter to Pantaleoni of December 1891, Pareto wrote:

> I am not an opponent of the new school. . . . However, I am an opponent of all the reasoning based on false assumptions. . . . According to me, the true enemy of the science is the reasoning that seems rigorous but, as a matter of fact, is based on false premises.
>
> (Letter to Pantaleoni of 9 December 1891, in Pareto 1984, vol. I: 118)

In the letter quoted above to Pantaleoni of 7 October, Pareto had clearly expressed his thoughts on mathematics: 'I agree with those who think that mathematics is a sort of a complicated-syllogism-making machine. The important thing is to correctly pose the problem. Then a mathematician can solve it' (letter to Pantaleoni of 7 October 1891, in Pareto 1984, vol. I: 74).

In the meantime, Pareto was broadening his knowledge of the new economics and filling in his previous gaps, thanks to books and journals that Pantaleoni gave him. Pareto was particularly struck by Edgeworth's *Mathematical Psychics* and by the dispute between Walras and the pair Auspitz and Lieben. Pareto considered *Mathematical Psychics* to be fundamentally important for the foundation of the new political economy. He considered the Walras–Auspitz and Lieben dispute of such an importance that it needed to be discussed in an article he would write 'before the publication of the paper on the principles of the new science' (letter of 25 December 1891, in Pareto 1984, vol. I: 129).

By 1 January, 1892 Pareto had read Walras' criticism of Auspitz and Lieben but not their reply. In a letter to Walras on this date, he expressed his agreement with his observations, which rightly showed 'the mistake made by these men claiming that protection is a benefit! According to me, this is absolutely false' (letter to Walras of 1 January 1892, in Walras 1965, vol. II: 473). Walras then sent him Auspitz's and Lieben's reply, which he judged as inadequate. Pareto then informed Pantaleoni that he was going to write the article on the controversy in a month (letter of 20 January 1892), but he actually finished the article in about ten days. Later, he stressed that 'the series of articles on the principles of the new science will not be ready until a few months from now. I am not yet completely satisfied with it'. He added: 'as the ideas mature, I will write the great paper on the principles' (letter to Pantaleoni of 31 January 1892, in Pareto 1984, vol. I: 173). On 17 February 1892, Pareto informed Pantaleoni: 'On the final degree of utility there are still some points around which I see some mist. Notwithstanding, I think that I will be able to send to you the first part of the paper by March because it all seems ready to go' (letter to Pantaleoni of 17 February 1892, in Pareto 1984, vol. I: 183).

On 4 March 1892, Pareto informed Pantaleoni that 'the first part of the article is ready' (letter to Pantaleoni of 4 March 1892, in Pareto 1984, vol. I: 193). It contained his introductory remarks, including his beliefs on method. Pareto further wrote that he did not understand 'why Walras does not like neither Edgeworth nor Marshall' (ibid.: 194). He supposed that there was some 'rivalry' between them, probably referring to a letter from Walras of 23 February 1892, that contained a strongly negative judgement of Marshall, Edgeworth, Launhardt, Auspitz and Lieben. In fact, Walras called their works 'lucubrations', laborious studies that showed that 'one could elaborate a great number of false systems in a mathematical form' (letter to Walras of 23 February 1892, in Walras 1965, vol. II: 483). In the end, Pareto did not deal with the Edgeworth–Walras dispute.

Pareto's second article was completed before mid-April and published in the June issue of the *Giornale degli Economisti.* Here Pareto supported Walras's position on the issue of the marginal utility of money in a stronger way than he had done in his article on Auspitz and Lieben. He wrote to Walras on 20 March 1892: 'I think that I found a way of presenting and stressing the proposition you established that the utility of all the goods has to be taken into account. A consequence of this proposition is that the final utility of money cannot be considered constant' (letter to Walras of 20 March 1892, in Walras 1965, vol. II: 491).

While Pareto was writing his third article, he realized that new issues should have been raised, so much so as to call for a fourth and 'perhaps' a fifth article (letter of 22 May 1892). He finished the third article at the beginning of July and had it published in the August issue of the *Giornale.* The important and new points discussed in the article include the calculus of the final degree of utility; the mean of these degrees; and the maximum of the total utility in repeated exchanges. The article implicitly criticized Walras's handling of the calculus of the average utility, something he explicitly criticized in a letter to Pantaleoni of 3 July 1892:

> Walras would like to take the arithmetic mean as the degree of average utility. You see that he did not study this issue. I did not talk of him about it, because there were already too many occasions when I had to contest some of the things he said.
>
> (Letter to Pantaleoni of 3 July 1892, in Pareto 1984, vol. I: 236)

Pareto was not surprised by the inaccuracies and the mistakes he found in the economic theory of his times. In fact he realized that 'mathematical economic science is being born now. No wonder if it is still very imprecise. This is what happened in all the sciences' (letter to Pantaleoni of 6 July 1892, in Pareto 1984, vol. I: 240).

After the publication of his third article Pareto received complimentary letters from Edgeworth (letter of 28 August 1892) and Walras (letter of 18 October 1892). We can surmise that he had been admitted to the club of the new mathematical economists.[6]

The last two articles were finished and published after a certain lapse of time. The fourth was completed in the early autumn and published in January 1893. It treated the calculus of the final degree of utility of money as well as an interesting discussion of Bernoulli's Petersburg paradox. The fifth and last article, on the theory of rational consumer, was finished at the beginning of August 1893 and published in October 1893.[7] At that point Pareto looked ahead: 'We must now – it seems to me – stop trying to explain the exchange in many ways and start going on ahead to establish new theorems' (letter to Pantaleoni of 17 October 1892, in Pareto 1984, vol. I: 301).

After he had made his long in-depth analyses of the new economic theories, he was well aware that pure economics issues 'are things which move slowly' (letter to Walras of 22 January 1893, in Walras 1965, vol. II: 540).

The concrete deductive method at work in the 'Considerazioni': some methodological considerations on how to deal with the fundamentals of pure economic theory

The articles that make up Pareto's 'Considerazioni' plot out a many-faceted analytical discussion. They contain several theoretical contributions to the field of pure economics that reveal the outstanding level of Pareto's mathematical qualification, which readers may appreciate even today.[8] However, we think that the lasting contribution of the 'Considerazioni' is methodological. Pareto clearly poses the issue of the conditions for political economy to be a science and, as opposed to Walras, he maintains the importance of the experimental method for making valuable demonstrations in economics.[9]

The first article starts with some preliminary considerations on method and on the use of mathematics in economics. These are to be recurring leitmotifs in Pareto's later works. Pareto maintains that the correct method in economics is Mill's 'concrete deductive method'. Mill's method is one that brings together the empirical quantitative method and the deductive method. This principle was by then universally known in the scientific community, as Pareto notes. Nevertheless, Pareto stresses it in order to criticize a tendency in the new economics that Walras exemplified: this is the tendency 'to lead science on a metaphysical path, where reasoning dominates experience'. This is the path 'that no follower of the experimental method will be able to tread after him'. On the other hand, the quantitative method 'could only lead to empirical propositions' if it is used alone. Therefore it must be flanked by the deductive method.

The first article's second issue is the use of mathematics in political economy. Above all, Pareto writes, the mathematical method allows for 'the higher degree of rigour in demonstration' (p. 7, this edition). In later works Pareto is to emphasize that the essential reason for using mathematics in economics is that mathematics is needed to solve the system of equations of the general economic equilibrium. In other words, mathematics is needed to treat problems far more complicated than those generally solved by ordinary logic. As he writes some years later (1906a [1902]: p. 427; see also *Cours* § 584 and the letter to Pantaleoni of 15 September 1907):

> We refer to mathematical analysis in order to have an idea of the links of economic circulation and to establish its fundamental characteristics. On the contrary, if restricted to a special and numerical problem ... the utility of mathematics is limited.... Its utility becomes great when we have to deal with a general and qualitative problem, for example, the exact knowledge of the conditions determining economic equilibrium.

In the 'Considerazioni' Pareto also emphasizes that economists must use mathematics with caution. Although he appreciates the work of the new economists, he thinks that there are still some unresolved issues to clear up.

The greater rigour of the demonstrations, 'which is typical of this type of logic', may be 'only apparent' (p. 7, this edition). Like Marshall and Edgeworth, Pareto stresses that economists's caution should be extreme in the use of mathematics in economics. He comments, in fact: 'the more the reasoning tends to become almost a mechanical operation . . . the greater become the probabilities of errors, which derive from the uncertainty of the premises' (ibid.). Therefore the central question becomes the question of the validity of the premises upon which the theorems that yield the conclusions are built. Thus, only 'by sticking very closely to observation' (p. 10, this edition) is it possible to avoid errors.

After these general remarks, Pareto examines the fundamental hypothesis assumed by the new economists – i.e. the *homo oeconomicus* who is a perfect hedonist. This hypothetical *homo oeconomicus* is a concept that is very similar to the concept of material point in theoretical mechanics. In fact, *homo oeconomicus* is a 'pleasure machine', in Edgeworth's (1889a) words. Pareto notes: 'Edgeworth has succeeded in expounding the new theory in the most general way and with the rigour of mathematics' (p. 14, this edition). He adds:

> this concept [*homo oeconomicus*] is wonderfully simple and grand at the same time, . . . there is much truth in it [but] it is necessary to proceed very carefully [following the concrete deductive method] in order not to draw conclusions which, should they be found to be contrary to experience, could spoil and be cause for the rejection of both the good and the bad that the new theories contain.
>
> (p. 14, this edition)

Here Pareto questions the generality and abstractness of the concepts used. First, he critiques the expression of the concept of utility. Second, he critiques the adoption of implicit qualities of the *homo oeconomicus*. He is supposed to be a perfect hedonist endowed 'to a certain extent' with foresight and reasonableness. First, Pareto judges that utility is expressed 'in very general terms' in the works of the new economists. The result is that basic questions remain unsolved, so that we still do not know whether utility really exists or whether it is merely an abstraction. Moreover, individuals are very seldom aware of the total utility of an economic good. They are usually aware only of its utility for small variations – i.e. they are aware of the final degree of utility. Second, Pareto thinks that the theorems of pure science can be applied to a perfect hedonist who is perfectly foresighted and reasonable. However, these *extreme* hypotheses have a very limited significance, as he stresses: 'When dealing with economic phenomena, it seems to us that by considering men as perfect hedonists we do not stray too far at all from reality; this would not be the case, however, if they were to be considered entirely provident and reasonable' (p. 20, this edition).[10]

This assumption of perfect foresight and reasonableness has to be considered an important flaw in the hedonistic theories. This flaw becomes extremely serious when applied to the study of phenomena that are not exclusively economic or in successive approximation to reality. In those cases we are running the risk of producing 'fairy tales', as Pareto puts it.

The points that we have just reviewed are the methodological principles that Pareto applies in his theoretical work in the 'Considerazioni'. Pareto focuses his theoretical reflections on the concept of the final degree of utility, the key issue of the new political economy. He starts off with his claim that the final degree of utility has to be drawn from the observation of real facts, as he states in his first article and develops in his third article. The third article takes up how final degrees of utility could actually be calculated. Pareto indicates the steps in this calculation. First, economists should choose the units of economic goods. Second, they should observe consumption in relation to the prices of those commodities in various cases, and use these observations to obtain the law of demand. Third, they should infer the final degrees of utility. Then, there is a second level of inquiry that requires the use of statistical interpolation. Here Pareto emphasizes a fundamental point in his research: the fact that the first step of economists' analysis is to identify the empirical regularities that can serve to define realistic hypotheses upon which to build the theoretical model. Hence Pareto's approval of the realism of the theoretical hypotheses and disapproval of unjustified abstractions, can be interpreted as a corollary of his experimental method. Theory grows through the acquisition of more knowledge upon the principles underlying its reasoning. This is the point that is missing in the new economic theories, according to Pareto. Therefore statistics can play a fundamental role to make up for this gap.[11]

Pareto then goes further into the problem of the measurement of the final degree of utility. He argues against the objection that pleasure and utility cannot be directly measured. This objection 'does not hold [because] in the natural sciences we have many quantities that are impossible to measure directly and are indirectly measured' (p. 58, this edition). Economists can measure the final degree of utility indirectly by relying 'on the accuracy of the observer' and 'collect[ing] a large quantity of precise data on prices and on the consumed commodities' (p. 59, this edition). According to Pareto, the best formulas for calculating the final degrees of utility in the most general case are those proposed by French mathematician Cauchy and French astronomer Le Verrier. More sophisticated methods, like the least squares method, could be used only if the data available on prices and consumption were more precise than it was in Pareto's days. Pareto emphasizes that 'knowing even with rough approximation the numerical value of the quantities at hand greatly increases our scientific wealth' (p. 59, this edition). This can help economists avoid many mistakes. Pareto illustrates his reasoning with an example taken from the history of astronomy: 'Newton thought that Saturn's orbit was significantly altered at every conjunction with Jupiter, whereas observations by later astronomers showed it to be almost insignificant' (p. 59, this edition). The data available in political economy in Pareto's days were less precise than the data in astronomy in Newton's days. This gives us a good idea of how easy is to make mistakes, Pareto notes. In any case, once economists have some 'numerical idea, no matter how approximate' of the final degree of utility, 'we shall have to go back and deal again with pure theory, correct it, improve it, advance it' (p. 73, this edition), following the procedures of experimental sciences.

The Paretian path of research in pure economics after the 'Considerazioni': concluding remarks

The articles in the 'Considerazioni' were followed by the *Cours d'économie politique* in 1896–1897, which represents a sort of interlude in Pareto's theoretical reflection. The section of the *Cours* devoted to pure theory is basically a re-explanation of Walras's theory from the *Eléments*. However, it does contain many autonomous and original points (see Marchionatti and Gambino 1997b). Pareto essentially retains the cardinal theory of utility from the 'Considerazioni'. He expresses his dissatisfaction with the concept of utility, though, by introducing a new term to take its place – i.e. 'ophelimity' (*ophélimité*) – in order to avoid the misunderstanding derived by the different meanings of the term utility in the ordinary language (see *Cours*, §§ 4,5).

He reopened his critique of hedonism in 1898, one year after the publication of the second volume of the *Cours*. This critique appears in a paper presented at a conference hosted by a Lausanne students association, the Société Stella, entitled 'Comment se pose le problème de l'èconomie pure' [How the problem of pure economics should be posed]. Pareto puts the measurability of utility under discussion. He recognizes that the economists do not need to measure utility in order to explain consumer behaviour.[12] Walras had argued that utility was not measurable in practice but nevertheless remained quantifiable like physical quantities such as temperature and mass. As we have seen, Pareto initially had defined the field of application of utility measurement along Walrasian lines. However, since he was an experimentalist, he was dissatisfied with a mere hypothetical possibility of measuring utility. Yet, in order to explain consumer behaviour, economists still seemed to need the hypothesis that they could measure utility. As Pareto wrote in 1900:

> Choices have been explained as man's aim to achieve maximum pleasure. Between two things, man chooses the one that provides more pleasure. The point of equilibrium is obtained by expressing the conditions mathematically that enable the individual to enjoy the maximum pleasure compatible with the obstacles he meets. . . . The use of this point of view forces us to consider pleasure as a quantity. And this is what the economists who have established pure economic theories have done and what we ourselves have done in the *Cours*.
>
> (Pareto 1900a: 221)

Pareto recognizes that 'this is not a thoroughly rigorous method'. How can this hypothesis be replaced? If it is not possible to measure pleasure exactly, what kind of science is it that bases itself on such a measurement? He then answers his own question: 'In order to examine general economic equilibrium, this measurement is not necessary. It is sufficient to ascertain if one pleasure is larger or smaller than another. This is the only fact we need to build a theory' (Pareto 1898: 108).

This idea and the critique of the theory presented in the *Cours* first appear in a systematic form in the paper 'Sunto di alcuni capitoli di un nuovo trattato di economia pura del Prof. Pareto' [Summary of some chapters of a new treatise on pure economics by Professor Pareto], published in the *Giornale degli Economisti* in 1900.[13] This summary introduced the new theory of value, which was later developed in the *Manuale* and then refined by Slutsky, and by Hicks and Allen. Pareto writes:

> In reality and in the most general way, pure economic equations simply express the fact of a choice, and can be obtained independently of the notion of pleasure and pain. This is the most general point of view and also the most rigorous. . . . For us, it is sufficient to note the fact of individual choice, without investigating the psychological or metaphysical implication of such a choice. . . . We do not inquire into the causes of men's actions: the observation of the fact itself is sufficient. . . . Pure economic equations and their consequences exist unchanged whether we start from the consideration of pleasure as a quantity, or we limit our investigation . . . exclusively to the fact of choice.
>
> (Pareto 1900a: 221–224)

Pareto develops his theory of value on this basis by using the indifference curves introduced by Edgeworth (1881) and already discussed in the fifth article of the 'Considerazioni'. He first discusses the meaning of his own indifference curves in detail as well as the points that differentiate him from Edgeworth in the letter to Pantaleoni of 28 December 1899:

> Edgeworth and the others *start* from the concept of marginal utility and *arrive* at the determination of indifference curves (which, by the way, is what I myself did in the articles in the *Giornale*). Now I am leaving marginal utility completely aside and I am starting from the indifference curves. That is the only new departure. It is strange that such a step has not been taken before. The reasons are, I believe: 1) the mania of always trying to go *beyond* experience; 2) science began by considering marginal utility and everybody has continued on these lines. I do not think that the first motive had any influence on me when I wrote the articles in the *Giornale* discussing indifference curves. It is probably the second motive which operated. Lastly, however that may be, the principles of pure economics have hitherto been based on final degree of utility – scarcity

> [*rareté*], ophelimity, etc. Well, there is no point in that. One can start from the indifference curves which are a direct result of experience.
>
> (Letter to Pantaleoni of 28 December 1899, in Pareto 1984, vol. II: 288)

In this way Pareto abandoned the path of research that was central in the 'Considerazioni'. This abandonment was due to the rigorous application of the experimental method, the thread which connects all the Paretian research.

Notes

1 Over the last decade there has been a wave of studies on Pareto's 'Considerazioni'. See Marchionatti and Gambino (1997a), Mornati (1997) and Weber (2001). After the early isolated case of Chipman (1976), they first consider the role of the 'Considerazioni' in the development of Pareto's thought. More recently Marchionatti and Mornati (2003) offer an extensive discussion of Pareto's reflection at the beginning of the 1890s, which the present introduction extends.

2 The controversy is extensively examined in Marchionatti (forthcoming, 2007).

3 For Pareto's biographical details see Busino 1987 and 1989 and Mornati 2007.

4 In particular, he considered Pantaleoni's work *Dell'ammontare probabile della ricchezza in Italia* [On the probable total of private wealth in Italy] 'the best study of political economy that has been published in Italy in many years' (letter to Pantaleoni, 17 October 1890, in Pareto 1984, vol. I: 14–15).

5 Pareto writes: 'Our reading of this book [*I Principi di Economia pura* by Prof. Pantaleoni] has prompted many of the considerations we are putting forward in this article, and has greatly clarified for us some ideas that other books had left obscure' (note 16, pp. 143–144, this edition).

6 In the meantime Pareto had read Irving Fisher's *Mathematical Investigations* and judged this book positively but thought that 'it added little to the existing knowledge' (letter to Pantaleoni of 17 October 1892, in Pareto 1984, vol. I: 301).

7 Pareto had became professor of political economy at the University of Lausanne to succeed Léon Walras, who had retired – he was appointed *professeur extraordinaire* on 25 April 1893 and delivered his first lecture on 12 May 1893.

8 The more relevant analytical issues discussed are: the assumption of constancy of the final utility of money; the determination of demand and supply in relation to price assuming that the final degrees of utility are known; the determination of the final degree of utility when the laws of demand and supply are known; the maximization of the utility of a community; Gossen's law of diminishing marginal utility; the existence of total utility function; the case of general non-additive utility functions. These points are considered in Chipman (1976), Weber (2001), Marchionatti and Mornati (2003).

9 On the dissent on method between Walras and Pareto see Marchionatti (1999) and Mornati (1999).

10 A similar criticism of the hypotheses adopted by new economics was made some years later by the eminent French scientist Henri Poincaré in reply to a letter that Walras wrote him asking his opinion of the *Eléments*. Poincaré wrote: 'You consider men perfect egoist and perfectly clear-sighted. As a first approximation, the first hypothesis may be accepted, but I have some reservations about the acceptance of the second' (letter of Poincaré to Walras of 10 September 1901, in Walras 1965, vol. III).

11 Schumpeter (1954) numbers Pareto among the figures from the marginalist period

who are aware of the importance of statistical treatment, together with Jevons, Marshall and Edgeworth.

12 In a letter to Pantaleoni of 19 November 1899 (in Pareto 1984, vol. II: 278) he writes: 'I am writing a treatise on mathematical economics in which I develop the idea to which I have already referred in my article "Comment se pose le probléme de l'économie pure". And I formulate the basic conclusion without using marginal utility, or utility, or even prices.'

13 Pareto thinks that 'Comment se pose . . .' represents an intermediate level in his process of analysis: 'We must not let the metaphysical entities, driven out through the door, come back through the window. I had not completely freed myself from them in my study: "Comment se pose le probléme de l'économie pure." There are three different degrees in the reasoning: 1st degree, the reasoning of all the economists, including my own in the *Cours*; the whole theory is subordinated to a concept of an entity: pleasure, final degree of utility, scarsity [*rareté*], ophelimity; 2nd degree, the little work to which I have just referred: I begin by freeing myself from these entities, but I do not put them completely aside; 3rd degree: they disappear completely, and all that is left is the fact' (letter to Pantaleoni of 28 December 1899, in Pareto 1984, vol. II: 290–291).

References

Auspitz, R. and Lieben, R. (1889) *Untersuchungen über die Theorie des Preises*, Leipzig: Ducker & Humblot.

Auspitz, R. and Lieben, R. (1890) 'Lettre' [Reply to Walras], *Revue d'économie politique*, 4: 599–605.

Bortkievicz, L. (1890) 'Review of Léon Walras, *Eléments d'économie politique pure*', *Revue d'économie politique*, 4: 80–86.

Busino, G. (1987) 'Vilfredo Pareto (1848–1923)', in J. Eatwell, M. Milgate and P. Newman (eds), *The New Palgrave: A Dictionary of Economics*, vol. III, London: Macmillan, pp. 799–804.

Busino, G. (1989) *L'Italia di Vilfredo Pareto. Economia e società in un carteggio 1873–1923*, Milano: Banca Commerciale Italiana.

Chipman, J. S. (1976) 'The Paretian Heritage', *Revue européenne des sciences sociales. Cahiers Vilfredo Pareto*, 14 (37): 65–173.

Edgeworth, F. Y. (1881) *Mathematical Psychics: An Essay on the Application of Mathematics to the Moral Sciences*, London: Kegan Paul & Co.

Edgeworth, F. Y. (1889a) 'On the application of mathematics to political economy', *Journal of the Royal Statistical Society* 52: 538–576. Republished in R. Marchionatti (ed.) (2004) *Early Mathematical Economics 1871–1915*, vol. II, London: Routledge, pp. 126–157.

Edgeworth, F. Y. (1889b) 'The mathematical theory of political economy' [Review of Walras], *Nature* 40 (5 September): 434–436. Republished in R. Marchionatti (ed.) (2004) *Early Mathematical Economics 1871–1915*, vol. II, London: Routledge, pp. 168–170.

Edgeworth, F. Y. (1891) 'La théorie mathématique de l'offre et de la demande et le coût de production', *Revue d'économie politique* 5: 10–28. Republished in R. Marchionatti (ed.) (2004) *Early Mathematical Economics 1871–1915*, vol. II, London: Routledge, pp. 177–191.

Fisher, I. (1892) *Mathematical Investigations in the Theory of Value and Prices*, Transactions of the Connecticut Academy of Arts and Sciences No. 9, New Haven, CT: Connecticut Academy of Arts and Sciences.

Hicks, J. R. and Allen, R. G. D. (1934) 'A reconsideration of the theory of value', *Economica*, 1. Part I: February, 1(1): 52–76; Part II: May, 1(2): 196–219.

Jaffé, W. (1977) 'A centenarian of a bicentenarian: Léon Walras's *Eléments* on Adam Smith's *Wealth of Nations*', *Canadian Journal of Economics*, 10: 19–33.

Malandrino, C. and Marchionatti, R. (eds) (2000) *Economia, sociologia e politica nell'opera di Vilfredo Pareto*, Firenze: Olschki.

Marchionatti, R. (1999) 'The methodological foundations of pure and applied economics in Pareto. An anti-Walrasian programme', *Revue européenne des sciences sociales. Cahiers Vilfredo Pareto*, 37: 277–294.

Marchionatti, R. (ed.) (2004) *Early Mathematical Economics, 1871–1915*, four vols, London: Routledge.

Marchionatti, R. (forthcoming, 2007) ' "On the application of mathematics to political economy". The Walras–Bortkievicz–Edgeworth controversy, 1889–1891', *Cambridge Journal of Economics*.

Marchionatti, R. and Gambino, E. (1997a) 'Pareto and political economy as a science: methodological revolution and analytical advances in the 1890s', *Journal of Political Economy*, 105: 1322–1348.

Marchionatti, R. and Gambino, E. (1997b) 'The contributions of Vilfredo Pareto to the new theories of economics in the years of the *Cours d'économie politique*', *History of Economic Ideas*, 3: 49–64.

Marchionatti, R. and Mornati, F. (2003) 'Pareto et l'économie mathématique au début des années '90. Quelques réflections à propos des "Considerazioni sui principii fondamentali dell'economia politica pura" ', in *Histoire et théorie des sciences sociales. Mélanges en l'honneur de Giovanni Busino*, sous la direction de Mohamed Cherkaoui, Geneva: Librairie Droz.

Marshall, A. (1879) *The Pure Theory of Foreign Trade. The Pure Theory of Domestic Values*, Cambridge: privately printed.

Marshall, A. (1890) *Principles of Economics*, London: Macmillan.

Marshall, A. (1891) *Principles of Economics* (2nd edn), London: Macmillan.

Mill, J. S. (1843) *A System of Logic, Ratiocinative and Inductive, Being a Connected View of the Principles of Evidence and the Methods of Scientific Investigation*, London: Parker.

Mornati, F. (1997) 'The pure economics of Pareto before the *Cours d'économie politique*', *History of Economic Ideas*, 3: 89–102.

Mornati, F. (1999) 'Le début des différends entre Pareto and Walras vu à travers leur correspondence et leur ouvrages, 1891–1893', *Revue européenne des sciences sociales. Cahiers Vilfredo Pareto*, 37: 261–275.

Mornati, F. (2000) 'Gustave de Molinari e Yves Guyot nella formazione del pensiero paretiano fino al *Cours d'économie politique*', in C. Malandrino and R. Marchionatti (eds), op. cit., pp. 247–271.

Mornati, F. (2007) 'Vilfredo Pareto's correspondence as a significant source for the knowledge of his economic thought', in R. Leeson (ed.) (forthcoming) *Archival Insights into the Evolution of Economics*, New York: Palgrave Macmillan.

Pantaleoni, M. (1890) 'Dell'ammontare probabile della ricchezza privata in Italia dal 1872 al 1889', *Giornale degli Economisti*, August: 139–176.

Pareto, V. (1892), 'Di un errore del Cournot nel trattare l'economia politica colla matematica', *Giornale degli Economisti*, 4: 1–14.

Pareto, V. (1892–1893), 'Considerazioni sui principi fondamentali dell'economia pura', *Giornale degli Economisti*, 4: 389–420, 485–512; 5: 119–57; 6: 1–37; 7: 279–321.

Pareto, V. (1896–1897), *Cours d'économie politique*, 2 vols, Lausanne: Rouge.

Pareto, V. (1897) 'The new theories of economics', *Journal of Political Economy*, 5: 485–502.

Pareto, V. (1898) 'Comment se pose le problème de l'économie pure', Lausanne: Société Stella. Reprinted in *Marxisme et économie pure*, vol. IX of *Oeuvres complètes*, ed. Giovanni Busino, Geneva: Droz, 1966.

Pareto, V. (1900a) 'Sunto di alcuni capitoli di un nuovo trattato di economia pura', *Giornale degli Economisti*, 25: 401–433.

Pareto, V. (1900b) 'Sul fenomeno economico. Lettera a Benedetto Croce', *Giornale degli economisti*, 21: 139–162. Reprinted in *Ecrits d'économie politique pure*, vol. XXVI of *Oeuvres complètes*, ed. Giovanni Busino, Genève: Droz, 1982. English translation: 'On the economic phenomenon: a reply to Benedetto Croce', in *International Economic Papers*, vol. 3, London: Macmillan, 1953.

Pareto, V. (1906a) 'Applicazioni della matematica all'economia politica', *Giornale degli Economisti*, November: 545–574. [Originally the article was published in 1902 in *Encyklopedie der Matematischen Wissenschaften*, Leipzig: Teubner, and then translated into Italian by Guido Sensini].

Pareto, V. (1906b) *Manuale d'economia politica*, Milano: Società editrice libraria. New edition ed. A. Montesano, A. Zanni and L. Bruni, Milano: Università Bocconi Editore, 2006.

Pareto, V. (1909) *Manuel d'économie politique*, Paris: Giard et Brière. English translation: *Manual of Political Economy*, ed. A. S. Schweir and A. N. Page, New York: August M. Kelley, 1971.

Pareto, V. (1911) 'Economie mathématique', in *Encyclopédie des sciences mathématiques*, Paris: GauthierVillars. English translation: 'Mathematical economics', *International Economic Papers*, 5 (1955): 58–102.

Pareto, V. (1984) *Lettere a Maffeo Pantaleoni 1890–1923*, vol. XXVIII of *Oeuvres complètes*, ed. G. De Rosa, Genève: Droz.

Schumpeter, J. A. (1954) *History of Economic Analysis*, New York: Oxford University Press.

Slutsky, Eugen (1915) 'Sulla teoria del bilancio del consumatore', *Giornale degli Economisti*, 51: 1–26. English translation: 'On the theory of the budget of the consumer', in G. Stigler and K. Boulding (eds) (1952) *Readings in Price Theory*, Homewood, IL: Irwin, pp. 27–56.

Walras, L. (1889) *Eléments d'économie politique pure* (2nd edn), Lausanne: Corbaz.

Walras, L. (1890) 'Observations sur le principe de la théorie du prix de MM. Auspitz et Lieben', *Revue d'économie politique*, 4: 320–323.

Walras, L. (1965) *Correspondence of Léon Walras and Related Papers*, ed. W. Jaffé, 3 vols, Amsterdam: North Holland.

Weber, C. E. (2001) 'Pareto and the 53 per cent ordinal theory of utility', *History of Political Economy*, 33: 541–576.

Note on the translation

Dr Vincenzo Savini (University of Western Australia) and Prof. John Kinder (University of Western Australia) translated the 'Considerazioni' under the supervision of Roberto Marchionatti (University of Torino) and Fiorenzo Mornati (University of Torino and Centre Walras-Pareto, University of Lausanne), together with the help of Michael McLure (University of Western Australia), in the context of a two-year research programme on economics and mathematics in the history of economics directed by Roberto Marchionatti and financed by the Italian Ministry of Education, University and Research, in 2004–2005.

Also, please note that the editors' notes run sequentially through both Pareto's text and his original notes.

1 Considerations on the fundamental principles of Pure Political Economy, I

(*Giornale degli Economisti*, May 1892)

Introductory remarks

In keeping with the general propensity of natural sciences to progress towards a higher degree of perfection, Political Economy has for some years now been showing a tendency to replace the qualitative method used in its beginnings with the quantitative one.

In fact, one could not say that economists have until now neglected the quantitative principle, in the same way ancient physics never totally did; but its use by economists was always limited, whereas now it is increasing and becoming prevalent in the study of economics.

If we consider what has happened to the other sciences, we shall easily come to the conclusion that Political Economy would not extract a lesser benefit from the use of the quantitative method than the one they attained. However, if we do not wish to forgo all necessary prudence, we must at the same time add that one should not deem any method as good or any theorem derived from it as true only because it carries the 'quantitative' label.

In our view, all arguments regarding the method that should be adopted in a particular science are somewhat useless. Only from experience can one find out the benefit that can be attained from using a given method. Employ whatever reasoning method you prefer, seek the support of history, physics, mathematics, accept or reject the evolutionary theories, and, if ancient logic does not satisfy you, apply the new mathematical logic; all is allowed, all is fair, provided you can discover new truths, or shed new light on old ones, and rectify errors; in short, if you can increase the quantity or the quality of human knowledge. Here the public lies in wait, and your work will be judged according to the new ideas it divulges.

If it is to be found later, that it is possible to arrive at the goal that you have reached through an easier path, such a path will replace the method you used, but without taking anything away from the praise you deserve for having increased our scientific wealth. Celestial mechanics treatises no longer make use of the synthetic form of Newton's demonstrations,[1] but this has not detracted from the reverence and admiration that every mathematical scientist feels for that man, whose genius was certainly equal, if not greater than any of the most outstanding human beings.

On the other hand, considerations on methodology are not only legitimate, but also necessary, when they arise as a consequence of the quest to find whether a proposition is true or not. If a theorem seems right to some scientists but is not, it is not a waste of time to search for the reasons for their mistake, in order to avoid it in the future.[1] It is still necessary diligently to examine the premises of any new proposition, and the quantity and the quality of the rigour of the deductions that stem from it.

Difficulty of the topic

Anyone who wishes to learn any science, such as physics or mathematics, knows that it will imply hard work, and while they can ask the author whom they are studying to ease the burden, they cannot expect it to be completely removed, as some people seem to expect in the study of Political Economy, which is accused by Thiers[III] of being 'a kind of boring literature' – as if in the study of any science one should pursue one's personal enjoyment, rather than the usefulness and pleasure of acquiring the knowledge of new truths.

The reader who wishes to acquire wholesome and precise concepts of the theorems of economics must shed all such prejudices. In turn, the author must make sure that the difficulties of the topic are not increased through his fault, and that the reader is not subjected to more hard work than is required by the very nature of the subject matter.

Explanation of the ways that have been followed in this work

In order to fulfil this duty of ours, we have deemed it appropriate to make use of some little devices that we shall now explain to the reader.

There is no mathematics used in the paragraphs printed in large font, which we have attempted to construct in such a way that they may stand alone, without the mathematical part, which is printed in small font. In doing this, we have followed Marshall's example; he consigns the exposition of the mathematical propositions to the footnotes.[IV]

Those who do not wish to read the parts where mathematics is used, will have to accept their conclusions as they would accept the testimony of a trustworthy witness. But it is necessary, for that, to have another principle, which we have tried to apply consistently, by giving space exclusively in the paragraphs written in large font to anything that might [not] be the object of economic controversy. From time to time this has not been possible, and in those cases, we have pointed it out to the reader.

We should also say a few words about the comparisons, whose number some may perhaps see as excessive. Since it is only from the experience of the past that men can find reliable guidance for the future, we believe it necessary to take into account the tests and trials made in other sciences by various methods of reasoning, so that we may discern a correct way of using that method in the science of economics.

Such comparisons could have been taken either from the moral sciences, or from the sciences of physics and mathematics. In favour of the former kind of comparisons is the advantage of being easily understood by all; against, that it is not easy to find any that may not lead to controversy. We have therefore chosen the latter kind of comparisons; they are much more reliable, though with the drawback that fewer people can easily understand them. The paragraphs containing such comparisons will be marked with an asterisk [*].

Various quantitative methods

It is necessary to distinguish between essentially different things, such as: the use of quantitative considerations in general, the higher degree of rigour in demonstrations, the use of mathematical methods in demonstrations and, in particular, the use of analytical and geometric methods.[V]

* Not all quantitative sciences are also mathematical. With its atomic theory, chemistry has become an almost entirely quantitative science, after having already come close to becoming one with the theory of definite proportions, but it is not yet a mathematical science. Statistics is definitely a quantitative science and it is on the point of becoming mathematical as well, but on this subject there are still treatises that make little or no use of mathematical symbols.

An empirical quantitative method is already in use in the science of economics, with the ever-increasing habit of verifying the propositions of this science through statistically derived information. For example, one can no longer simply state that a very heavy tax causes a decrease in the consumption of the targeted goods, but one is also required to know of practical cases where that effect of the law has actually been observed.

The treatise on Political Economy published in 1887 by Mr Yves Guyot[VI] has nearly half of its pages taken up by diagrams and by numerical tables. Quite rightly, Prof. Marshall states that 'many of the faults, many of the injustices that are the consequence of the economic policies of governments arise from the lack of statistical information'.[2]

But this method, however excellent in verifying theorems found in other ways, taken by itself could only lead to empirical propositions;[3] consequently, it is crucial to take advantage of the deductive method first. It is therefore natural that many economists are turning to the most perfect form of the latter, i.e. the quantitative method, and are looking for help in it.

As we all know, by acting in such a way other sciences obtained great benefit. The path they followed was always the same. Some hypotheses were put forward; from them, through logical or mathematical deductions – which is the same thing, since mathematics is nothing but a type of logic – some consequences were obtained; the latter were then compared with information gathered from observation or from experience, and were acknowledged to be true. Only from that, and nothing else, did the postulated hypotheses acquire credit and authority.

To recall these things, when they are by now universally known, might seem redundant, but we need these principles to help us wholly to understand some of the statements of the new science of economics.[4]

For instance, after demonstrating how one can infer the way of achieving price equilibrium from the principles of Pure Economics, Prof. Walras goes on to say:

> Quelques critiques se sont pourtant égayés du nombre de pages que j'employais à démontrer qu'on doit arriver au prix courant en faisant la hausse en cas d'éxcédent de la demand sur l'offre, et la baisse en cas d'éxcédent de l'offre sur la demande.
>
> Et vous, ais-je dit une fois à l'un d'eux, comment le démontrez-vous? – Mais, me répondit-il, un peu surpris, et même assez embarassé, cela a-t'il besoin d'être démontré? Il me semble que c'est une chose évidente. – Il n'y a d'évident que les axiomes, et ce n'en est pas un.[5]
>
> [Some critics, nevertheless, have laughed at the number of pages that I found necessary to demonstrate that one must arrive at the current price by making it increase in the case of excess demand relative to supply and making it diminish in the case of excess supply relative to demand. And you, I once said to one of these critics, how would you demonstrate it? But, he responded to me a little surprised and also rather embarrassed; is there a need to demonstrate it? It seems obvious to me. Only the axioms are obvious and this is not.]

Now if, by saying that, Prof. Walras simply meant to attack those who have the impudence of passing off as demonstrations the expression of their feelings, then he was right. However, his words would rather seem to indicate a wish to lead science on a metaphysical path, where reasoning dominates experience; in this case we must confess that it was his interlocutor who was right, only he did not defend himself well. He should have said that it is from direct observation that we deduce the law about prices rising when demand is greater than supply, and vice versa. And he should have added:

> Since these are elementary, simple, direct observations, if you no longer wish to take them as the basis of your reasoning, but as its consequences, then you must show that the replacements are more elementary, simpler and more direct.

We are not saying now whether this is true or not, but Prof. Walras does not ask the question in these terms, and when he shows his belief[6] that the day will come when 'all sciences will blend together into a science that will be metaphysics', he sets off on a path that no follower of the experimental method will be able to tread after him. He would therefore prove Dr Ingram[XIII] right, who in the new science of economics detects the fault 'of restoring the metaphysical entities that had already been purged from science'. As for us, if we were convinced of this, we would side with the opponents of the new science, such is the light we see radiating from the experimental method, from which alone men have learned the few truths they now know. In fact, we prefer to believe Prof. Edgeworth's opinion to be true, according to which one should deem mathematical economics to be as far from Dr Ingram's interpretation as it is from Gossen's, who compares the new science to astronomy;[7] these considerations are indeed aimed at illustrating the opinion of that learned English professor.

Various degrees of rationality in the principles assumed as the basis of this science

The experimental method should not be confused with the empirical method, and it is not necessary for us to dwell on something that can be ascertained by reading any treatise on logic.

In Political Economy, therefore, as in any other science, one must always find a way to go back to the more general and more rational causes, but every step must be taken with the utmost caution, leaving the firm ground of observation to soar into the unreliable realm of abstraction only for the shortest possible time.

Marshall takes a big step, and he builds the science of economics on few principles; but Walras and the German school[XIV] go even further. They create a whole science from nothing, out of a single postulate – the hedonistic one. In this respect, the science of economics could be seen as being similar to astronomy, which rests entirely on a single principle.

This attempt is worthy of great consideration and careful study. Even if this work does not turn out to be perfect, one can rest assured that it will be of some benefit to the science of economics, were it only for the increased rigour and precision that the demonstrations of that science will derive from it.

However, all this does not detract from the merit of economists such as Smith, Mill, J.-B. Say,[XV] Ricardo, Ferrara,[XVI] and many others, to whom we owe all the truths we know in the science of economics. The new school does not always do them justice, and though understandable – since, being under attack, it strives to return blow for blow – this is not acceptable.

Classic economics is found wanting in the areas of form, precision and demonstration rigour, but in actual fact we think these are very small flaws.

The metaphysical concept of absolute perfection, which played a major role in preventing the ancients from considering concrete truths, and led them into the dreams of metaphysics, continues to cause damage in many sciences, among which we must include Political Economy. Recognizing a truth and providing a perfect proof of it are two quite different things. Almost every theorem we know was demonstrated in ways that were later replaced by better ones, without taking anything away from the discoverer's merit.

* Among the countless examples, suffice it to mention that until the beginning of this century, mathematicians used series without trying to demonstrate their convergence. But this is certainly not a good enough reason to detract from the fame of scientists such as D'Alembert,[XVII] Bernoulli,[XVIII] Euler, Lagrange[XIX] and Laplace.[XX]

* In his course of analysis,[8] Mr Hermite[XXI] does a calculation in which he says that he is using a well-known method devised by Laplace for certain approximate integrations. But anyone who checks that method in the *Teoria Analitica delle Probabilità*,[XXII] will soon find that, while Hermite's demonstration is rigorous – as any by every other modern mathematician – Laplace's demonstration is not rigorous at all. Nevertheless, Hermite does not even mention this fact, rightly judging, in our opinion, that the few words that must be added to Laplace's demonstrations to give them the necessary rigour are of little importance, compared to the results achieved by that most accomplished mathematician.

It is especially the concept of value that the new school sees as being wrong in the economists of the classic school. And we believe that many of the remarks made by Walras about the theories of Smith's and J.-B. Say do hit the mark. But if these economists did not use perfectly correct expressions, if they even made mistakes in looking for the true cause of value, this did not prevent them from discovering its laws, and after all, this is essentially what mattered most.

The times of ontology have gone, and all sciences now study the concrete properties of things without caring much about knowing their essence. It is necessary to abandon the concept, found in Plato, that in order to discuss correctly about any thing, one must first know its true nature. The value that goods have on the market is a fact; we can look for its laws without knowing from where that fact originates. It goes without saying that if someone is able to connect that fact to another, more general fact, that will be all the better for our science.

* Astronomers do not care much at all about the true nature of gravity, and one day much bigger mistakes will perhaps be found in some of their ideas on this topic, than those for which Prof. Walras reproaches Smith and J.-B. Say.

* Carnot, who is credited with the second principle of thermodynamics,[XXIII] did not express himself correctly in expounding it, and, not knowing the first principle,[XXIV] he made the mistake of believing that heat would not transform into work. Nevertheless, that second principle still bears the name of its illustrious discoverer, whose work was later brought to perfection.

Use of mathematics in Political Economy

The German school has above all else turned its attention to investigating from where value originates. Jevons[XXV] and Cournot[XXVI] have started using mathematical analysis in Political Economy, and this use has been vastly expanded by Walras, whose work is and will always be worthy of great consideration. In his book *Mathematical Psychics*,[XXVII] Prof. Edgeworth elegantly shows the merits of the mathematical method in the moral sciences. In his studies on Political Economy, Prof. Marshall uses it sparingly, but often to great effect; and there is no dearth of excellent scientists who are following the same path.[9]

This fact alone should suffice to give authority to the mathematical method, and one cannot read the *Pure theory of foreign trade*[XXIX] by Marshall without admiring the elegance and the effectiveness of its demonstrations, and without acknowledging that by now, that theory can be positively said to have been brought to perfection by the illustrious English author.

In the mathematical method one has to take great care in distinguishing three things: the greater rigour of the demonstrations, which is typical of this type of logic; the use of the analytical method; and the use of the geometric method.

The greater rigour of the demonstrations may often be only apparent; on this topic, we refer the reader to those words of Poinsot's[XXX] which we quoted in a previous article,[10] where we also stated our opinion on the merits of the geometric method, and we shall not go back to it.

Precautions required by the use of the mathematical method

The use of this method, both analytical and geometric, must always be accompanied by extreme caution, and the more the reasoning tends to become almost a mechanical operation – as happens when using algebraic symbols – the greater become the probabilities of errors, which derive from the uncertainty of the premises.

When we are reasoning according to usual logic, in passing from one proposition to another we can examine it, and if we find it to be in contrast with the concepts we hold true, we stop and decide whether we must modify the concepts or reject the proposition. But the use of the mathematical method – especially the algebraic, less so the geometric – prevents us from doing so. The intermediate propositions escape our perception; we only know the two extreme ones. We can state that one logically follows from the other, but we do not know if along the way we have strayed too far from reality.

Now, and this is an important point to make, all any science can do is to approximate reality, without ever being able wholly to encompass it.

The phenomenon studied by science is always an ideal phenomenon, which sometimes comes extremely close to the real phenomenon, but never entirely coincides with it; hence the necessity to compare our deductions with experience or with observation as often as possible, to make sure that we have not strayed too much from the facts of nature.

This is all that is true in the common remark that theory and practice are two different things. But to conclude that theory should be rejected is a foolish thing, if not ignorance or bad faith. In this way every human science would be discredited, and there is no need to recall all the sophisms at which the ancients arrived through this path. The true conclusion is that it is necessary to proceed cautiously and always to go back to experience and observation.

* We shall express our concept in a better way by reasoning on a concrete example. Let us consider the fall of bodies, which is precisely the example chosen by Walras[XXXIII] to show how mathematics is used in the study of natural phenomena.

The problem of the fall of bodies to the surface of the earth looks extremely simple, but not even that problem is completely solved. We have only studied various abstract phenomena that more or less approximate the real one.

* The first and simplest is the case of a material point, or even, if one wishes, of a sphere falling in a vacuum, assuming that the intensity of gravity is constant for the whole duration of the fall, and that the part played in the phenomenon by the rotation of the earth is irrelevant.

* The formulae recalled by Prof. Walras in the introduction to his book *Elements d'Economie Politique* are in relation to this very case. The real phenomenon of a platinum sphere falling to the surface of the earth is very close to the abstract phenomenon.

* But the latter differs from the natural phenomenon in two ways. First of all we must take into account that the body is not falling in a vacuum but through air. The air causes the body to lose some of its weight, and in the case of the oscillations of a pendulum, it has also been calculated how such loss varies according to whether the body is at rest or swinging. All these phenomena depend on the temperature of the air and on that of the body. Furthermore, we have the resistance of the air; and we are stopped here in our very first few steps by the difficulty of the topic. The rational theory of the phenomenon is very imperfect, the empiric theory is worth little more. If we take away the case of spheres and of a few more bodies of very simple shapes, we do not know anything about the resistance of the air.

* Then, even ignoring the air, we see that the study of this phenomenon becomes progressively more difficult. Let us even not bother with fixing the direction of the vertical, which gives rise to important studies, but gravity varies according to latitude and to the distance of the body from the earth. The main parts of these phenomena can be easily known through calculations, but studying them in such a way as to exhaust the subject in all its details involves considerable difficulties. One has also to take into account the

rotation of the earth. Finally, in theory, one should also consider the attraction of celestial bodies. And then, if we are dealing not with a material point, but with a solid body, the study becomes even more difficult. Luckily, in practical terms many of these phenomena are absolutely negligible, but this does not mean they do not exist, demonstrating that the real phenomenon is different from the abstract phenomena we can study.

* The example we are now dealing with is also very good for allowing us fully to appreciate the difference between the empirical method and the experimental – or *concrete deductive*, as Mill calls it – method.[XXXIV]

* Theory tells us that a mass falling from a great height must deviate to the east of the vertical. There is also a deviation to the south, but it is in the order of the square of the speed of the rotation of the earth, and it is therefore too small to be observed. The deviation to the east falls instead within the limits of quantities we can actually observe. Many attempts were made to verify the conclusions of the theory through experience. Abbot Guglielmini[XXXV] managed to discover these deviations in 1790, by conducting experiments in the *Torre degli Asinelli*, in Bologna. Other experiments were conducted by Dr Benzenberg[XXXVI] in Hamburg and in a mine at Schlebush, and more still by Prof. Reich[XXXVII] in the mines at Freiberg. All these experiments show a tendency by falling bodies to deviate to the east, but none of them can be said to agree entirely with the theory,[11] so that yet again one should repeat Laplace's words about the objections that were once moved against Galileo:[XXXIX] 'In recording the influence of the rotation of the earth in the fall of bodies, we find as many difficulties now as were found then in trying to demonstrate that that influence was not significant'.

* However, no physicist has any doubt whatsoever about the results of the theory. Is the experimental method being abandoned because of this? Most certainly not. But, even without taking into account direct experiences such as Foucault's[XL] pendulum or the gyroscope, the movement of the earth is proved by such a large number of observations, that we must accept the consequences that derive from it, even when they perchance escape our direct observation.

Similarly, we accept that theoretical Political Economy may set up theorems that cannot be directly verified through observation, provided that these are a necessary consequence of principles that elsewhere find broad and effective demonstration from experience, which is therefore always guiding us, either by directly leading us to the truth, or by indirectly letting us know it.

We have seen that our premises are never entirely, but only approximately true; we must add that conclusions are not always as close to reality as premises, but may sometimes end up very far from it.

We believe it is possible to give examples of this proposition without making use of the science of quantities; but here we are on the boundaries of its domain, and therefore we cross them without hesitation.

An equation

$$y = \varphi(x)$$

is nothing but the conclusion of a reasoning, whose premises are some qualities and the measurements of x and y. Now, it is generally true that to a slight variation of x corresponds a slight variation of y, but it is also known that this is false in many cases. Let us suppose, for instance, that by indicating with a the quantity of one kilogram, one has found[12]

$$y = e^{\frac{1}{x-a}};$$

then, if x is equal to one kilogram and one milligram, it will be possible to conclude that y is very large, since it will be equal to 2.71828 . . . to the power of one thousand. Who would believe now, if they did not know any mathematics, that by changing the premise in a minimal way, namely by supposing that x is equal to one kilogram minus one milligram, the conclusion changes completely and y becomes very small? And yet this is exactly how things are, and y is equal to one divided by 2.71878 . . . to the power of one thousand.

In this case, mathematics also shows us the reason for the difference between the conclusions, since it tells us that beside the absolute value of x, one must also bear in mind the crucial circumstance whether that value is greater or smaller than a.

* Theoretical mechanics teaches us how to calculate the pressure on each foot of a three-legged table. But if the legs are four, the problem becomes indeterminate. The geometricians who first confronted the question found this fact quite puzzling. How could indeterminateness ever exist in nature, with regard to the weight supported by each of the four feet of a table? The answer can now be found in any basic treatise of mechanics. The indeterminateness ceases to exist when one stops considering rigid bodies, as theoretical mechanics would like them to be, and starts considering elastic bodies instead, as they are in nature.

Who could deny, now, that similar cases may arise, when one considers people not as shrewd and perfect hedonists, as pure Political Economy would like them to be, but with that mixture of hedonistic and altruistic qualities of shrewdness and carelessness as we observe them in real life?

The theorem that the pressure on each of the four feet of a table is indeterminate is not more or less close to reality, it is actually false. How, then, can we ever make sure that the theorems of Pure Economics will not lead us to similar mistakes, other than by sticking very closely to observation?

A priori objections to the new theory

On the other hand, by pushing such fear too far, some fall into the opposite mistake. 'Your principles' they say to the followers of the new science, 'are not true in an absolute way, therefore your conclusions are not worthy of credit, and we do not care about them.'

We do not believe that to state that the mathematical method does not have to be subject to experience is an appropriate answer to this objection.

* Physicists who study the theory of light would avoid a great deal of hard work, if they could do without having to confirm their deductions through experience.[13] The theory of vibrations in ether tells us that in an anisotropic elastic environment, every plane wave gives rise to three types of vibrations parallel to the axes of the polarization ellipsoid. Experience confirms the existence of two of these types of vibrations, but the third cannot be found. No geometrician has ever entertained the thought of dominating experience with his theories. On the contrary, all have looked for ways to change the theory, in order to obtain exactly what experience provides. This is why the theory of light is still imperfect, and it would not be surprising if the time should come when the ether hypothesis were abandoned. But if this hypothesis is to survive in the world of science, it will only be by having all of its conclusions justified by experience.

The right answer for those who condemn the new science a priori is to remark that such an objection could be levelled at any science. Even in mathematics, the doubt arises whether the three-dimensional space we know is the only one that exists! The principles of no science are true in an absolute way, and even if one wishes to argue about this matter, one must discuss it in general terms, but there is no reason specifically to target Political Economy.

Value

Object of a theory of value

The real facts which we can observe are the sales of some commodities for which certain prices are paid. The object of a theory of value cannot consist in anything but explaining these facts, connecting them, and showing them as a consequence of one or a few principles.

The empirical path is the one that would lead us to gather a great amount of data on the prices, to put them together, and to see if it is possible to infer any law from them. We agree that by using this method, which Mill calls *chemical*,[14] it is not possible to achieve any truly rational law, although it is still always very useful to have such data and the empirical laws, which can be of assistance as a first step in the search for truth.

The geometrical or abstract method[15] does not care about those facts; it sets certain axioms on the nature of men and it infers how the phenomenon of value *must* follow. Not even through this path do we believe that it is possible to achieve the truth; on the contrary, we judge it more fallacious than the previous one.

Finally, the 'concrete deductive' method assumes certain hypotheses in order to ascertain whether they are true or not. To this end, it infers from them the laws of value, which it then compares with the natural facts, and, according to whether they agree or disagree, it accepts or modifies or totally rejects the hypotheses.

As long as we stick to a general outlook, no one will perhaps oppose these observations, which in fact will be deemed superfluous here, being well known. But when it comes to the details, things are not going be so smooth, and one will easily end up using those reasonings that would earlier have been excluded in general terms. In the new school there is a certain tendency to subordinate experience to the school's theories, and this is where the greatest danger for the new school lies; it is therefore a good thing to try in every possible way to avoid it.

It will be better for us to reason on a real example. Figure 1.1 shows the prices of cast iron (warrants) in Glasgow over many years.

A perfect theory of value would be one that, when all the circumstances of the market were known, with the only exception being the prices of cast iron, would allow us to calculate those prices in such a way as to replicate the diagram precisely.

* Astronomy had to act in a similar way, in order to rise to the degree of perfection it has achieved in our times. Without Kepler, or some other person

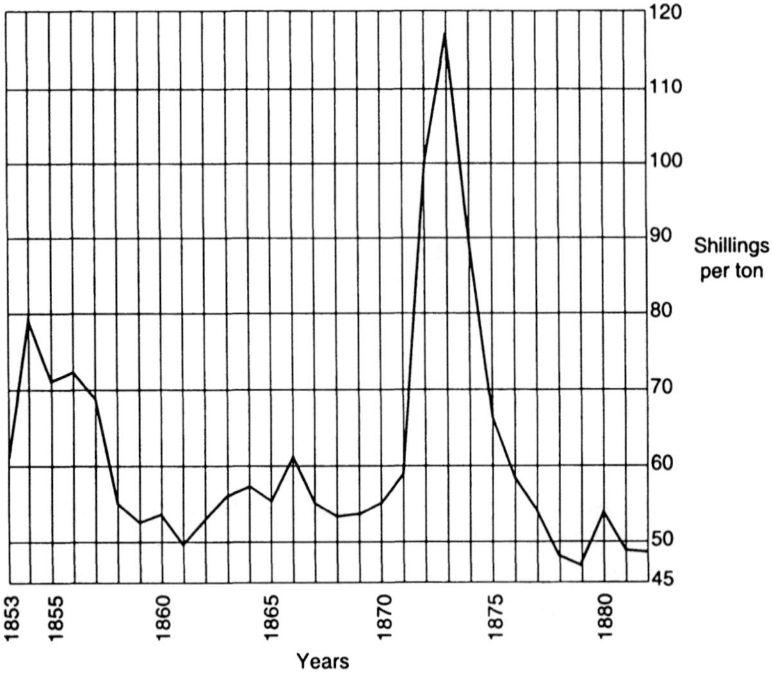

Figure 1.1 Average annual prices of warrants

who might have done the work he did in his stead, astronomy would not exist. The price diagram we have outlined does not look, and is not, very regular, but neither was the trajectory of Mars easy to know. See in Kepler's works the vivid description he gives of the hard work he had to endure:

> At the moment when, with this half triumph about the movements of Mars, and in the belief that I had conquered it, I am preparing diagrams and equations to lock it up, I am told it is somewhere else. Empty victory! One must go back and renew the terrible fight, since the enemy I had captive, in chains, like a neglected prisoner, has snapped the ropes of my equations and has escaped from my numerical diagrams.

On the other hand, we are far from being able to do for the value curves, what Kepler did for the curve traced by Mars; in fact, one could perhaps say that it will never be humanly possible to do so. It is therefore necessary to find some way to make the problem easier.

Let us remark, in the meanwhile, that as irregular as our diagram may be, the real facts are even more so. They consist of individual sales, and whatever average we calculate is arbitrary, and it replaces a real phenomenon with an ideal one. But it is necessary to follow this path, and we would be quite happy, even if we could only find the law of variations pertaining to very broad averages, ignoring any particular fact.

But this is not enough. A general law of value should include as particular cases the law of the value of wheat, as well as that of bread and that of pastries; the law of the value of coal, as well as that of the value of that handful of diamonds whose extraordinary worth has gained them worldwide fame. Is it possible to find such a law? And if it is not, is it not helpful to divide the subject into categories and examine each of them separately?

This is what has always been done, and is still being done, both by classic economics and by the new school, but is at times forgotten, as it happens with Thornton,[XLIII] who levels many objections at the theory of value, some of which stem only from his extending laws to retail sales, that only apply to wholesale.

But, besides the study of the various parts of the phenomenon, there has also been a search for general laws. The new school is clearly showing a tendency to venture on this path further than the classic school.

The new school considers a *homo œconomicus* that is a perfect hedonist, and studies the Political Economy of this abstract being.[16] This method is logically irreprehensible, provided one does not forget that every time we revert to the real world, we have to show that the laws we have found in the case of the abstract men we studied are valid in it.

* Pure Political Economy is somewhat similar to theoretical mechanics. The latter defines the abstract entity it calls *material point*, and then the other entity that goes by the name of *rigid system*, or *solid body*; these definitions are enough to warn us that the conclusions of that science will apply to a

natural phenomenon only to the extent that the quality studied by theoretical mechanics is paramount in it. As we progressively want to consider other properties of natural bodies, we are forced to create new abstractions. The perfect elastic body has no more real existence than the perfect rigid body. In nature, there are some bodies that are almost isotropic, but none that is perfectly so.

It is advisable, therefore, that we analyse very closely what are the explicit as well as the implicit postulates of the arguments of the new Political Economy, in order to know how far, and when, its laws will be applicable in the real world.

The hedonistic theory

Prof. Edgeworth has succeeded in expounding the new theory in the most general way and with the rigour of mathematics, and, whatever change time may bring to it, his book, entitled *Mathematical Psychics*, will always be worthy of careful study.

Prof. Edgeworth[17] openly states that he considers man as a *pleasure machine*. He divides the calculus of pleasure in two parts: the economic calculus, which investigates the equilibrium of a system of hedonistic forces, each tending to procure the greatest good for each individual; and the *utilitarian calculus*, which investigates the equilibrium of a system where each and all of the forces tend to procure the greatest benefit for all.

In this way, not only Political Economy, but also the science of human society becomes a branch of the calculus of variations.

This concept is wonderfully simple and grand at the same time. And it seems to us that there is much truth in it, but for this very reason it is necessary to proceed very carefully, in order not to draw conclusions which, should they be found to be contrary to experience, could spoil and be cause for the rejection of both the good and the bad that the new theories contain.

We shall say nothing on altruistic feelings since they are opposed to the egoistic feelings that the hedonistic theory assumes, not because the topic is irrelevant, but only because it seems to us almost exhausted, after all that economists and philosophers have already said about it. At this point, we would rather make two general remarks, to which we shall often have to come back in particular cases.

The first is that it would be useful to explain more clearly what is meant by *pleasure*, that is, to consider what is found pleasing in *general*, or in average terms.

Otherwise one runs the risk of being caught in circular reasoning. If we define a thing as 'pleasing', provided any one man likes it, only from the actions of that man shall we be able to know what is and what is not pleasing to him; and it is not acceptable, later, to explain those very actions through the pleasure they afford the man.

The second remark is that it is not enough to give *homo œconomicus* the quality of being a perfect hedonist, but it is also necessary to decide what qualities of foresight, reasonableness, etc. are to be granted to him. We shall see that he is implicitly supposed to be endowed with such qualities to a certain extent. And we do not think this is right, since postulates must always be stated in an explicit way.

Total utility and final degree of utility

Let us consider an individual and two economic goods *A* and *B*, of which he owns a certain quantity. He can directly enjoy *A*, or indirectly *transform* it into *B*. And similarly for *B*. Barter is one way to achieve that transformation, but not the only one.

This principle of the transformation and equivalence of goods informs the geometrical method with which Prof. Walras demonstrates the fundamental theorem of barter,[18] and the elegance and the lucidity of his exposition are superb.

In the transformation of *A* into *B*, the number of units of *A* that must be transformed in order to have one unit of *B* will be called the price of *B* in *A*.

* The use we make here of this general consideration of the transformation is not very useful for those who are only studying Political Economy; but those who have also studied thermodynamics, or, more in general, physics, find themselves using an already known language. The transformation of energy, the equivalence of heat with work, etc., are similar to economic transformations, of which barter is one case.

The *total utility* that an individual has from the ownership of *A* and *B* is represented by Prof. Edgeworth as a function of the owned quantities.

Jevons, Prof. Walras, Prof. Marshall and others consider *total utility* as the sum of two functions – one of the quantity of *A*, the other of the quantity of *B* – rather than as any one function of the quantities of the two owned goods.

However, this restriction still leaves *utility* expressed in very general terms; this can be adequate for most economic problems, while for some of the others nothing will later prevent us from abandoning such a definition.

Does *total utility* really exist? Is *homo œconomicus* aware of it? Or is it merely an economists' abstraction? We shall discuss this later; at this point, we only point out that the economists agree that the individual considers instead another quantity, called by them *final degree of utility*, or *rareté* (by Walras), or *marginal utility* (by English authors), which strictly speaking is the utility relating to the unit of a very small quantity of a good that is added to the quantity already owned.

Let us assume that economic goods are indefinitely divisible. The consideration of non-divisibility beyond a certain limit does not create major difficulties with the general principles of quantity sciences.

It will perhaps be useful, here, to recapitulate the notations used by the illustrious economists we have mentioned, so that the reader may more easily compare our remarks with the texts by those authors.

Economic goods	A	B
Owned quantities: Edgeworth[19]	$a + x$	y
Owned quantities: Jevons	$a - x$	y
Owned quantities: Walras	$q_u - 0_u$	d_b

These notations refer to the case where A transforms into B.

Total utility: Edgeworth	$U = P = F(x, y)$
Total utility: Walras	$\int_0^{q_a - 0_a} \varphi_a(q)dq + \int_0^{d_b} \varphi_b(q)dq$
Final degree of utility: Edgeworth[20]	$\frac{\partial P}{\partial x}, \frac{\partial P}{\partial y}$
Final degree of utility: Jevons	$\varphi(a - x), \quad \psi(y)$
Final degree of utility: Walras	$\varphi_a(q_a - 0_a), \quad \varphi_b(d_b)$

It should be noted that in Edgeworth's formula x is essentially negative and corresponds to Jevons' $-x$.
Infinitesimal variation of total utility

Edgeworth	$\frac{\partial P}{\partial x} dx + \frac{\partial P}{\partial y} dy$
Jevons	$\psi(y)dy - \varphi(a - x)dx$
Walras	$\varphi_b(d_b)d.d_b - \varphi_a(q_a - 0_a)d.0_a$

The final degree of utility of a commodity is the partial derivative, with regard to that quantity of commodity, of the total utility.
The utility of an infinitesimal portion of good dy, added to the quantity y already owned, is equal to the final degree of utility multiplied by dy. Of course, if the quantity of owned good decreases, dy is negative.
Total utility is the sum of the utility of successive infinitesimal portions of good, in other words, it is the integral of infinitesimal utility.
This integral is usually calculated starting from zero, but this gives rise to two problems. First: this integral can easily become infinite. For example, if

$$\varphi_a(q) = \frac{a}{q}$$

– which is a form one does not come across, because it should be excluded a priori – one has

$$\int_h^{d_a} \varphi(q)dq = a\log\left(\frac{d_a}{h}\right),$$

which becomes infinite for $h=0$.
Second: considering the elements of the integral corresponding to zero quantity of economic good always makes the integral more abstract.

How many men in a country are aware of the sufferings caused by an absolute lack of food? And yet, when the integral is calculated from zero, one is considering the utility deriving from removing such sufferings.

We believe therefore that it is better to calculate the integral starting from a positive quantity h, which will be determined according to the various cases. This does not change the substance of the demonstrations of the authors who calculate that integral from zero.

When one considers the profit in the transformation of economic goods, the variables x and y are not independent, but the conditions according to which the transformation is carried out establish a relationship between them. For example, in the case of a barter, such as the one considered by Jevons and Walras, where each successive portion of bartered good has the same price, one has:

$$\frac{y}{x} = p.$$

Marshall and Edgeworth have considered the case where the successive portions of bartered goods can have different prices. In that case x and y remain independent until the law that those successive barters must follow has been established.

Fundamental principle of hedonistic calculus

This principle can be formulated in two ways.

First: every man continues the transformation of the economic goods in his possession until he obtains maximum total utility from them.

Second: every man continues the transformation of the economic goods until by so operating he can procure a positive infinitesimal final degree of utility.

From an analytical point of view the two formulations are generally equal, since total utility is the integral of the infinitesimal final degree of utility, which is the same as saying that the former is maximal, or that the latter is zero. It is true that this second condition also includes the case of the minimum, but this can easily be excluded by adding supplementary considerations.

But if we look at the real facts, the difference between the two formulations is this, that with the first one, one could assume that an individual is aware of the total utility of an economic good. In our opinion, this seems to happen very seldom. None of us has a clear idea of the utility of eating, drinking, dressing, having a house where one can shelter, but we only understand its advantages for small variations, positive or negative, in other words, our mind only comprehends the concept of final degree of utility.

From an analytical point of view too, there are special cases, in which it is not without importance to apply one formulation instead of the other.

For positive or negative increments dx and dy of the commodities owned, let the infinitesimal variation of utility be

$$Qdx + Rdy.$$

Surely, until this equals zero it will be useful, if possible, to continue the transformations one way if positive and the other way if negative. This is the second formulation, which is shown therefore to be always true.

If Q and R are the partial derivatives of the same function P*, that is, if it is possible to assume

$$\frac{\partial P}{\partial x} = Q, \quad \frac{\partial P}{\partial y} = R,$$

then the equation, for which the infinitesimal variation of utility equals zero, is the condition according to which P is a maximum (or a minimum), and the first formulation is equivalent to the second.

But it could well be that Q and R are not the partial derivatives of the same function; in this case, the function for which the first formulation would be valid does not exist.

* It is known that, if Q and R are partial derivatives of the same function P, this is a maximum in the case of stable equilibrium, and it is a minimum in the case of instable equilibrium.

We conclude therefore that the second formulation of the theorem is preferable, with regard both to real facts and to analytical reasoning.

* The reader who is familiar with theoretical mechanics will have already noticed the perfect correspondence between these formulae and those of mechanics.

* If Q is the force acting on a material point along the x axis, and P is the force acting along the y axis, and if δx and δy are the movements afforded to the point by its restrictions, Lagrange's equation for the equilibrium of the point,

$$Q\,\delta x + R\,\delta y = 0,$$

is identical to the equation we obtain by making the infinitesimal variation of utility equal to zero.

The economics of the individual

The transformation of economic goods must be studied, first of all, by considering the reasons why it is carried out by an individual; then, we have to add the condition that in a barter we have to harmonize the wishes of the contracting parties.

The theory of barter was first formulated by Jevons and Walras for a special type of market.[XLIV] We have already pointed out, among other things, that these authors assume the existence of a single price for the various portions successively bartered.

With his famous barter problem,[21] Prof. Marshall started considering cases, in which successive portions of commodity are bartered at different rates.

Prof. Edgeworth considers the more general case of barter at different rates.

Reasons at play in determining a barter

All the theories we have just mentioned assume that the only reason is that of continuing the transformation of economic goods until, by doing so, one obtains a positive increase of utility.

Let us ignore the ethical reasons, which everybody agrees are not the responsibility of Political Economy to deal with, but are there not other economic reasons?

We believe such reasons do exist. One of the most important is the consideration of price variations. It is enough to glance over any stock exchange or market report, be it wheat, or wine, or coffee, or other commodities, to realize immediately that in the contracts, beside considering intrinsic utility, one also takes into account the market trend, as indicated by price variation. If prices are falling fast, buyers seldom come forward; most times they prefer to pull out instead. If, on the contrary, prices are going up, sometimes it is the sellers who come forward, but very often people are attracted to buy by the very upward movement of the prices.

These phenomena can be observed also in retail markets. A peasant comes to the market with some bunches of asparagus. He does not even dream of equating the profit he would have by eating them with the profit he can achieve from the money he will obtain by selling them. His only aim is to guess what is the highest price he can make out of them. If at the market he learns that asparagus bunches are selling in great quantities at 60 cents each, he will probably be satisfied with that price. If, however, he is told that they started at 60 cents, but then the price went quickly up to 80 cents, perhaps he will not want to put his bunches for sale at less than 90 cents.

Such facts can be observed in all markets. It is enough, for instance, to spend some time listening to the conversations that go on in a market where silkworm cocoons are sold, in order to understand how influential is the consideration of the prices that have already been put into effect.

The above-mentioned reason can also be seen as included in other more general ones.

In general, barters do not take place in order to satisfy current needs, such that they cannot be deferred, but to provide for future needs. Thus, in deciding today's barter, the following are of great weight: first, the forecast about the future conditions of the market; second, the effect that the idea of a future need has on our thoughts and feelings.

The latter kind of considerations is in connection with the qualities of foresight of the men. It is a known fact that savage peoples lack these qualities to an extent that is almost beyond belief for those who live among civilized people.

American natives are described as only thinking of what is useful to them at the time they purchase it, since they are totally unconcerned about anything that is not immediately useful to them. Labat[XLVII] tells us that a Caribbean native would never sell his *hamac* at night, whatever price was offered to him, but in the morning, after sleeping, he would give away that same *hamac* for whatever object of very little value he might fancy at the time.

Barter laws cannot obviously be the same for him, as for the shrewd trader, who buys wheat taking into account every possible forecast of future harvests.

The great majority of people, who are neither totally careless, nor totally provident, are between these two extremes; it is therefore between these two extremes that the barter law that is applicable to them must also lie.

Mill rightly observed how on the European continent competition did not determine value in the same way as happened in England; similar considerations were taken into account by Classical Economics. We believe that the new Political Economy must also do the same. We believe that the proposition according to which the theorems of pure science have absolute value, even if only for the perfect hedonists, is wrong. At most, they could govern the actions of perfect hedonists, who at the same time happen to be perfectly provident and perfectly reasonable. Now, when dealing with economic phenomena, it seems to us that by considering men as perfect hedonists we do not stray too far at all from reality; this would not be the case, however, if they were to be considered entirely provident and reasonable.

Limit of the hedonistic theories

In our view, the above-mentioned flaw becomes extremely serious, when one tries to apply the principles of the new science to the study of phenomena that are not exclusively economic. For instance, one would make mistakes, even blunders, in many cases, if one tried to use them in the science of finance, and nearly always, if one tried to use them in the science of government. And when they are also combined with postulates, such as the one on the ethical nature of the State, or the other about the government being considered as the expression of the people's will, they end up producing fairy tales that are less entertaining but not more real than Astolfo's[XLVIII] voyage to the moon.

If a vinedresser repeatedly barters a certain number of litres of wine for a certain number of kilograms of wheat, we can certainly say that, according to his judgement, the utility of the last of those litres of wine is for him equal to the utility of the last of those kilograms of wheat. But if one said that voters deem the damage they suffer because of protectionism and the other robberies that the politicians commit against them, to be lesser than the damage they would suffer if they opposed such bad practices, and if one wanted to prove such a proposition by saying 'the parliament represents the majority of the voters, the laws are approved by the majority of the parliament, therefore protection is approved by most in the country', one would produce a reasoning that contains as many mistakes as it does words.

It is true that in England, the consideration of the questions that have to be resolved in parliament has some influence on the election of its members, but on the European continent that influence is minimal. Even ignoring the intrigues, the corruption, the prejudices and other similarly powerful reasons that determine how members of parliament are chosen, there is perhaps not one voter in a thousand who, in casting his vote, may consider and solve the questions that will have to be solved by the parliament's vote. And if ever the voters did so, how close their judgement could be to the truth remains to be seen. Any man who is not completely stupid can judge if a litre of wine is more useful to him than a kilogram of bread, but intelligence and culture are needed to understand the subtle ways that allow politicians to steal the riches of the country and share them with their friends. And it should be added that in the economic order, repetition of the evidence is a good substitute for the lack of intelligence and culture. You might perhaps be swindled when buying a pound of sugar; but then, by going around and seeing a number of grocers, you will find someone who will give you good produce at a convenient price. But one does not elect member of parliaments every day, the same way one visits a shopkeeper every day.

It should also be pointed out that the parliamentary vote does not even represent the judgement of the majority of the representatives on a given question. How many members of parliament in Italy showed their opposition in theory against the levy on cereals,[XLIX] and then they approved it because it was convenient for them and their friends not to antagonise those who had power!

But there is no point in dwelling any longer on this topic; it is enough for us to have mentioned it as an example to justify the way we interpret the hedonistic theories, which we think can be valid only in the case of very frequently repeated acts, such that their consequences may be easily understood by the class of people who perform them.

As for the forecast of the future conditions of the market, and for the degree of foresight of the hedonists, they can be taken into account by suitably modifying the expression of the final degree of utility. By doing so, we are not eliminating the difficulty, but we are only pushing it away; it will resurface when we deal with the final degree of utility.

2 Considerations on the fundamental principles of Pure Political Economy, II

(*Giornale degli Economisti*, June 1892)

Fundamental theorem of the transformation of any given number of goods

Let us assume, with Prof. Edgeworth, that the reasons causing an individual to transform one economic good into another depend exclusively on the quantities he owns of those goods. We have seen that he will continue the transformation until it no longer brings him any profit, and this corresponds to the highest level of utility he can obtain from those economic goods through the transformation. This theorem is obviously valid regardless of the number of economic goods considered.

Strictly speaking, one should take into account the ratio of the transformation (i.e. the price) of any one commodity compared with all the others, but it is convenient from the very beginning to assume a common measure, that is a money,[1] in which case the number of ratios of transformation (i.e. the prices) is only equal to the number of economic goods, or, in fact, to that number minus one, if, as we shall do, one uses one of those goods as money.

Jevons and Prof. Walras consider these prices constant for the whole quantity being transformed, whereas Prof. Edgeworth and Prof. Marshall consider them also variable for the parts of goods that are subsequently transformed.

Let us assume that an individual owns n economic goods	$A \ldots B \ldots C \ldots$
of which he owns the quantities	$r_a \ldots r_b \ldots r_c \ldots$
the first of these goods is used as money, and the prices are	$1 \ldots p_b \ldots p_c \ldots$

P = Total utility obtained from the consumption of those quantities of goods

The final degree of utility of those quantities will be[2] $\quad \dfrac{\partial P}{\partial r_a} \ldots \dfrac{\partial P}{\partial r_b} \ldots \dfrac{\partial P}{\partial r_c}.$

According to Walras's and Jevons's notations, these final degrees are

indicated by $\quad \varphi_a(r_a) \ldots \varphi_b(r_b) \ldots \varphi_c(r_c) \ldots,$

and they are only functions of one variable each, whereas the previous ones can contain all the variables.

In order for the individual who owns the goods to stop the transformations – i.e. in order for these quantities to coincide with those that correspond to the state of equilibrium – it is necessary for the utility of any one infinitesimal transformation to be zero.

Let us assume that the quantities	r_a	r_b
increase by the infinitesimal quantities	dr_a	dr_b

one of these two increments will have to be negative, since the quantity of one commodity increases if the quantity of the other decreases, as one commodity is being transformed into the other. Since p_b is the transformation ratio, we shall have

$$dr_a + p_b dr_b = 0,$$

and therefore[3]

$$p_b = -\frac{dr_a}{dr_b} \tag{1}$$

The utility of this transformation must be zero, and consequently:

$$\frac{\partial P}{\partial r_a} dr_a + \frac{\partial P}{\partial r_b} dr_b = 0, \tag{2}$$

that is

$$\frac{\partial P}{\partial r_a} = \frac{1}{p_b}\frac{\partial P}{\partial r_b};$$

and similarly one would obtain the other equations of the following system

$$\frac{\partial P}{\partial r_a} = \frac{1}{p_b}\frac{\partial P}{\partial r_b} = \frac{1}{p_c}\frac{\partial P}{\partial r_c} = \ldots . \tag{3}$$

According to Jevons and Walras, the final degree of utility of A is a function of r_a only, and the final degree of utility of B is a function of r_b only, and one has

$$\varphi_a(r_a) = \frac{1}{p_b}\varphi_b(r_b) = \frac{1}{p_c}\varphi_c(r_c) = \ldots . \tag{4}$$

Many important inferences stem from these formulae; we shall therefore briefly dwell on them. First of all, let us see how they would be expressed in everyday language.

Formulae (3) and (4) correspond to Gossen's,[1] or Jevons's, theorem on final degrees of utility: *Whenever the available means are used up, all the needs that have been fulfilled with those means have equal degrees of intensity, and these are the highest possible the individual can perceive at that given moment.*[4]

It is possible to give a more tangible form to this theorem by using a chart (see Figure 2.1).

The successive cells of the vertical column *A* represent equal and equally-priced portions, at one lira each, for example, of commodity *A*. The cells included in column *B* denote successive portions of commodity *B*, each of which has the previously set price, i.e. one lira.

Similarly, the cells of columns *C*, *D*, . . . represent portions of commodities *C*, *D*, . . . all at the price of one lira. We also assume that the numbers written in the cells show the utility, for the individual, of the portions of commodity they represent.

This chart has been conceived in a somewhat artificial way, to make demonstrations easier. To verify how the hypotheses that have been tacitly accepted in the chart agree with the facts, see, in this chapter, the section on 'The variety of human needs'.

Now, if we look at Figure 2.1, it is evident that an individual who only has one lira to spend buys the commodity of cell 4(*A*). An individual who has three lira to spend also buys the commodities of cells 3(*A*) and 3(*B*), and, going on in this way, an individual with 10 lira to spend buys 4(*A*), 3(*A*), 3(*B*) – 2(*A*), 2(*B*), 2(*C*) – 1(*A*), 1(*B*), 1(*C*), 1(*D*). But what if he only had 9 lira to spend? In this case, if the commodities in the cells marked with 1 are divisible, he should buy 3/4 of each of them, as 3 lira is all he has left after satisfying his more urgent needs, which correspond to cells 2 and above.

This chart can be represented in a different way (see Figure 2.2).[5]

Let us assume that a number of vertical holes, or small wells, have been drilled in a solid rock; the wells *A*, *B*, *C* . . . are communicating with each other and have different depths. Let some water be poured in them; it will settle at a level *XY*. Let the depth *h*, at which the slice *uv* is situated, be directly proportional to the intensity of the need satisfied by the portion of commodity represented by that slice. We shall then have the image of the distribution of a certain quantity of goods available for the purchase of some commodities. And it is also possible to take into account the case of commodities that are not indefinitely divisible, by assuming we pour sand, instead of water, into the wells; only the wells that are broad enough to let a grain of sand pass through will be filled, whilst the narrower ones will remain empty.

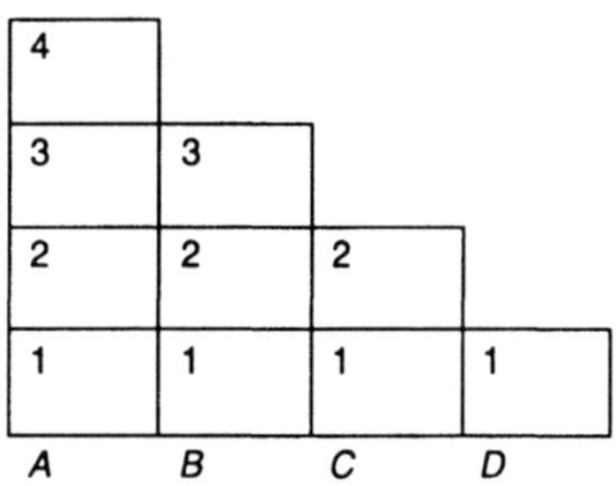

Figure 2.1

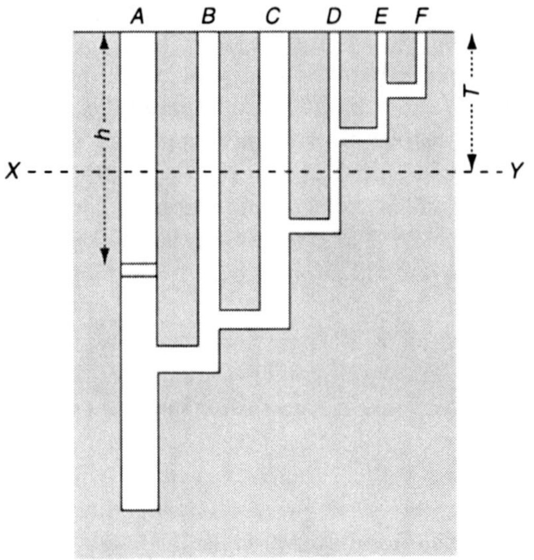

Figure 2.2

Wicksteed[II] has given a very clear explanation of this problem. He says:[6]

> In the same way, in a family, the father or a good housewife sees to it that the last penny (or shilling, or pound, or whatever the **smallest perceivable amount** in each case may be) spent towards each good procures the same utility or the same pleasure. If such a goal is not obtained, then the money is not being spent in the most convenient way. But how can one achieve this goal? Obviously, by adjusting the purchases of each commodity in such a way that the final degree of utility (*marginal utilities*) of the quantity that can be had for a penny is equal for each commodity.

Final degree of utility of instrumental goods

It is necessary to keep in mind that the final degrees of utility being discussed here are exclusively those of consumable commodities. In the case of an economic good that cannot be directly enjoyed, but can only be used to obtain other economic goods that are consumable, i.e. in the case of a good that is **exclusively** *instrumental*, the latter does not have a final degree of utility of its own, which may appear in the above formulae, but its degree of utility is simply equal to the common value of the degrees of utility of the goods, which are obtained with it.

Let us indeed consider an individual who owns some wheat and, having gone to the market, barters it for some wine. He does not drink a single drop of the latter, but uses it instead to acquire oil, meat and vegetables. For that individual, then, the utility of a litre of wine is only the utility of the oil, the meat and the vegetables for which he can barter it. There is therefore this crucial difference, between the utility of the wine an individual drinks and the utility of the wine he uses **only** to acquire other commodities: the former is determinate only for the individual under consideration, the latter remains for him indeterminate, until he knows the ratios (the prices) at which he can barter that wine for oil, meat and vegetables.

Theorem

The final degree of utility of instrumental goods varies with the prices of the consumable commodities and with the other market conditions, except in very special cases. Thus, that final degree of utility can never, in theory, be assumed as constant.

The importance of this theorem prompts us to give various demonstrations of it. The first demonstrations, where mathematics is not used, are imperfect and must be regarded as explanations, rather than actual demonstrations.

I. Let us go back to the previously shown diagram (Figure 2.1). Let us assume that the commodities represented by the various cells are obtained by bartering for them an instrumental good, which is not directly consumed. Then, if we have one unit of that good, we shall purchase the commodity in cell 4, and the degree of utility of that unit of instrumental good is precisely 4.

If we have three units of this good, we shall purchase the commodities of cells 4–3–3. The utility of the last portion of the instrumental good is nothing but the utility of the commodity purchased using that portion, that is, 3. And so it goes on; eventually, one will find that the final degree of utility of the instrumental good, when we have 10 units of it, is 1, since 1 is the utility of the commodity that is purchased with the last portion of that good, and since the latter is not supposed to be used for any other purpose. And if instead of 10 units we had 9, the final degree of utility of the instrumental good would be 3/4, provided the commodities in the last cells are divisible.

That degree of utility varies, therefore, with the variation of the owned quantity, and consequently cannot be assumed to be constant.

Also, let us suppose that, thanks to a discovery, or an industrial improvement or, in short, whatever reason, a new commodity is brought onto the market; let us suppose that with one unit of the instrumental good one can buy a portion of this new commodity that has utility 1; one cell is added to the last row of the diagram, and the final degree of utility of the instrumental good of which we have 10 units, which was 1 before the new commodity came out, is reduced to 4/5, since we shall divide the last 4 units by purchasing 4/5 of the commodity of each cell 1.

Finally, if the price of commodity D varies, for instance, in such a way that the smallest quantity one can buy with one unit of the instrumental good is 2, instead of 1, then one cell is added to the second-last row, and only 3 units of the instrumental good are left to purchase the commodities of the four cells 1, and the final degree of utility is therefore 4/3.

In conclusion, any variation of the market conditions triggers a variation of the final degree of utility of a changed quantity of the instrumental good.

II. The theorem takes tangible form through the considerations given in relation to Figure 2.2.

The water that is poured into the wells represents the instrumental good, by means of which we purchase the goods for direct consumption represented by the parts of the wells that are full. Since the instrumental good has no utility of its own, its final degree of utility is equal to the final degree of utility of the last slice *XY* of the various goods we are obtaining with it. Such final degree of utility is therefore represented by the level *T*.

Now, if new wells are opened, if any of the old ones are closed, if the depth or the cross-section of any of the remaining wells is changed – all of which represent changes in the state of the market – then the level *XY* also changes; and, consequently, the final degree of utility of that quantity of instrumental good changes.

Only in the very particular, and very improbable, case, in which all the above changes balanced each other, would the level *XY* be left unchanged.

III. If, as Jevons and Wicksteed say, we must use the money we own so that the final degree of utility of all the commodities we buy with the last bit of money spent is equal, it is clear that if those commodities change in number, price, etc., the way of using that last bit of money will also change, and so will its utility, which is the final degree of utility of the amount of money we spend, when the latter is exclusively considered as an instrumental good.

IV. Let us suppose that A is an instrumental good whose quantity q_a is used to

purchase the commodities	B	C	E
and the purchased quantities are	r_b	r_c	$r_e \dots$
and the prices calculated in A are	p_b	p_c	$p_e \dots$

First, let us suppose, with Prof. Walras, that these prices are constant for all the subsequent portions of the same commodity; we shall have

$$q_a = p_b r_b + p_c r_b + \dots \tag{5}$$

In order to make use of the previously written formulae, we shall assume

$$dr_a = -dq_a$$

since q_a decreases when $r_b, r_c \dots$ increase.

The equations (4) become

$$\varphi_a(q_a) = \frac{1}{p_b}\varphi_b(r_b) = \frac{1}{p_c}\varphi_c(r_c) = \dots \tag{6}$$

Let us suppose, if it is possible, that the final degree of utility of the instrumental good is constant and equal to m; we shall have

$$\varphi_a(q_a) = m,$$

and the previous formulae will allow us to calculate r_b, r_c . . . as functions of m and of p_b, p_c . . .; that means that we shall be able to write

$$r_b = \psi_b(mp_b),\ r_c = \psi_c(mp_c), \ldots \tag{7}$$

By introducing these values in equation (5), we shall have:

$$q_a = p_b\psi_b(mp_b) + p_c\psi_c(mp_c) + \ldots$$

and since p_b . . . are independent one after the other, it will not be possible to have q_a constant, unless the quantities

$$p_b\psi_b(mp_b),\ p_c\psi_c(mp_c), \ldots$$

are constant too; that is, if we recall equations (7), and if with A_b, A_c . . . we indicate constants, it will have to be

$$p_br_b = A_b,\ p_cr_c = A_c, \ldots \tag{8}$$

It should be pointed out that if q_a were not constant, this would imply that a certain value of q_a corresponds to certain values of m, p_b, p_c . . .; and vice versa various values of m would correspond to various values of q_a, p_b, p_c . . ., which would go against the hypothesis that the degree of utility of the instrumental good is constant.

By combining the previous equations with (6), we have

$$\varphi_b(r_b) = mp_b = \frac{mA_b}{r_b},\ \varphi_c(r_c) = \frac{mA_c}{r_c}. \ldots$$

It would therefore be necessary that the final degrees of utility of **all** the commodities had that *very particular* expression, to make it possible for the final degree of utility of an instrumental good to remain constant. This amounts to saying that it will never be so.

It should be noted that the conditions (8) are tantamount to considering *the elasticity* **of the demand** as constant.[III] We can therefore say that *the final degree of an instrumental good cannot be considered as constant, except for the case where the elasticity of the demand of* **all** *the commodities that are being purchased using that instrumental good is constant.*

Note that in this case, from the combination of formula (8) with (5), one has

$$q_a = A_b + A_c + \ldots;$$

thus, if some new commodity appears on the market, or if any disappears from it, q_a varies; therefore not even the condition about the elasticity of the demand is sufficient, but it is also necessary for the number of commodities not to change.

V.[7] Let us assume, with Prof. Edgeworth: first, that the final degree of utility of a commodity is a function not only of the owned quantity of that commodity, but also of the other commodities; second, that the price of a commodity changes with successive bartered portions.

We have

$$dq_u = \frac{\partial q_u}{\partial r_b} dr_b + \frac{\partial q_u}{\partial r_c} dr_c + \ldots.$$

And with equation (1), which, since

$$dr_u = -dq_u,$$

becomes

$$p_b = \frac{\partial q_u}{\partial r_b},$$

we obtain

$$dq_u = p_b dr_b + p_c dr_c + \ldots; \qquad (9)$$

p_b, p_c . . . are *known* functions of r_b, r_c . . .; and to make them vary independently of r_b, r_c . . . we shall introduce a parameter for each of these functions,[8] by writing

$$p_b = f_b\,(r_b, r_c, \ldots u_b)$$

$$p_c = b_c\,(r_b, r_c, \ldots u_c)$$

By integrating equation (9),[9] one has

$$q_u = \int_0^{r_b} p_b dr_b + \int_0^{r_c} \underset{(r_b=0)}{p_c} dr_c + \int_0^{r_d} \underset{\left(\frac{r_b=0}{r_c=0}\right)}{p_d} dr_d + \ldots; \qquad (10)$$

where the expression

$$\underset{(r_b=0)}{p_c}$$

indicates that in p_c one has to make $r_b = 0$, and similarly for the other similar expressions.

If the total utility of instrumental good A, i.e. if

$$\frac{\partial P}{\partial r_a},$$

is constant, it is necessary that for a given value of that quantity there is only one corresponding value of q_u; or, in other words, it is necessary for q_u not to be a function of $u_b, u_c, \ldots$, since otherwise, by eliminating those quantities between the previously found equation and equations (3), one would have a relationship[10] between the final degree of utility $\frac{\partial P}{\partial r_u}$, and q_u, which is contrary to the hypothesis put forward.

It is therefore necessary that in q_u we give $r_b, r_c \ldots$ values that are functions of u_b, $u_c \ldots$, and of such a kind that they cause the latter quantities to disappear.

With the exception of this very particular case, therefore, the final degree of utility of the instrumental good will vary with the quantity of the latter.

Corollary

Since the money made of precious metals that we use possesses the quality of instrumental good to the highest degree, *its degree of utility can never be theoretically taken as constant.*

On the other hand, in many cases one can approximately consider it so.

Cases where the final degree of utility of money is approximately constant

Strictly speaking, any alteration, however slight, of the conditions of the market alters the final degree of utility of money, but this alteration can often be negligible. For example, when not long ago, in order to restore the national finances, the Italian government decided to increase the levy on nutmegs, strictly speaking this measure altered the final degree of utility of the Italian money, but it is evident that this alteration is imperceptible, almost as much as the profit the Treasury obtained from it. On the contrary, the levy on wheat[IV] that has been imposed in Italy has significantly altered the final degree of utility of our national currency. It is therefore clear that there are some phenomena for which the final degree of utility of money can be considered constant without incurring noticeable errors, and other phenomena where this alteration is the main part that should be studied.

Some may think that we have been dwelling too long on a question whose solution is obvious. And those who do not like the theories of Pure Economics will probably even joke about it, and say: 'Was it necessary to pull out so many formulae, number diagrams, and even little wells!, to let us know that one lira is more useful to the individual who has few of them, than to the one who has many!'

But we never intended to give a demonstration of that fact; our aim was to give a rigorous expression of it, which is a quite different proposition. It is not our formulae that demonstrate the fact; rather, it is the fact that adds to the authority of our formulae, by being susceptible to be expressed by them.

On the other hand, this objection could be levelled at the principles of any science. They nearly always seem to be obvious, but it is only by expressing them in a rigorous form that one can extract any consequences from them.

* For instance, Lagrange's principle of virtual velocities basically reiterates that a body is in equilibrium when it is not moving in any of the directions in which it could. And in this form, perhaps even prehistoric men knew it. But one was not going any further. On the contrary, in the rigorous form of Lagrange's equations, it embraces the whole of Statics and, when one expresses D'Alembert's principle[V] by means of them, the whole of Dynamics! Those many pages which the treatises on mechanics spend to explain and make clear Lagrange's principle are therefore anything but useless.

One should also add that while the principle of the variability of the final degree of utility of money is one of the seemingly obvious principles, in practice it is also one of the most easily forgotten.

We have seen an example of this fact in the analysis carried out in a previous article[11] of the controversy between Prof. Walras and Messrs Auspitz and Lieben on the theory of prices. The crucial point of the argument regards precisely the final utility of money.

In that article, we purposefully avoided following the deductive path, which would have required us first to demonstrate the variability of the utility of money, and then to deduce its consequences, but we decided instead to proceed according to the analytical path. We assumed, at first, that the final utility of money was constant and it was the facts that compelled us to add the condition about its variability.

Some may deem this way less scientific, but the followers of the experimental method will understand why we alternate the use of analysis and synthesis in an attempt, so to speak, to move around the topic in order to consider its every side.

And even after doing so, we are always afraid that the truth may escape us; but our fear would be much greater, were we to consider the question from only one point of view.

Relationship between the final degree of utility of money and the prosperity of a people

The prices of commodities on the international market certainly depend on the consumption of each population, and possibly even of each individual. But it is easily understandable that if an individual eats one loaf of bread more than usual, this will not cause the price of wheat to rise. Similarly, a variation, even substantial, in the consumption of a **single** population will not change much the price of wheat on the **world** market.

As for the commodities that are sold on the international market, the prices can therefore be supposed to be fixed according to general circumstances; consequently, one can say that *the smaller the final degree of utility of their gold is, the more affluent their people are.*

For a small degree of utility of gold, **when prices are fixed**, indicates small degrees of utility for all commodities, which means that that society has almost enough of every economic good.

If, on the contrary, we are dealing with commodities that are only traded on a restricted market, then the prices can no longer be supposed to be approximately constant while consumption varies, and a small degree of utility of gold could be stemming not from a small degree of utility of those commodities, but from the fact that their price has risen a great deal.

The above proposition is the same proposition that Cairnes[VII] expressed by saying that 'A nation's interest lies not in having its prices high or low, but in having its gold cheap, where "cheap" does not mean low value, but *low cost*, i.e. a small sacrifice in terms of ease and comfort.'[12]

He also explains that

> among countries that are commercially connected, there is a great class of commodities – all those, that is, which constitute the great sources of trade, such as wheat, flour, tea, sugar, metals, and raw industrial materials – whose prices cannot vary much in different places. As a rule, the difference between the prices will not be greater than the cost of transportation between the countries of production and the countries of consumption, provided of course that the items in question do not fall under the action of local fiscal laws. In the exchange against commodities of this kind, the value of gold, though not the same throughout the world, does not change much within the sphere of international trade. But beside the commodities constituting the source of trade, there are those that, by being unsuitable for long distance trading, or because of some other obstacle, are not included in international trade. With regard to these, there is nothing preventing the widest divergence in their prices in gold . . . .[13]

Even without taking into account the ambiguity of those words, '*value of gold*', which does not add to the clarity of Cairnes' reasoning, one cannot deny that the theorem is not formulated and demonstrated by him in a much less clear and rigorous way than is possible by using the principles of rational economics. And even if these principles had the only merit of adding to the rigour of the demonstrations, they should still be deemed very useful within science. But beside such greater rigour, the precise knowledge of the terms within which the theorem applies will help us inferring its consequences.

It could be argued that all these theoretical considerations do not achieve much in actual terms. And it is true that as it is not only through their ignorance of the teachings of ethics that evil-doers appropriate other people's property, similarly, it is not only through their ignorance of the truths of the science of economics that politicians are led to act in the wrong way.

It is manifest that with this kind of people there is no logic that works: neither mathematical nor usual logic, nor any other logic man could ever find;

the language they understand is of an entirely different nature! But they take advantage of the ignorance of the public, and getting rid of this is the best way, and perhaps the only way, as Molinari[VIII] says, to destroy their power.

See, for instance, what follows with regard to money. In ancient times and in the Middle Ages, governments altered it by adding base metals to precious metals. Modern politicians would like to do the same, but the public's improved knowledge compels them to disguise the same fraud with subtler artifices, and they print paper money. The day will come when even this ruse will not be possible, the people's knowledge having expanded further.

It is obvious that the populace will never study the science of economics, with or without the use of mathematics, but it is also true that the same populace did not have to study astronomy in order to get rid of the prejudices and fears caused in other times by celestial phenomena, and it was enough that some scholars found the laws that governed them. Therefore, pure theory is not useless because it can only be studied by a few and, if not directly, at least indirectly it increases and improves popular knowledge.

The variety of human needs

The law of the variety of human needs, which Jevons rightly describes as the most important law of Political Economy, is very well known; equally known is also the fact that a large number of sophisms have arisen from disregarding it.

In order to avoid these sophisms, we must include in our formulae the condition about the various and growing needs of men.

Together with the invaluable advantage of the unrivalled rigour of inference, mathematics also has the serious disadvantage that from time to time, some conditions one was not contemplating stealthily find their way into the formulae. Then, as a consequence, science seems to give answers that are out of tune with the questions.

* Among the best-known purely mathematical examples, we find the case of multiple solutions, and negative or imaginary solutions of equations. Let us assume a question that obviously admits only one solution; we seek it from the science of mathematics and end up with an equation that has more than one solution! But this happens because in submitting the problem, we have inadvertently considered another more general question beside the question we had in mind.

In order to avoid the danger of false interpretations, it is therefore necessary for us to look carefully not only at what we put into the equations, but also at what we leave out.

The chart (Figure 2.3) which illustrates Gossen's law shows us various noteworthy facts. Let us ignore the fact that the final degrees of utility decrease when the quantity of commodity increases, which is something we shall have to discuss at length later; for the moment, let us note that with a lower degree of utility comes a higher number of cells, as shown in I. If the

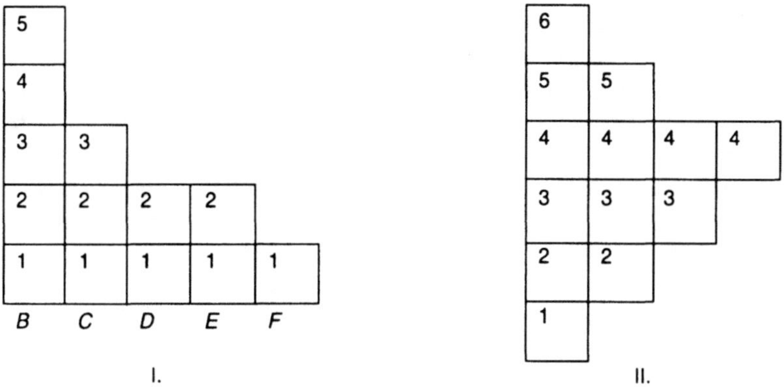

Figure 2.3

law of human needs were instead illustrated by diagram II, Political Economy would be totally different from the science that goes by this name, as we know it today. We shall therefore limit our comments to the case shown in diagram I. And we intend now to give a more rigorous and scientific form to this way of illustrating that phenomenon.

Discontinuity of the phenomenon

Let us start by looking for a way to remove a difficulty that confronts us from the very outset.

We have assumed that the degrees of utility were decreasing gradually, so that all of the last cells could be full; if however the quantity of commodity *B* that can be bought for one lira in order to extinguish need 2 not only extinguished that need, but also entirely satisfied us with regard to that commodity, what would happen? Cell 1-*B* would disappear, and what becomes then of the theorem that requires all the final degrees of utility to be equal?

These difficulties, which stem from the necessity to consider discontinuous functions, are greater in Political Economy than in the physical sciences, because economists usually have not prepared themselves to handle the subject matter by studying mathematics.[14] If Political Economy is to become a mathematical science, the need will arise for treatises to be published, where those who study Political Economy may easily find all they need to know about mathematics and mechanics.[15]

And at this point we shall allow ourselves a small digression. Gossen's law does not apply only to Political Economy, but it would be very useful if it were taken into consideration also with regard to education.

Without referring to this law, which he was probably not bearing in mind, Bain[X, 16] shows how every man has only a certain amount of mental faculties available for learning, which must therefore be wisely spent; and obviously, the best way of spending them is by ensuring that the last pieces of knowledge to be acquired all have the same degree of utility for the individual. At present, this is almost never achieved, and when the way is found to perform such a deed, the effectiveness of human intellectual work will perhaps grow beyond the boldest guess we can possibly envisage today.

The criticism levelled at the use of mathematics by saying that the latter is unknown to the majority of economists – see Block,[XI] among others – could therefore be easily removed, because many of the other pieces of knowledge economists acquire are pushed to such extremes that they have a very small degree of utility, which means that by reducing them there would be enough time left for the study of physics and mathematics.

But let us go back to our problem. In actual fact, things happen as we have supposed, and Wicksteed was right in his judgement when he spoke of the *perceptible minimum*, because we can never regulate our expenditure with such precision, as not to satisfy some needs while others are still remaining.

For all wealthy persons the final degree of utility of bread is zero. It is impossible for these people to take from the amount they spend for bread that one cent, or that fraction of a cent, which would be necessary to trigger in them a need to eat bread equal to their need of luxury items and superfluous objects.

In order to remove these difficulties, the method that is usually adopted consists in making the discontinuous functions continuous, ensuring that the error generated by doing so is negligible. There are a number of reasons for this, one of the main ones being the fact that discontinuous functions are much more difficult to deal with than continuous functions, which is also the case when using mathematics.

* We have already pointed out that in calculating Newtonian attraction and in other cases, mechanics considers matter as continuous, and the error arising from it is absolutely negligible.

Let us see what we will be able to do by following these ideas.

Let us assume that the functions $\varphi_b(r_b)$, $\varphi_c(r_c)$ . . . of formulae (4) are continuous, and let us represent with curve A in Figure 2.4 the quantity

$$\frac{1}{p_b}\varphi_b(r_b).$$

What Gossen's law really tells us, and what is expressed by formulae (4), is that the ordinate y, corresponding in this curve to the abscissa r_b, is equal to the ordinate y that corresponds to the abscissa r_c in the curve

$$\frac{1}{p_c}\varphi_c(r_c);$$

and so on for the other curves.

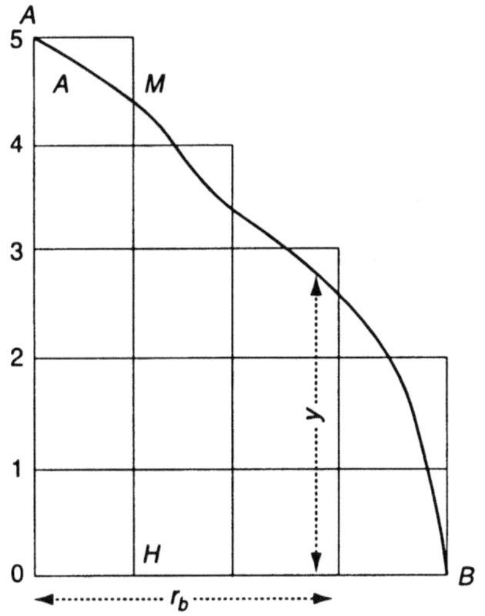

Figure 2.4

But the diagram expresses something totally different. We have assumed that the line *0A* in the illustration has been divided in 5 equal parts, which are proportional to $\varphi_b(r_b)$, and so to the needs of the individual. With one unit of money one buys a quantity of commodity *B* represented by *0H*, and the maximum need *0A* and all the intermediate needs from *0A* to *HM* are satisfied at the same time. And only in a very particular case will *HM* happen to be exactly equal to 4/5 of *0A*, as it is assumed in the diagram. And at the end of the curve, in *B*, one can see how by buying the last portion, need 2 and every other need up to zero are satisfied at the same time.

Let us draw two perpendicular lines *0X* and *0Y* (see Figure 2.5). On the axis of ordinates *0Y* we shall record lengths equal to the final degrees of utility of money, equal, that is, to the common values of

$$\frac{1}{p_b}\varphi_b(r_b), \frac{1}{p_c}\varphi_c(r_c) \dots$$

On the axis *0X* we shall record the small segments

$$\overline{ob} = p_b\Delta u, \overline{bc} = p_c\Delta u, \overline{ce} = p_e\Delta u \dots$$

where u is a parameter of which $p_b, p_c \dots r_b, r_c \dots$ are functions; and Δu is the increase of that parameter when passing from one commodity *B* to another commodity *C*, from *C* to *E*, etc. Let us draw through *0Y* a plane *0YZ* perpendicular to the plane of the diagram. *0Z* will be a straight line passing through *0*, and is perpendicular to the plane of the diagram, so that *0X*, *0Y*, *0Z*, form a system of three orthogonal axes. Let us assume that $\overline{0B}$ is the length that measures the final degree of utility of money when $r_b = 0$. Moving from point *B*, let us trace a curve *BG* on plane *0YZ* such that the

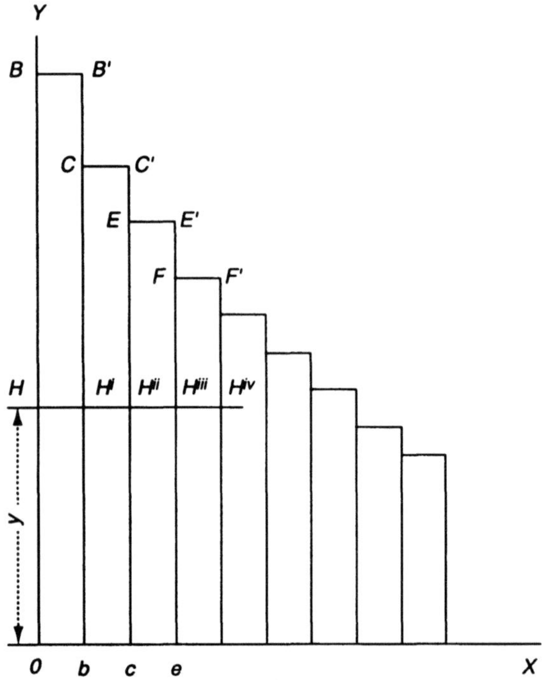

Figure 2.5

area included between B and the ordinate z, which corresponds to any value of the final degree of utility of money, is equal to r_h. We must therefore have

$$\int_z^0 z\,dy = r_h$$

and, by differentiating,

$$-z\,dy = dr_h.$$

But since

$$y = \frac{1}{p_h}\varphi_h(r_h),$$

we have

$$dy = \frac{1}{p_h}dr_h\varphi_h'(r_h);$$

and therefore

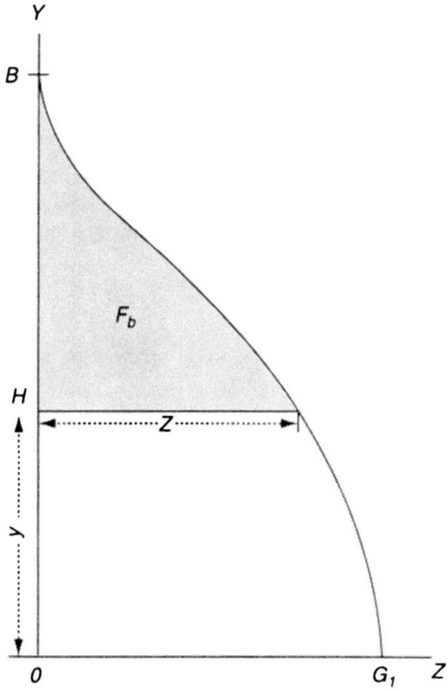

Figure 2.6

$$z = -\frac{p_b}{\varphi_b'(r_b)}.$$

Let us consider a cylindrical surface, generated by a straight line parallel to $0X$ that moves passing all the time through curve BG. The volume included between this surface, plane $0XY$, and the planes perpendicular to plane $0XY$, having as traces HB, $H'B'$, HH', is equal to

$$r_b p_b \Delta u,$$

because it a portion of a right-angled cylinder which has the area shaded in Figure 2.6 as base and $p_b \Delta u$ as height.

Let us suppose that the needs are in decreasing order with regard to their intensity. Then bC will be smaller than $0B$. By acting in a way similar to the one we have followed so far, we shall have in $H'CC'H''$ a volume equal to

$$p_c r_c \Delta u.$$

By continuing in this way we shall have a series of cylindrical slices which will form the solid $HH'''F'E'C'B'B$, whose volume is

$$p_b r_b \Delta u + p_c r_c \Delta u + p_e r_e \Delta u.$$

We have supposed that u was such a parameter that by giving it

the values	u_0	$u_0 + \Delta u$	$u_0 + 2\Delta u$	...
a certain function p would assume the values	p_b	p_c	p_e	...
and another function r would assume the values	r_b	r_c	r_e	....

The functions p and r, especially the former, will generally be discontinuous, i.e. an increase however great of p, or of r, can correspond to a small increase of Δu of u.

The volume of the solid we have just considered will be more simply indicated with

$$\Sigma\, pr\Delta u,$$

with the sum extending, in the case of the figure, from u_0 to $u_0 + 3\Delta u$, and in general from a certain value u_0 to another value u; this is written as

$$\sum_{u_0}^{u} pr\Delta u$$

and equation (5) becomes

$$q_u = \sum_{u_0}^{u} pr\Delta u.$$

In order to express equations (4), which give Gossen's law, by using the new notations, it is necessary to introduce a function φ that changes shape with the changing in the value of u, so that

for the values	u_0	$u_0 + \Delta u$	$u_0 + 2r\Delta u$	...
the function $\varphi(r)$ may become	$\varphi_b(r_b)$	$\varphi_c(r_c)$	$\varphi_e(r_e)$	...

Therefore Gossen's law is expressed by saying that the expression

$$\frac{1}{p}\,\varphi(r)$$

must remain constant when u varies. That constant value is the final degree of utility of money $\varphi_u(q_u)$, and equations (4) are replaced by

$$\varphi_u(q_u) = \frac{1}{p}\,\varphi(r).$$

Let us imagine now that the volume indicated by an *upside down* Figure 2.6 is excavated in a solid rock, in such a way, that is, that plane $0XZ$, which we shall regard as horizontal, is the uppermost plane of the rock. Then if one pours into that cavity a volume of water equal to q_u, the distance y between its level and the uppermost horizontal plane will give us the final degree of

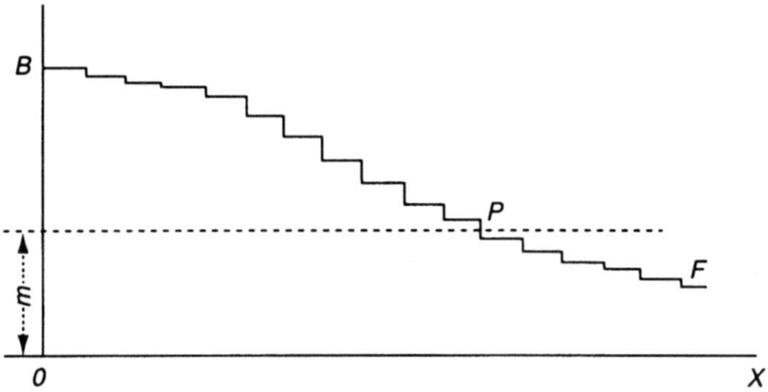

Figure 2.7

utility of the money that corresponds to that quantity q_a, whilst the volume of water contained in each of the cylindrical slices will tell us the expenditure sustained in order to satisfy the need represented by that cylindrical slice.

The law of the increasing variety of human needs is indicated (in Figure 2.7) by the shape of line *BF*, which extends indefinitely in the direction *0X*. And the well-known theorem that there can never be a **general** excess of production is expressed by saying that the final degree of utility of money can never be too small, and in the figure one can see that whatever small utility *m* may the money have, there will always be the needs *P F* . . . to be satisfied.

When one is dealing with a large number of needs, the broken line *BPF* . . . can be replaced by a continuous line with little error.

In this way we would have obtained the continuity both for the quantities of the goods that satisfy each need, and for the needs themselves; which was the goal we had set for ourselves.

We can continue and try also to obtain continuity when considering the various individuals. It is evident that when we wish to study the political economy of a whole people – when, that is, we study the economy of several millions individuals – we cannot take into account individual differences, other than their cumulative effect on the general phenomenon.

In order to take into account the variations of the final degree of utility from one individual to another, we shall introduce a new parameter v. Thus, the function $\varphi(r,u,v)$ will represent and sum up the society under scrutiny.

The day will perhaps come when we are able to have an idea of the form of that function for our societies, and from the comparison of its values in various ages, we shall be able to learn precious lessons. Today, even though such knowledge is still beyond our reach, it is still not entirely useless to reflect on these functions because through them we can delineate ideal societies and infer conclusions which, when compared to the actual facts, will teach us how far our hypotheses are from the truth, and will therefore pave the way for us to introduce appropriate changes.

Final degree of utility of instrumental goods of various orders

Menger states:

> Our well-being is assured when we are in possession of goods that are suitable for the **immediate** satisfaction of our needs. For the sake of concision, we shall call this category of goods '*first-order good*'. In these the causal relationship between goods and satisfaction is immediate. Next we have goods inherently incapable of directly satisfying a need, but capable of being transformed in first-order goods. Their causal relationship with the satisfaction of human needs is mediated. They are called '*second-order goods*'. Similarly, one can have third- and fourth-order goods. The work of a miller who prepares the flour would be third-order, and the work of the farmer fourth-order, and so on.[XII]

The final degree of utility of all those instrumental goods, according to the theorem we have demonstrated, cannot but be considered equal to the final degrees of utility of the first-order goods into which they are transformed.

This fact is true, and in some circumstances it is very useful to keep it in mind in order to dismantle many of the sophisms that clog the science of economics, but it cannot be denied that by following that path, when we really wish to know those final degrees of utility, we are led into a very prickly jungle, so thick with difficulties that we can no longer extricate ourselves.

Let us suppose we have to investigate the utility of sheet iron produced in England. That sheet iron will be bought by a shipbuilder. The ship will be acquired by a shipowner. A trader will charter the ship and load her with cotton. That cotton will be spun in Manchester, the yarn will be taken to Italy and used to make some fabric, which, to cut a long story short, will end up in the hands of the consumer. The degree of utility of that sheet iron is nothing but the degree of utility of that fabric and other similar direct consumption objects that will be procured by means of the ship!

It can be easily understood how, when they see themselves being pushed into such a thick jungle, many resist and reject the theories of Pure Economics. In our opinion, it is necessary to study diligently all that is reasonable in their objections and treasure it, and it is not beneficial to reject them haughtily as contrary to our theory; for a theory that cannot bow to practice is not only useless, but also noxious. And for this reason no praise will ever do justice to the careful use that Marshall makes of it in his treatise, his mind being always focused on the actual facts. When pure theory has grown in size and authority, then it will also be able to claim a more important role for itself in the study of the science of economics.

* General theorems in the science of economics, like the theorems that reduce the final degree of utility of any given economic good to the degrees of utility of the goods that satisfy direct consumption, are very similar to general theorems generated by the science of dynamics.

* For instance, it is very useful to know the principle of the preservation of the movement of the centre of gravity. We know that the movement of the centre of gravity of the solar system must be uniform, if we assume that no celestial body external to the solar system acts on it. But this is not enough for the science of astronomy. We also need to know the movements of the bodies of which the system is constituted.

For Political Economy it is not enough to reduce the utilities of all the other goods to the utility of first-order goods, it is also necessary to know how those reductions are carried out through various degrees. And this corresponds to reality. The person who produces sheet iron does not care about knowing the utility of the individual who will use the cotton fabric, he only cares about the needs of the shipbuilder.

We must therefore recognize that free competition is a way of obtaining through trials the solution to the equation that equates the final degree of utility of goods of higher order to the degrees of utility of first-order goods.[17]

The shipbuilder assumes as the final degree of utility of his ship a function that he ensures is as close to reality as possible. The trader does the same for the cotton he imports from America, the spinner for the yarn he produces, and so on.

The inevitable mistakes made in these calculations are the main source for the crises that cyclically affect industries and trades.

If the shipowners have made a mistake in setting the degrees of utility of the ships and have assumed them too high, the charter fees will drop, and this will possibly trigger a crisis in the shipbuilding industry.

When these facts happen at the same time for a number of industries, they give rise to the false belief that there is an excess of **general** production, whereas in fact all there is an excess of production in those industries, and this is the tangible manifestation of a mistake in the calculations made in order to equate the utility of goods of a higher order to first-order goods.

A *general* excess of production is impossible because of the shape that the diagram of the needs has, as we have previously seen. However large the sum total of all production is, it will always be equal to consumption, provided it is proportionally distributed among the various needs; in fact, from this generic point of view, production and consumption are two words used to indicate the same thing. When they are considered for some of the parts included in the total, however, they can instead be vastly different.

In this way we see how, far from being overcome by the difficulties it encounters, the theory extracts from them the explanations of facts that are known to be true from experience. And in this we must see a reason, one of the best possible, to hold the theory true.

Analytically, let us assume that $B, C, E \ldots$ are first-order goods, A is a second-order good, and S a third-order good, and let us also keep notations similar to those previously used.

The final degree of utility of A will be given by the equation

$$\varphi_a(q_a) = \frac{1}{p_b}\varphi_b(r_b) = \frac{1}{p_c}\varphi_c(r_c) = \ldots$$

and that of S by

$$\frac{1}{p_s}\varphi_s(q_s) = \varphi_a(r_a) \tag{11}$$

But if we wish to study *only* the phenomenon of the transformation of S into A, we shall have to replace

$$\varphi_a(r_a)$$

with another function

$$\psi_a(r_a),$$

which **in the mind** of the purchaser of A should be equal to the function φ_a, but actually is not. And the difference between ψ_a and φ_a acts like a force on a material point, and causes the prices and the bartered quantities to oscillate around the central positions that would be obtained from equation (11).

3 Considerations on the fundamental principles of Pure Political Economy, III

(*Giornale degli Economisti*, August 1892)

Supply and demand

The demand of a commodity at a certain price, and similarly its supply, depend on the final degree of utility of that commodity.

One usually starts by dealing with the case of two economic goods that are transformed into each other, but since, as we have seen, it is necessary to consider all the goods that are needed for direct consumption, it is better, when possible, to take this circumstance into account.

Supply can be considered as negative demand. And the law of their variations is simply the law of the variation of the quantities of economic goods in relation to prices.

The variation of the demanded (or supplied) quantity of a commodity can be considered either in relation to its price, while the prices of the other commodities remain unchanged; or in relation to the prices of the other commodities, which vary while the price of the commodity under consideration remains unchanged.

One may examine, by way of example, how much more or how much less bread an individual buys when the price of bread goes down or up; or one may investigate how the quantity demanded by that individual changes when the price of the individual's work, or of his clothes, or of his lodging, or some other price of economic goods varies, while the price of bread remains unchanged.

In mathematical terms we shall say in few words that it is necessary to consider the partial derivatives with regard to the prices of the various economic goods.

Let us maintain the notations illustrated in the section 'Fundamental theorem of the transformation of any given number of goods (chapter 2, pp. 23–26) and let us remember formulae (4) and (5), in the latter of which we shall revert to using $-r_a$ instead of q_a; we shall therefore have

$$r_a + p_b r_b + p_c r_c + \ldots = 0 \tag{12}$$

$$\varphi_a(r_a) = \frac{1}{p_b}\varphi_b(r_b) = \frac{1}{p_c}\varphi_c(r_c) = \ldots. \tag{13}$$

If the commodities are n, as we shall assume, the equations (13) will be $n-1$, and with equation (12) we shall have n equations, which is indeed all that is needed to determine the n unknowns

$$r_a, r_b, r_c \ldots,$$

if the prices $p_a, p_b, \ldots$ and the functions $\varphi_a, \varphi_b, \ldots$ are known.

By replacing in equation (12) the values of $p_b, p_c, \ldots$ inferred from equations (13), we shall have

$$r_a\varphi_a(r_a) + r_b\varphi_b(r_b) + r_c\varphi_c(r_c) + \ldots = 0. \tag{14}$$

From this equation we can obtain the value of one of the r, for example of r_a, as a function of the others, which are then independent variables. Using that value of r_a we shall calculate $\varphi_a(r_a)$, and we shall find that it is equal to a certain function ψ, that is

$$\varphi_a(r_a) = \psi(r_b\varphi_b(r_b) + r_c\varphi_c(r_c) + \ldots).$$

Then from equations (13) we shall have

$$\begin{cases} p_b = \varphi_b(r_b)\ /\ \psi(r_b\varphi_b(r_b) + r_c\varphi_c(r_c) + \ldots) \\ p_c = \varphi_c(r_c)\ /\ \psi(r_b\varphi_b(r_b) + r_c\varphi_c(r_c) + \ldots). \\ \ldots \end{cases} \tag{15}$$

Thus we obtain the expression of the laws of demand (or supply) of the various commodities.

Law of the variation of supply and demand

This is a very important problem, that will be solved directly by considering equations (12) and (13), without first obtaining the equations (15).

For the sake of greater symmetry, let us also assign a price p_a to commodity A. Prices will be measured in any given *ideal* money. We shall therefore suppose that

for the commodities	A	B	C	E	$\ldots$
the prices are	p_a	p_b	p_c	p_e	$\ldots$

The equations (12) and (13) will become

$$p_ar_a + p_br_b + p_cr_c + \ldots = 0 \tag{12 bis}$$
$$m = \frac{1}{p_a}\varphi_a(r_a) = \frac{1}{p_b}\varphi_b(r_b) = \frac{1}{p_c}\varphi_c(r_c) = \ldots \tag{13 bis}$$

For commodity A, the quantity

$$\frac{\partial r_a}{\partial p_a}$$

gives us the variation of the demand (or of the supply) when the price of that same commodity changes, while all the other prices remain unchanged. And the quantities

$$\frac{\partial r_a}{\partial p_b}, \frac{\partial r_a}{\partial p_c} \ldots$$

show us the variations of r_a that depend on the variations of the prices of the other commodities, with the exception of *A*.

There are obviously similar expressions for the other commodities *B*, *C*. . . .

Let us differentiate (13 *bis*); we shall have

$$\begin{cases} \dfrac{\partial m}{\partial p_a} = \dfrac{1}{p_a}\dfrac{\partial r_a}{\partial p_a}\varphi'_a - \dfrac{1}{p_a^2}\varphi_a \\ \dfrac{\partial m}{\partial p_a} = \dfrac{1}{p_b}\dfrac{\partial r_b}{\partial p_a}\varphi'_b \\ \dfrac{\partial m}{\partial p_a} = \dfrac{1}{p_c}\dfrac{\partial r_c}{\partial p_a}\varphi'_c \\ \ldots \end{cases} \tag{16}$$

Therefore[1]

$$\begin{cases} \dfrac{\partial r_a}{\partial p_a} = p_a\dfrac{\partial m}{\partial p_a}\dfrac{1}{\varphi'_a} + \dfrac{1}{p_a}\dfrac{\varphi_a}{\varphi'_a} \\ \dfrac{\partial r_b}{\partial p_a} = p_b\dfrac{\partial m}{\partial p_a}\dfrac{1}{\varphi'_b} \\ \dfrac{\partial r_c}{\partial p_a} = p_c\dfrac{\partial m}{\partial p_a}\dfrac{1}{\varphi'_c} \\ \ldots \end{cases} \tag{17}$$

Let us multiply the first of these equations by p_a, the second by p_b, the third by p_c . . ., and let us assume

$$S_a = p_a\frac{\partial r_a}{\partial p_a} + p_b\frac{\partial r_b}{\partial p_a} + p_c\frac{\partial r_c}{\partial p_a} + \ldots$$

$$T = \frac{p_a^2}{\varphi'_a} + \frac{p_b^2}{\varphi'_b} + \frac{p_c^2}{\varphi'_c} + \ldots;$$

we shall have

$$S_a = T\frac{\partial m}{\partial p_a} + \frac{\varphi_a}{\varphi'_a}.$$

But differentiating equation (12 *bis*), gives

$$S_a + r_a = 0,$$

and by combining this equation with the previous one, one obtains

$$\frac{\partial m}{\partial p_a} = -\frac{r_a + \dfrac{\varphi_a}{\varphi'_a}}{T} \qquad (16\ bis)$$

This is the variation of the utility of the money; by inserting its value in equations (17), one will know the quantities

$$\frac{\partial r_a}{\partial p_a}, \frac{\partial r_b}{\partial p_a}, \frac{\partial r_c}{\partial p_a} \ldots$$

and our problem will be solved.

Law of supply and demand assuming that the final degree of utility of an economic good decreases when the quantity of the latter increases

If we suppose that this law exists for final degrees of utility, the quantities

$$\varphi'_a, \varphi'_b, \varphi'_c \ldots$$

will be negative, so T will always be negative, and therefore the sign of the left-hand side of equation (16 *bis*) will be equal to the sign of

$$r_a + \frac{\varphi_a}{\varphi'_a}.$$

If commodity A is supplied then r_a is negative, and since φ'_a is also negative, it follows that the sign of

$$\frac{\partial m}{\partial p_a}$$

is negative, and equations (17) show that the sign of

$$\frac{\partial r_b}{\partial p_a}, \frac{\partial r_c}{\partial p_a} \ldots$$

will be positive. As for the sign of the derivative of r_a, it still cannot be determined, since that derivative is equal to a difference and it can therefore be positive or negative, according to the case. Now if we recall that the positive derivative of a positive quantity indicates that the latter increases as the variable increases, and of a negative quantity indicates that the latter decreases in **absolute value**, and vice versa, we shall have the following proposition:

Theorem

If the price of a commodity supplied by an individual increases while the prices of the other commodities remain unchanged, the quantities that are demanded of the latter will increase, and the quantities that are supplied will decrease.

Let us assume that A is required. Then r_a is positive and the sign of the derivative of m with respect to p_a remains uncertain; nothing can be decided for the derivatives of r_b, r_c . . .; but for the derivative of r_a we have[I]

$$\frac{\partial r_a}{\partial p_a} = \frac{-p_a r_a + \frac{\varphi_a}{p_a}\left(\frac{p_b^2}{\varphi'_b} + \frac{p_c^2}{\varphi'_c} + \ldots\right)}{T\varphi'_a}$$

and one can see that this derivative is negative; hence the following proposition.

Theorem

If the price of a commodity required by an individual increases, the quantity demanded decreases. With regard to the other commodities, whose prices do not change, one can only state that: either the quantities of all supplied commodities will increase, while the quantities of the required commodities decrease;[II] or vice versa.[III]

However, this analysis is still incomplete, even though we conducted it in a more general way than usual. The possible variation in the number of transformed commodities was not taken into account. The price variations of a commodity do not alter only the quantities of the commodities consumed by the individual, but they may allow him to satisfy new needs, or they may prevent him from continuing to satisfy as many needs as before.

All this is taken into account by observing how the new needs one can satisfy, or the old ones one must cease to satisfy, simply alter some quantities and S_a and T. It will be necessary, on the other hand, in our equations, to replace the derivatives

$$\frac{\partial m}{\partial p_a}, \quad \frac{\partial r_a}{\partial p_a}, \quad \frac{\partial r_b}{\partial p_a} \ldots$$

with the quotients of the finite differences

$$\frac{\Delta m}{\Delta p_a}, \quad \frac{\Delta r_a}{\Delta p_a}, \quad \frac{\Delta r_b}{\Delta p_a} \ldots$$

since it would be hard to imagine that the needs that appear and disappear could correspond to infinitesimal variations of price p_a.

The introduction of finite differences renders the previous equations only approximate. But apart from that, the whole reasoning proceeds on as before, and one deduces theorems like those we have already demonstrated.

We have supposed that only one of the prices varied; let us now consider instead the case where they all vary.

In this case the variation of one of the quantities, for example r_u, will be

$$dr_u = \frac{\partial r_u}{\partial p_u} dp_u + \frac{\partial r_u}{\partial p_b} dp_b + \dots$$

$$dm = \frac{\partial m}{\partial p_u} dp_u + \frac{\partial m}{\partial p_b} dp_b + \dots$$

and so on.

The first of equations (16) gives us the partial derivative of m with respect to p_u; for reasons of symmetry, the others, with respect to $p_b, p_c \dots$, can be written immediately, and so we have

$$\frac{\partial m}{\partial p_u} = -\frac{r_u + \frac{\varphi_u}{\varphi'_u}}{T}$$

$$\frac{\partial m}{\partial p_b} = -\frac{r_b + \frac{\varphi_b}{\varphi'_b}}{T}.$$

$$\dots$$

Let us substitute these values in the equation that gives us dm, let us assume

$$d\sigma = p_u dr_u + p_b dr_b + \dots$$

$$d\tau = \frac{\varphi_u}{\varphi'_u} dp_u + \frac{\varphi_b}{\varphi'_b} dp_b + \dots$$

and we shall have

$$dm = -\frac{d\sigma + d\tau}{T}. \tag{18}$$

This is the total variation of the utility of money.

Equations (17) and the other similar equations found for the derivatives with respect to $p_b, p_c \dots$, in combination with the equation that gives dr_u and with the other similar equations that give $dr_b, dr_c \dots$, allow us to find that

$$\begin{cases} dr_u = \frac{p_u}{\varphi'_u} dm + \frac{1}{p_u} \frac{\varphi_u}{\varphi'_u} dp_u \\ dr_b = \frac{p_b}{\varphi'_b} dm + \frac{1}{p_b} \frac{\varphi_b}{\varphi'_b} dp_b \\ \dots \end{cases} \tag{19}$$

And these equations can be more easily obtained by *totally* differentiating equations (13 *bis*).

By replacing in equations (19) the value of dm given by equation (18), one will find the values of the total variations of r_a, r_b. . . .

Determination of the final degree of utility when the laws of demand and supply are known

This problem is the opposite of the previous one, and dealing with it will lead us to consequences that appear to be very important.

First of all we observe that whilst, with the formulae we have assumed, the demand – or the supply – is determined as a function of the price when the final degrees of utility are known, the latter are instead not wholly determined when only the demand – or the supply – is known.

From an analytical point of view, one can immediately see how the matter stands.

We have one equation (12) and $n - 1$ equations (13), that is a total of n equations. Therefore, if one knows the functions φ_a, φ_b, φ_c . . ., one can eliminate the $n - 1$ quantities r_b, r_c, . . . among those n equations and have a relationship between r_a and p_a (besides p_b, p_c . . . that are considered constant), which shows precisely the law of demand (or supply).

But when, instead, the quantities r_a, r_b, . . . p_a, p_b . . . are given, and one has to determine φ_a, φ_b . . ., one of the equations, i.e. (12), is no longer necessary for the determination of the unknowns because it only establishes a relationship between known quantities. Thus only $n - 1$ equations are left, and therefore one cannot determine all n quantities φ_a, φ_b . . ., but only $n - 1$ of these as functions of one of them chosen arbitrarily.

It will be useful to explain the same thing without analysis; we shall therefore reason on a more simple case.

A worker gives a certain number of hours and receives in exchange a certain quantity of food. For him the final degree of utility of work is known, and so is that of food. Then everything is determined and we can find the law of supply of work and of demand of food. But if the latter is instead known, we shall only be able to find the relationship between the final degree of utility of work and that of food.

Today, a worker gives two hours of work for one kilogram of bread. We can say that the utility of the last minute of work is equal to the utility of one one hundred and twentieth of one kilogram of bread. Next day, bread has gone up in price and the worker gives three hours of work to have half a kilogram of bread. The utility of the last minute of work is equal to that of one three hundred and sixtieth of one kilogram of bread. But it would be a mistake to infer that the final degree of utility corresponding to one kilogram of bread is to the final degree of utility corresponding to half a kilogram as 120 is to 360. This would be right if the final degree of utility of the last minute were the same when one works one hour or half an hour. But this is not so. And until we do not know what relationship exists between those degrees of utility of work, we shall never be able to know the relationship between the degrees of utility of bread.

All this applies when, generally, the final degrees of utility can be functions of all the quantities of consumed commodities. When the final degree of utility of a commodity is only a function of the consumed quantity of it, one must take this condition into account.

The latter case is not different from the former if there are only two economic goods.

Indeed, thanks to equation (12), since r_a is a function of r_b, any more general function of these two quantities can be expressed as a function of only one of these quantities, by eliminating the other.

But in the case of three or more economic goods there is a difference between considering each of the final degrees of utility as a function of only one quantity, or of all of them.

In equations (12) and (13) we have assumed as independent variables the $n-1$ quantities

$$p_b, p_c \ldots,$$

but one could instead assume $n-1$ of the other quantities

$$r_a, r_b \ldots .$$

Let us suppose that they are $r_b, r_c, \ldots$

The condition that φ_b depends only on r_b will be expressed with the $n-2$ equations

$$\frac{\partial(p_b\varphi_a)}{\partial r_c} = 0 \,, \frac{\partial(p_b\varphi_a)}{\partial r_d} = 0 \ldots \qquad (20)$$

and since the $\varphi_b, \varphi_c \ldots$ are $n-1$, all together there are $(n-1)(n-2)$ similar equations.

Furthermore, from observation we shall have the expressions of the $n-1$ quantities

$$\frac{\partial p_b}{\partial r_b}, \frac{\partial p_c}{\partial r_c} \ldots$$

and therefore $n-1$ equations which, added to the previous ones, give a total of

$$(n-1)^2$$

equations. There are n unknowns, namely the derivatives

$$\varphi'_a(r_a), \varphi'_b(r_b) \ldots;$$

by subtracting this number from the number of the equations one has

$$N = n^2 - 3n + 1. \tag{21}$$

If there are two commodities, that is if $n = 2$, one has

$$N = -1,$$

and we are one equation short of being able to determine the unknowns. If there are three commodities, that is if $n = 3$, one has

$$N = +1.$$

In conclusion we shall therefore say that when the final degree of a commodity depends only on the consumed quantity of that commodity, if we only consider two commodities, the final degrees of utility remain indeterminate, and it will be possible to know one only when the other is known. And every law of demand, or of supply, can be arbitrarily fixed.

If there are three or more economic goods, not all the laws of demand are compatible with the posited condition for the expression of the final degrees of utility, but it is necessary for those laws to satisfy certain conditions as indicated by the theory.

The final degrees of utility are then entirely determined when the law of demand is known.

Need for new phenomena to be considered

What is the reason for the indeterminateness we observe in the case of two economic goods? There is nothing indeterminate in nature. If our theory is well constructed, by giving us as an answer that the problem is not determinate, it must be telling us that we should have taken into account some circumstances that we ignored.

Let us point out that up to this point we have considered isolated phenomena. And it could well be that this theory applies to men so improvident that they only work when need drives them to it, and stop as soon as their need is satisfied. And this seems to be the case for some primitive peoples, but in our societies the majority of men work to provide not only for their present needs, but also for their future. If nothing else, by working for six days every worker provides also for his sustenance on the seventh.

This phenomenon of *saving* was not taken into account in our formulae; let us see what consequences follow from considering it.

Here one must consider saving independently from the idea of capital, as Prof. Walras does,[3] as a mere surplus of past consumption which is used to provide for future contingencies. With this quality, saving has a degree of utility of its own that depends mainly on the individual's foresight.

Let us go back to our previous example. If the worker in question has a certain quantity of bread put aside, and if we know that the degree of utility of bread, considered only as savings, does not vary from one day to the other, and if we observe that the saved quantity has not been increased or decreased, we shall infer from these facts that the final degree of utility[4] of the work of the last minute of the first day is equal to the final degree of utility of the work of the last [minute of the] second [day]. Indeed those final degrees are both equal to the final degree of the last small saved quantity of bread because if they were smaller, the individual would have continued working to increase the quantity of bread put aside; he would have consumed some of it, if the pleasure of abstaining from work had been greater than the pleasure afforded by putting bread aside.

In this way we have obtained the relationship between the final degrees of utility of work, which we needed in order to infer from it the value of the final degree of utility of bread.

But things do not proceed so smoothly in nature. Our observations do not show that perfect equilibrium, but the changes which the quantity of saved economic good undergoes. Perhaps even this case can be explained in plain language; we do not know whether one day we shall be able to overcome the difficulties that confront us when we attempt to do so, but today we are compelled to seek the help of mathematics.

And the discussion flows more easily when using the latter. The savings made by the individual can actually be of one or more of the commodities A, B . . ., but we can always calculate them in terms of A; we shall indicate them with s, and they will be positive if they are actual savings, negative when we are instead dealing with the consumption of the economic goods that have been put aside. We shall have

$$r_a + p_b r_b + p_c r_c + \ldots = s \qquad (22)$$

for the equation that must replace equation (12).

This replacement increases by one the number of independent variables, of which there will now be n; it will therefore be possible for them to be the n quantities

$$r_a, r_b, r_c \ldots .$$

The number of equations given by the partial derivatives, which previously was

$$(n-1)^2,$$

now becomes

$$(n-1)n,^{\text{IV}}$$

and by subtracting the number of unknowns, one obtains

$$n^2 - 2n$$

equations. This number is equal to zero for $n = 2$; there are therefore enough equations to determine the unknowns. When there are three commodities, there will be three condition equations.

Since the unknowns are variations of final degrees of utility, the initial values are still arbitrary, i.e. they must be determined with other considerations.

By taking saving into account the problem is therefore perfectly determined, even in the case of two commodities, though always with arbitrary constants.

Let us see even more closely how the matter follows.

Without considering saving, we have the equations

$$r_a + p_b r_b = 0, \ \varphi_a(r_a) = \frac{1}{p_b}\varphi_b(r_b).$$

We can observe the various values of r_a, of r_b, of p_b, and in this way we can have the variations of r_b and p_b when r_a varies. But the former of the previous equations shows that one will always have

$$1 + p_b\frac{dr_b}{dr_a} + r_b\frac{dp_b}{dr_a} = 0;$$

and so observation does not really give us anything but one of those variations of which the other is a consequence. We have therefore only one equation

$$\varphi'_a = \frac{1}{p_b}\varphi'_b\frac{dr_b}{dr_a} - \frac{1}{p^2_b}\frac{dp_b}{dr_a}\varphi_b,$$

which is not enough to determine the two unknowns

$$\varphi'_a, \varphi'_b.$$

In our previous example of the worker who bartered his work for bread, we availed ourselves of the consideration of saving to recognize that

$$\varphi'_a = 0,$$

thus obtaining the second equation we needed to determine the two unknowns.

In general, saving can have various values, in which case the previous equations no longer apply, but must be replaced by the equations one obtains by observing the variations of p_b when r_a and r_b vary independently from one another. And this is possible because the expression

$$r_a + p_b r_b$$

does not necessarily have to be equal to zero, but can take all the values corresponding to the various values of saving. We shall therefore infer from observation the values of

$$\frac{\partial p_h}{\partial r_u}, \frac{\partial p_h}{\partial r_h}$$

and by inserting them in the equations[V]

$$\varphi'_u = -\frac{1}{p^2_h}\frac{\partial p_h}{\partial r_u}\varphi_h,$$

$$0 = \frac{1}{p_h}\varphi'_h - \frac{1}{p_h^2}\frac{\partial p_h}{\partial r_h}\varphi_h,$$

we shall be able to calculate the successive values of φ_u and φ_h starting from arbitrary initial values, or we shall be able to obtain them directly by integrating those equations. And, as is well known, integration will introduce two arbitrary constants.

These constants will then be reduced to one by using the equation

$$\varphi_u = \frac{1}{p_h}\varphi_h,$$

since the initial value of φ_u will be inferred from it, once the value of φ_h that corresponds to a certain value of p_h has been arbitrarily fixed.

We would like to know how those people, who, while approving of the convenience of considering the final degrees of utility, bitterly criticize the use not only of formulae but also of any mathematical reasoning, would deal with these problems.

And if others will even refuse to incorporate the final degrees of utility in the study of economics, they will admittedly avoid the hard work of reasoning, with or without mathematics. But even lighter will the effort be of those who forsake the study of any economic theory, though they will not reach that minimum of work that is the rightly deserved prize of those fortunate mortals who abstain from any reasoning.

It should be pointed out that the economic goods we have so far discussed are such that the consumed quantities are independent of each other. The dependence of those consumed quantities, or the possibility of substituting one economic good for another makes the final degree of utility of each commodity depend on more than one quantity. We shall discuss these goods later, as we shall also come back to examine the above-mentioned condition equations. But we must stop for a moment here, to see how final degrees of utility could actually be calculated.

Numerical calculation of the final degrees of utility

The first difficulty confronting us is that of choosing the units for economic goods; however, this difficulty is not specific to this study, and one faces it every time one wants to measure economic goods.

In statistical surveys relating to international trade, for instance, heterogeneous quantities that are arbitrarily reduced to the same unit are added together. One says that a country exported a certain number of hectolitres of wine, and by doing so one uses the word 'wine' to indicate both a liquid worth two hundred lire per hectolitre, and one worth ten, but the two are still quite different commodities. For this reason some statistical surveys give further details: in French statistics, for instance, the export of Gironde wines is shown separately from the export of wines from other regions. On the other hand, it is sometimes convenient to gather various commodities together and create large categories, and one speaks of the export of foodstuff and of industrial products. Finally, commodities must be sorted according to the particular purpose one has in mind, and must therefore be measured using different units.

Let us assume that the present study has been completed and that, for the purpose of achieving our goal, the categories of commodities and their measurement units have been fixed. What will be left for us to observe in various cases is consumption in relation to the prices of those commodities; and once the law of demand has been obtained in this way, the final degrees of utility will be inferred from it.

Let us consider, for example, a small company of workers, for each of whom it is possible to think that the final degrees of utility have virtually equal values,[5] and who do piece-work here and there in various towns, where both their remuneration and the prices of the commodities they consume vary.

In this way one obtains separate bits of information divided among various quantities, which one must try to collate through *interpolation.*

Here lies the second difficulty of a practical nature that we encounter. Whole treatises have been written on interpolation in general, and there are many considerations one must keep in mind in order to obtain sufficiently approximate results.

One could have other examples by considering a whole town when the prices of some commodities suddenly change, but perhaps it will be better to try first with monographs of working families and of small companies, according to Le Play's[VI] system, applied to our present purpose.

At any rate, let us suppose that we have obtained the data regarding consumed quantities and prices.

It is probably more convenient to interpolate the logarithm of the price, rather than the price itself, since the very little we know about price variations seems to indicate that the price curve is closer in shape to a logarithmic curve, rather than to a parabola.

Unfortunately, the data that for a long time to come we will be able to gather on prices and consumption will not be quite so precise as to suggest, for interpolation, the use of the least squares method. Cauchy's[VII] method will be more than adequate, with Le Verrier's modifications, perhaps, for those who desire a more precise method.[6]

Let us suppose that there are two economic goods. Through interpolation we shall obtain

$$\log p_b = M_0 + M_1 r_a + N_1 r_b + M_2 r_a^2 + p_2 r_a r_b + N_2 r_b^2 + \ldots.$$

There is no point in extracting the differential coefficients of p_b from this formula; they have been considered only for ease of demonstration; we can more easily obtain the values of φ_a, φ_b. Let us therefore posit

$$\log\varphi_a = A_0 + A_1 r_a + A_2 r_a^2 + \ldots$$

$$\log\varphi_b = B_0 + B_1 r_b + B_2 r_b^2 + \ldots.$$

From formulae (13) we have

$$\log p_b = \log\varphi_b - \log\varphi_a$$

and therefore, by equating the coefficients of the same powers of r_a and r_b,

$$B_0 - A_0 = M_0, \quad A_1 = -M_1, \quad B_1 = N_1, \quad \ldots.$$

In this way the coefficients of φ_a and φ_b will be determined, with the exception of the former, for which only the difference between them is known. This is in accordance with our previous remark that what is left is an arbitrary constant. Fixing it is the same as fixing the unit for those final degrees of utility, and since that unit is arbitrary, so is also the constant.[7]

When there are three or more commodities, the method to calculate the final degrees of utility is entirely similar to the method we have just demonstrated. One must also take into account the condition equations between the known quantities, as we shall shortly see.

Usefulness of measuring the final degrees of utility

Since the new Political Economy places the final degree of utility at the beginning of its every reasoning, it is clearly useful to acquire as much knowledge as possible about it.

The objection that pleasure, and therefore utility, cannot be directly measured does not hold. In the natural sciences we have many quantities that are impossible to measure directly and are indirectly measured.

* The simplest examples are those regarding the measurement of the distance of celestial bodies; but the artifice is less noticeable, because the measurements one can directly obtain and those one obtains indirectly are of the same kind. Less plain is the measuring with regard to the air vibrations from which sound originates, but at least we know the vibrating body. As for the luminous vibrations of ether, on the contrary, not even what vibrates falls under our senses. We can only say that if it exists it is ether, and that if it

vibrates as the theory of light requires, the waves must have certain lengths that demonstrate luminous phenomena.

Similarly, the observation of economic phenomena shows us what values the final degrees of utility must have. In both cases direct measurement is impossible, and indirect measurement intervenes.

As for the way of obtaining those measurements with precision, the science of optics relies on the perfection of the instruments and on the accuracy of the observer; Political Economy must rely on the latter too, and must also wait in order to collect a large quantity of precise data on prices and on the consumed commodities.

Jevons clearly saw how useful the measuring of the final degrees of utility could be to Political Economy. He says: 'We cannot really spell out the effect of any exchange in trade or in manufacturing until we can numerically express with some degree of approximation the laws of the variation of utility'.[8]

And he tries to break through in this way; but in order to calculate the final degrees of utility he assumes constant the utility of money. It is rather odd for him to make the latter hypothesis, when it was he who was quite rightly advising us to consider that utility variable.[9] By assuming it constant we have no way of adequately dealing with the most important issues of the study of the science of economics, such as, by way of example, the problems of international trade.

The formulae we have now found allow us to calculate the final degrees of utility in the most general case.

This topic is of the utmost importance for the science and deserves to be studied with great care by economists. Prof. Edgeworth is right when he remarks[10] that even without reducing mathematical formulae to numbers one can extract useful conclusions from them, but knowing even with rough approximation the numerical value of the quantities at hand greatly increases our scientific wealth, and we must therefore do our best to try to acquire that knowledge.

* And by so doing, not only shall we obtain new and precious bits of information, but we shall also avoid many mistakes. Among the countless examples, suffice it to mention here the following, which is notable for the standing of the person involved. Newton thought that Saturn's orbit was significantly altered at every conjunction with Jupiter, whereas observations by later astronomers showed it to be almost insignificant.[11]

One must realize how likely such errors must be in Political Economy, where we are now quite far from being able to have as precise data as those of which Newton could avail himself in the field of Astronomy.

But, some people ask, what is the use of all this? In this case it helps shed light on a theory that is of fundamental importance in the science of economics. And if the latter does not even have to bother with knowing what variations affect the consumption of a commodity when both the price of that commodity and the price of the other commodities vary, then one might as well stop studying it. Others add: what advantage shall we obtain from these theories? And it is true that there are more profitable theories; never will Political Economy be able to teach that most consummate skill with which bands of petty politicians play havoc with taxpayers' wealth in Italy. But perhaps the specific purpose of the science of economics is not this, in the same way that the study of chemistry does not aim at providing the best poisons to criminals. But even without going much further, he who only rejects the study of theorems that do not offer any direct benefit should consider that science must be studied only to know the truth,[12] and that from this knowledge often unexpectedly good and positive benefits follow that we could not even remotely imagine.

* The ancient geometricians who studied the properties of conical sections in Alexandria it could never have imagined that those properties were the fruitful seed from which the theories of modern Astronomy would sprout, thanks to which man can safely cross the oceans.

* When Newton was studying the solar spectrum, when Frauenhofer[XIII] was making its bands known in great detail, only a short time after Wollaston[XIV] had barely been able to see them, who would have dreamed that those bands would become a tool for chemistry to discover new substances; and that the light spectra of the stars would allow us to know the speed – a marvel to any true intellect – with which those heavenly bodies travel through space? But if one wanted to list all the benefits that mankind derived from scientific theories, one would have to tell the history of human civilization.

Necessary qualities that restrict the laws of demand

We have seen that in the case of three or more commodities not all the laws of demand are compatible with the fact that the final degree of utility only depends on the quantities of the commodity to which it refers. It is now necessary to examine this matter better.

In the case of equations (12) and (13), equations (15) give us the form that the expressions of

$$p_b, \quad p_c \ldots$$

must take.

These equations are the integrals of a system of partial derivative equations that it may be useful to know.

Let us indicate with *log* the Neperian logarithm; from formula (15) one has

$$\frac{\partial \log p_h}{\partial r_k} = \frac{\partial \log p_{h'}}{\partial r_k} \tag{23}$$

where h, h', k are any three of the letters b, c . . . provided they are different from each other.

Furthermore, if one recalls the value of r_u[XV]

$$\begin{cases} \dfrac{\partial \log p_h}{\partial \log r_k} = \dfrac{\partial r_u}{\partial r_{k'}} \\ \dfrac{\partial \log p_{h'}}{\partial \log r_{k'}} = \dfrac{\partial r_u}{\partial r_k} \end{cases} \tag{24}$$

These equations also include the previous ones, if one assumes that k' is one of the letters b, c . . . different from, *or even the same as*, k.

The total number of equations (23) and (24) is

$$(n-1)(n-2)-1 = n^2 - 3n + 1,$$

and one can verify that it is precisely the number of condition equations that had to be found.[XVI]

If there are two commodities, there are no condition equations. If there are three commodities, we only have the equation

$$\frac{\dfrac{\partial \log p_b}{\partial r_c}}{\dfrac{\partial \log p_c}{\partial r_b}} = \frac{\dfrac{\partial r_u}{\partial r_c}}{\dfrac{\partial r_u}{\partial r_b}}. \tag{25}$$

If there are n independent variables, which happens when one considers saving, the equations are simpler.

Prices must have the form

$$p_b = \varphi_u(r_u)\varphi_b(r_b), \quad p_c = \varphi_u(r_u)\varphi_c(r_c). \ldots \tag{26}$$

The derivative equations are: the $n-2$

$$\frac{\partial \log p_b}{\partial r_u} = \frac{\partial \log p_c}{\partial r_u} = \ldots$$

and the $(n-1)(n-2)$

$$\frac{\partial \log p_b}{\partial r_c} = 0, \quad \frac{\partial \log p_b}{\partial r_d} = 0 \ldots$$
$$\frac{\partial \log p_c}{\partial r_b} = 0, \quad \frac{\partial \log p_c}{\partial r_d} = 0 \ldots$$

for a total, therefore, of

$$n - 2 + (n-2)(n-1) = n^2 - 2n,$$

as we already knew.

Fungible economic goods

The consumptions of these goods are no longer independent from each other.

In this case, what is missing for the question to be entirely determined is precisely the knowledge of the proportions in which one of the economic goods can replace the other.

For example, the consumption of wine can partly replace the consumption of wine spirit. One has to know the proportions, either constant or variable, according to which this substitution takes place in order to be able to calculate the final degrees of utility of wine and wine spirit.

Let us assume that ten litres of wine replace one litre of wine spirit. One has to add the number of consumed litres of the latter commodity to ten times the number of consumed litres of the former. The total represents the quantity of a fictitious commodity, whose final degree of utility can replace the final degrees of utility of the first two. And to these fictitious commodities one will be able to apply all that has been previously said of the commodities whose consumption is independent.

Let us suppose in general that the consumption of commodity C may replace the consumption of commodity B, in a proportion that can vary with the variation of the quantities of the commodities. Let us therefore suppose that when one has already consumed r_b of B and r_c of C, it works out the same to consume dr_b of B, or $y_c dr_b$, where the coefficient y_c can be a function of r_b and r_c. The quantity dr_c, equivalent for consumption to the quantity dr_b, is therefore given by the equation

$$dr_c = y_c dr_b;$$

by integrating this equation we shall obtain

$$r_b = \psi_c(r_c), \quad r_c = \psi_b(r_b);$$

which give us the quantities of B that are equivalent to certain quantities of C, and vice versa. Hence, when one has consumed r_b and r_c, the final degree of utility for the consumption of B is

$$\varphi_b(r_b + \psi_c(r_c)),$$

and for the consumption of C

$$\varphi_c(r_c + \psi_b(r_b)).$$

Since the [relative benefit] from consumption of the quantity dr_b must be equivalent to that from the consumption of dr_c, it is necessary that

$$\varphi_b(r_b + \psi_c(r_c))dr_b = \varphi_c(r_c + \psi_b(r_b))dr_c;$$

but, because of equations (13),

$$\frac{1}{p_b}\varphi_b(r_b + \psi_c(r_c)) = \frac{1}{p_c}\varphi_c(r_c + \psi_b(r_b)) \tag{27}$$

and therefore

$$\frac{dr_c}{dr_b} = \frac{p_b}{p_c} = y_c, \tag{28}$$

which was moreover clear from the outset.

Indeed, if we go back to our previous example, it is evident that the prices of wine and of wine spirit must be in the exact ratio of 1 to 10, because if wine cost less, the consumption of wine spirit would cease, and vice versa.

This ratio is not constant in nature, and this is why a variation in price causes a variation in consumption; and the Swiss law on the monopoly on the sale of wine spirit had the specific purpose of reducing the consumption of liqueurs while increasing the consumption of wine and beer.

If other commodities existed whose consumption could replace the consumption of B, such as, for instance, commodities E, F . . ., then one would have the following equations

$$dr_e = y_e dr_b, \quad dr_f = y_f dr_b \ldots$$

$$r_b = \psi_e(r_e), \quad r_b = \psi_f(r_f) \ldots$$

and the consumption of r_b of B, plus the consumption of r_c of C, plus the consumption of r_e of E . . . would be equivalent to the consumption of

$$r_b + \psi_c(r_c) + \psi_e(r_e) + \ldots = t_b \tag{29}$$

of B, and so one would have

$$\varphi_a(r_a) = \frac{1}{p_b}\varphi_b(r_b + \psi_c(r_c) + \ldots).$$

It is therefore possible to consider a fictitious commodity, whose price is that of B and whose consumption is equal to that of (29), which in equations (13) will replace commodities B, C, E, F. . . . We are therefore brought back to the previous case, where consumptions were independent. Consumption (29) has still to be subdivided among the various commodities: B, C. . . . It will therefore be necessary to have the equations

$$\frac{p_b}{p_c} = y_c, \quad \frac{p_b}{p_e} = y_e, \quad \frac{p_b}{p_f} = y_f \ldots \tag{30}$$

which together with the equation obtained by equating expression (29) to the consumption of the fictitious commodity are precisely what is needed in order to determine

$$r_b, \quad r_c, \quad r_e \ldots$$

On the other hand, the equations similar to equations (27) are equivalent to equations (30) and will be solved with them.

The second problem, i.e. the determination of the final degrees of utility, remains to be solved.

The determination of the final degree of utility of the fictitious commodity, whose consumption is independent from the other commodities, will be carried out as before, whenever the consumed quantity of that commodity, i.e. quantity (29), is known. In order to find the latter quantity it is necessary to resort to observation and see how the consumption of commodities vary when prices change.

As previously explained, in this way we shall obtain through interpolation the expressions of

$$y_c, \quad y_e, \quad y_f \ldots,$$

from which we shall infer expression (29). We shall therefore know

$$\varphi_b(t_b)$$

which is the final degree of utility of *B*. Similarly, we shall have the final degrees of utility of *C*, *E*. . . .

We can therefore determine the final degrees of utility, even when we are dealing with economic goods that can be replaced with one another in consumption.

Average final degrees of utility for more than one person

So far, we have considered a single individual; let us instead assume that there are many. For the sake of conciseness we shall call such an aggregate *society*.

Let us consider it an entity distinct from the rest of humankind, let us ignore the bartering among the components of that aggregate, and let us instead concentrate only on bartering between that aggregate and the remainder of men.

The demand or the supply of that *society* will be the sum total of the demands and of the supplies of its various components.

The average final degree of utility of a commodity for that society can be defined: *that final degree of utility that for one individual*[XVII] *would have as a consequence the demand or the supply observed for the society.*

We believe that there is no advantage in considering the arithmetic mean, or the geometric mean, or any other similar mean, of the final degrees of utility.

Means are nothing but a creation of ours, and the way of putting them together must vary according to the goals we set ourselves. One of the main goals of Political Economy is to find the laws for the barter of commodities. For this purpose it must therefore be possible to replace the final degrees of utility of every single individual with the final degree of utility for a certain aggregate.

One should also look at the composition of those aggregates we are considering, for which the bartering within the aggregate itself, at least with regard to the commodities in question, must be negligible. In societies where the division of labour exists those aggregates can be made up of a great number of individuals. For instance, the bartering between people working in large factories is absolutely insignificant when compared to the bartering between them and the rest of the population. In primitive societies the socio-economic unit may be the individual, but with a better and more perfect organization of work the unit becomes an aggregate of many people, all of them offering certain commodities and requiring some others. And we must take this circumstance into account.

One should also add that Political Economy cannot but be a science of averages, and it cannot aspire at predicting and explaining merely acts of single individuals.

Let us attribute to the 'society' the notations we have used in formulae (12) and (13), which will therefore be characteristic of it. Let us indicate the single individuals with the indexes 1, 2, 3 . . . and let us add these indexes to the above notations in order to have the notations referring to the individuals, and so

for the commodities	A	B	C	. . .
whose prices are	1	p_b	p_c	. . .

the quantities required by the various individuals, whose number we assume to be θ, will be

expressed with	r_{1a}	r_{1b}	r_{1c}	. . .
	r_{2a}	r_{2b}	r_{2c}	. . .
	. . . .			

For those same individuals the final degrees of utility

will be indicated by	φ_{1a}	φ_{1b}	φ_{1c}	. . .
	φ_{2a}	φ_{2b}	φ_{2c}	. . .
	. . .			

while for the whole aggregate the required

quantities will be	r_a	r_b	r_c	...
and the final degrees of utility	φ_a	φ_b	φ_c	....

We immediately obtain n equations

$$\begin{cases} r_a = r_{1a} + r_{2a} + \ldots \\ r_b = r_{1b} + r_{2b} + \ldots \\ \ldots \end{cases} \tag{31}$$

Then, from equations (13), another $(n-1)(\theta-1)$, which indicate that the values of p_b, $p_c \ldots$ are the same for the various individuals

$$\begin{cases} \dfrac{\varphi_{1b}(r_{1b})}{\varphi_{1a}(r_{1a})} = \dfrac{\varphi_{2b}(r_{2b})}{\varphi_{2a}(r_{2a})} = \dfrac{\varphi_{3b}(r_{3b})}{\varphi_{3a}(r_{3a})} = \ldots \\ \dfrac{\varphi_{1c}(r_{1c})}{\varphi_{1a}(r_{1a})} = \dfrac{\varphi_{2c}(r_{2c})}{\varphi_{2a}(r_{2a})} = \dfrac{\varphi_{3c}(r_{3c})}{\varphi_{3a}(r_{3a})} = \ldots \\ \ldots \end{cases} \tag{32}$$

I. Let us suppose now that equations (12) are applicable, which must refer to each individual, and give us θ equations

$$\begin{cases} r_{1a} + p_b r_{1b} + p_c r_{1c} + \ldots = 0 \\ r_{2a} + p_b r_{2b} + p_c r_{2c} + \ldots = 0 \\ \ldots \end{cases} \tag{33}$$

All in all we have therefore

$$n + \theta + (n-1)(\theta-1) = n\theta + 1$$

equations. For the moment, let us exclude one of them: with the remaining $n\theta$ we shall be able to determine the $n\theta$ unknowns

$$r_{1a}, r_{2a}, \ldots r_{1b}, r_{2a}, \ldots r_{1c}, r_{2a} \ldots$$

which will be function of

$$r_a, r_b, r_c, \ldots$$

By substituting these values in the equations

$$p_b = \frac{\varphi_{1b}(r_{1b})}{\varphi_{1a}(r_{1a})}, \quad p_c = \frac{\varphi_{1c}(r_{1c})}{\varphi_{1a}(r_{1a})} \ldots$$

we shall have the values of p_b, p_c as a function of r_a, r_b. ... But these values will not necessarily have the form

$$p_b = \frac{\varphi_b(r_b)}{\varphi_a(r_a)}, \; p_c = \frac{\varphi_c(r_c)}{\varphi_a(r_a)} \ldots$$

and furthermore one equation has been left out, which in general will not be satisfied.
II. When we consider saving, as we previously did, we do not have to use equations (12) any longer. Then we can assume that the n quantities

$$r_{1a}, r_{1b}, r_{1c} \dots$$

are independent variables, and that

$$r_{2a}, r_{3a}, r_{4a} \dots$$

are functions of r_{1a}; similarly, that

$$r_{2b}, r_{3b}, r_{4b} \dots$$

are functions of r_{1b}; and so on. Equations (31) show that in this case r_{1a} becomes a function of r_a, r_{1b} of r_b, r_{1c} of r_c, . . . and by substituting those values in the equations

$$p_b = \frac{\varphi_{1b}(r_{1b})}{\varphi_{1a}(r_{1a})}, p_c = \frac{\varphi_{1c}(r_{1c})}{\varphi_{1a}(r_{1a})} \dots$$

one will obtain

$$p_b = \frac{\varphi_b(r_b)}{\varphi_a(r_a)}, p_c = \frac{\varphi_c(r_c)}{\varphi_a(r_a)} \dots \tag{34}$$

By doing so, we are acting as if we had been replacing equations (32) with the other $n(\theta - 1)$ equations

$$\begin{cases} \varphi_{2a}(r_{2a}) = H_2\varphi_{1a}(r_{1a}), & \varphi_{3a} = H_3\varphi_{1a}(r_{1a}) \\ \varphi_{2b}(r_{2b}) = H_2\varphi_{1b}(r_{1b}), & \varphi_{3b} = H_3\varphi_{1b}(r_{1b}) \\ \varphi_{2c}(r_{2c}) = H_2\varphi_{1c}(r_{1c}), & \varphi_{3c} = H_3\varphi_{1c}(r_{1c}) \\ \dots \end{cases} \tag{35}$$

where H_2, H_3 . . . are arbitrary constants.

These equations, together with the n equations (31) indeed give the $n\theta$ equations needed to determine the unknowns, which are in equal number.

We conclude therefore that the hypothesis put forward by considering many separate economic phenomena, in which each individual **necessarily** spends on the one hand nothing more and nothing less than he receives on the other, is irreconcilable (with the exception of particular cases) with the condition that if for every individual the final degree of utility of each commodity only depends on the quantity of that commodity, the final degree of utility referred to the aggregate of those individuals has the same property.

This condition can be satisfied if one admits that the individuals, either because they keep economic goods in reserve, or for any other reason, can avoid the need to conclude the contracts in question indiscriminately, and are able instead to offset less favourable contracts with more favourable ones.

If we remember, now, that we have already come across those two cases when dealing with the determination of the final degrees of utility, it will certainly strike us how our analysis has revealed the existence of a profound theoretical difference that corresponds to an equally great difference in the real world. This is reason for us to be hopeful about the application of similar theories to topics such as that of the influence of the Trade Unions, where the problem lies indeed in the evaluation of the differences in the economic phenomenon for workers who are at the mercy of those who pay them, and for others who may have acquired more independence thanks to the Unions.

There is nothing unusual in the fact that a theory may reproduce the fundamental ideas that were chosen for its formulation; in this way it is simply giving back what it received. But it should be noticed that here, in fixing our formulae, the idea of the difference between those two types of economic phenomena played no part whatsoever. Once the theory was formed – with totally different purposes – it happened that in moving forward some cases arose where it seemed that the concrete facts differed from our theoretical conclusions. That contrast had to be eliminated, and the theory would have been defeated, had it not been able to explain the facts; but as a matter of fact victory belongs to the theory since it plainly led us to find the real reasons.

* All deductions obtained through the experimental method behave in a similar way. In the science of chemistry, atomic theory gained great weight precisely from facts that at first seemed to elude it.[13] And *si parva licet componere magnis* [if one may compare small things to great ones],[14] one could recall the discovery of Neptune as a consequence of the study of the irregularities in the motion of Uranus. It seemed at first that they could not be explained through the theory of gravitation, but they ended up instead as a consequence of it, when Le Verrier and Adams[XIX] put forward the hypothesis of the existence of another planet. The latter was eventually discovered by Galle,[XX] following Le Verrier's indications, on 23 September 1846, in Berlin.

* Further irregularities remained in the motion of the planets; they were explained through 40 years of untiring work by Le Verrier, making use of Newton's theory.

As for those people who are intolerant of any delay and accuse the newborn science of Pure Political Economy of not having yet discovered new truths, they should consider the quality and the quantity of the work of which new truths were the prize in Astronomy. After people like Newton, D'Alembert, Euler, Laplace, and many other illustrious men, Le Verrier, whom Mr Airy[XXI] used to call *a scientific giant*, took 40 forty years to reform the analytical theory of planetary motion; and he had at his disposal a great wealth of observations by men who will always be the honour of humankind!

* Any theory that does not receive valid support from observation is unsafe and untrustworthy. When, in 1665–1666, Newton wanted to compare his theory with experience, he was compelled to use the very imperfect measurements that were then available for the earth's radius, and found that the

force that kept the Moon in its orbit was not the same as indicated by his theory. But then Picard[XXII] measured one degree of the earth's meridian with much greater precision, and in 1680 Newton did new calculations by using those measurements, and found then that his theory agreed with the facts, and that the same force, whose intensity is inversely proportional to the squares of distances, causes the fall of bodies at the surface of the earth and keeps our satellite in its orbit.

The data Political Economy has at its disposal are very imperfect; nevertheless, a study that followed rigorously scientific rather than empiric principles could even now derive great results from them.

For instance, for their number and precision, the existing data on the use of alcoholic beverages in various countries are already such that from them one might hopefully be able to infer, with some degree of approximation, the average of the final degree of utility of those commodities.

In Italy – where there are so many talented economists, not only among the teachers of this science, but also among the young, who by building on good and strong studies are intent on improving our scientific knowledge – it would be a good thing if someone became interested in this topic and wrote on it. He would produce a book that would be very useful to all those countries where variations to the taxes on those beverages are being studied.[15]

Of course the data we have are not homogeneous, and it is certain that with regard to the consumption of alcoholic beverages it is not possible to compare southern peoples with northern peoples; other imperfections could be found in the data that have been collected, but even so they can at least give us a roughly approximate idea, which is something we still do not have at the moment. And in France, where they are considering the possibility of increasing the duty on wine spirit in order to decrease the duty on wine, they do not seem to have any criterion to predict even very roughly how the consumed quantities will vary.

In experimental sciences it is necessary to keep equal distance from two extremes: one would consist in granting one's observations the precision they do not possess, the other would consist in never using them, because they are always imperfect.

Mr De Foville[XXIV] gives us a very lively account of how some people laugh at the science of statistics for data given with ridiculous precision, which he himself criticises.[16] But one should also add that he who does not do, does not err, and that any work, even if extremely imperfect, is better than none, while with the passing of time it is brought to ever-increasing perfection, by correcting mistakes and by suitably adding to it.

Total utility

It behoves us now to discuss the values taken by total utility in the various hypotheses we have mentioned.

There is no need to recall that here, as in this entire chapter, we assume that supply and demand of the 'society' in question have no significant effect to make the prices vary; which corresponds in general to the case where that demand and that offer are a very small part of the total demand and offer observed on the market.

When the degree of utility of a commodity is only a function of the quantity of this commodity, total utility is given by the formula

$$U = \int_a^{r_a} \varphi_a(x_1)dx_1 + \int_b^{r_b} \varphi_b(x_2)dx_2 + \ldots$$

$a, b \ldots$ being the initial values of $r_a, r_b \ldots$ which can also be equal to zero, as we have already explained.

Let us assume now that in every unit of time, for instance every day, those transformations are renewed. The total utility that one will have in a certain number of those units will be

$$\Sigma U$$

and if that number of units is large enough, we shall be able to consider that sum as not being significantly different from

$$V = \frac{1}{\Delta t} \int_{t_0}^{t_1} U dt$$

where t is time, Δt is the unit under scrutiny, t_0, t_1 the time limits within which total utility is considered.

We have already discussed this replacement of discontinuous with continuous functions, and there is no need to go back to it now.

If we assume that the functions φ do not change shape in the time under consideration, the various possible values of V will depend on the various values of $r_a, r_b, \ldots$

If one does not take saving into account, $r_a, r_b \ldots$ are determined when one knows $p_b, p_c \ldots$ which are functions of t, and V is entirely determined.

However, when saving is taken into account, it is according to its values that V varies.

Let us assume that within the given time span, the quantity of economic goods kept in reserve must neither increase nor decrease, with the increments compensating the reductions; and let us set ourselves the goal of finding what relationship there must be between successive portions of bartered commodities, in order for total utility to be maximum.

In calculating total utility one should take into account the total utility deriving from saving, but since the latter goes back to its erstwhile value, not only the variations of the quantities, but also their utilities balance each other, and the variation of the total utility that derives from saving is zero for the time span under consideration.

The condition that the total of the saved quantity must not change is expressed by

$$\Sigma(r_a + p_b r_b + \ldots) = 0;$$

which can be replaced by the equation

$$\int_{t_0}^{t_1} (r_a + p_b r_b + \ldots)dt = 0. \tag{36}$$

When this is satisfied, it is therefore necessary for

$$\int_{t_0}^{t} U dt = 0$$

to be a maximum.

The principles of calculus of variations[17] let us know that we shall achieve this by making maximum

$$\int_{t_0}^{t_1} \{U + \lambda(r_a + p_b r_b + \ldots)\}dt = 0;$$

where λ is an arbitrary constant.

It is necessary to equate to zero the variation of that integral. We shall assume that r_a is the unknown function, whilst r_b, r_c . . . are given by equations (12) as a function of r_a. The variation of the integral, equated to zero, will give

$$\frac{\partial U}{\partial r_a} + \frac{\partial U}{\partial r_b}\frac{\partial r_b}{\partial r_a} + \ldots + \lambda\,(1 + p_b \frac{\partial r_b}{\partial r_a} + \ldots) = 0$$

But

$$\frac{\partial U}{\partial r_a} = \varphi_a(r_a),\ \frac{\partial U}{\partial r_b} = \varphi_b(r_b)\ \ldots$$

$$\frac{\partial r_b}{\partial r_a} = p_b \frac{\varphi'_a}{\varphi'_b},\ \frac{\partial r_c}{\partial r_a} = p_c \frac{\varphi'_a}{\varphi'_c}\ \ldots$$

therefore

$$\varphi_a + \lambda + p^2_b(\varphi_a + \lambda)\frac{\varphi'_a}{\varphi'_b} + p^2_c\,(\varphi_a + \lambda)\frac{\varphi'_a}{\varphi'_c} + \ldots = 0$$

that is

$$(\varphi_a + \lambda)(1 + p^2_b \frac{\varphi'_a}{\varphi'_b} + p^2_c \frac{\varphi'_a}{\varphi'_c} + \ldots) = 0. \tag{37}$$

At this point it is necessary to make a very important remark. If φ'_a, φ'_b . . . have the same sign, the second factor of this expression consists of a sum of positive terms, and so it cannot have real solutions; therefore the real solutions of the above equation will only be those of the first factor, i.e. those deriving from the equation

$$\varphi_u + \lambda = 0. \tag{38}$$

This case occurs when all the final degrees of utility decrease with the increase of the quantity of commodity, which is often taken as a fundamental principle of the new science; but Prof. Edgeworth rightly observes[18] that there are exceptions. As we have already said, we have decided to deal with this topic later. Meanwhile, only once have we made use of that property of the final degrees of utility, in order to infer from it the law of the variations of demand and offer. We are recalling it here too, at least as a possibility.

For the commodities that have that property, equation (38) applies. For the other commodities there might be other solutions of equation (37), which would be obtained by equating the second factor to zero.

Equation (38) is worthy of notice. It allows us to know that the maximum will be obtained by ensuring that the final degree of utility of commodity A is constant. Let us assume

$$-\lambda = \beta,$$

we shall have

$$\varphi_u = \beta,\ \varphi_b = p_b\beta,\ \varphi_c = p_c\beta\ \ldots$$

From these equations we shall infer

$$r_u = \psi_a(\beta),\ r_b = \psi_b(p_b\beta),\ r_c = \psi_c(p_c\beta)\ \ldots$$

and equation (36) will therefore become

$$\int_{t_0}^{t_1} \{\psi_a(\beta) + p_b\psi_b(p_b\beta) + \ldots\}dt = 0.$$

This equation will be used to determine the value of constant β. And in order to have maximum utility it will be necessary to make use of saving in such a way that the final degree of utility of commodity A, which at least theoretically is used as money, may be as constant and close to the value of that quantity β as possible.

Such constancy in the value of the final degree of utility regards the successive values the latter acquires in the various barters under consideration, but has nothing to do with the variations that the final degree of utility can incur when the quantity of commodity varies. In other words, it is the values of $\varphi_u(r_u)$ that are obtained every day, that must be constant, and not the values of $\varphi_u(r_u)$ when r_u varies.

If saving is not taken into account, for a more symmetrical approach one can make use of the auxiliary quantity β_1, which will then be determined by the equation

$$\varphi_a(\beta_1) + p_b\psi_b(p_b\beta_1) + p_c\psi_c(p_c\beta_1) + \ldots = 0$$

and it will no longer be constant.

With those values of β and β_1 it will be possible to calculate the values of total utility

$$\int_{t_0}^{t_1} U dt,$$

both in the case of the maximum and in the case where saving is not taken into account.

We believe that the above problem, or more precisely, the problems of this kind, can have very important practical applications. In conjunction with the knowledge of the periods of industrial crisis, an improved and extended version of this theory could one day be as important for the Trade Unions and other workers' associations as the theory of mortality is for insurance companies.

Let those who reject the help not only of mathematics, but also of any type of pure theory, consider how one could solve the problem of making use of saving so as to have maximum utility. And this is not a simple matter regarding the direct use of saving, but the *Trades Unions*, which through their members' contributions put money aside for strikes, must aim at arranging income and expenses in such a way as to obtain maximum utility.

No individual can of course infer precise rules for his own behaviour from these theories. In the same way no one can find out how long he is going to live from the mortality tables, and only when dealing with a very large number of individuals it is possible to say, with Homer,

μοῖραν δ' οὔτινέ φημι πεφυγμένον ἔμμεναι ἀνδρῶν[19]

and this fate can only be known with very high probability.

The reader can see even better now why we took care to look for the average final degrees of utility for aggregates of individuals. In this way we extend to the aggregates the expounded theories, which would be useless if only applicable to single individuals.

We shall also remark that at this stage, before proceeding any further on this topic, it would be advisable for pure theory to be supported by observation. We have shown how the final degrees of utility could be calculated, and what is most pressing now is to obtain some numerical idea, no matter how approximate, of them. Once we have done that, we shall have to go back and deal again with pure theory, correct it, improve it, advance it.

In all experimental sciences the way of proceeding is not dissimilar, and theory and observation should lend each other help.

It would of course be possible to continue the theoretical study by putting forward various hypotheses on the form of the functions that illustrate the final degrees of utility, but since only one of them, and possibly none, would be true, one would waste a great amount of time for nothing.

* One could have studied various astronomies, by giving different forms to the law of gravitation. But if one reflects on how much hard work is necessary to study just one, it will soon be clear that in that way nothing much would have been achieved.

* Observation led men to postulate the law of gravitation, which in turn led to new observations, which in turn called for further theoretical research to be carried out. In this way our scientific knowledge has been, and is still being enriched.

And it is not unreasonable to hope that a similar method may bring similar benefits in the study of Political Economy.

4 Considerations on the fundamental principles of Pure Political Economy, IV

(*Giornale degli Economisti*, January 1893)

Fundamental property of final degrees of utility

Nearly all final degrees of utility decrease as the quantity of the consumed commodity increases. Some economists claim that all final degrees of utility have this property, and relate it to the physiological law according to which the more our sensations are protracted, the more their intensity decreases.

We find it difficult to agree that the consumption of an *economic good* may be considered similar to an uninterrupted sensation, as is required for that physiological law to be applicable.

It is true that to a naked man the first rag that protects him from the cold is most valuable, the second less so, the third even less so, until by continuing to cover himself he is too hot, and his pleasure turns into annoyance. But a man who already owns a cloak and buys another one is not at all compelled to put it on and go around wearing both cloaks.

To ride a horse for one hour is enjoyable, and if one keeps going it is obvious that the pleasure decreases in accordance with the above-mentioned physiological law. But the man who has two horses in his stable is certainly not compelled to ride for twice as long as he would if he only had one horse. And so, if the utility of a second horse is less than the utility of the first, this will be for an entirely different reason than the decreasing intensity of prolonged sensations.

A better advice would, in our opinion, be directly to accept such decrease of the final degree of utility as an experimental fact, all the more so since, as Prof. Edgeworth rightly pointed out, there are many exceptions.

The main one is saving. Admittedly, if we exclude the not inconsiderable host of the miserly, the final degree of utility ends up decreasing whenever the saved amount grows beyond certain limits. But such limits are quite broad, and therefore a substantial part of the phenomenon of saving escapes the law of the decrease of the final degrees of utility.

The French peasant's passionate desire to own land increases and becomes more intense, rather than decreasing, with the expansion of his land holdings.

Among the other cases where the law of the decrease of the final degrees of utility does not apply one could point out the artificial monopolies, i.e. the *syndicats* of the French, the *kartelle* of the Germans and the *corners* of the Americans where, in fact, the last quantities have much greater utility than the first quantities acquired. But these cases must be excluded because they do not refer to first-order goods. To the shopkeeper, the commodity he buys to sell is always an instrumental good, and such goods, as previously noted, do not have a utility of their own, but their utility depends on that of first-order goods.

Daniel Bernoulli's theorem

When economists began to study the theory of the final degrees of utility, they immediately noted that it did not substantially differ from Daniel Bernoulli's theory of *moral hope.*

Favourably received by profound thinkers and outstanding mathematicians such as Buffon,[I] Laplace, and Quetelet,[II] the latter theory has now found a fierce opponent in the person of Prof. J. Bertrand, who is an illustrious mathematician himself.

In a separate work of his he has also criticized the new economic doctrines, and therefore the opponents of the latter invoke his authority as their last resort. Their way of reasoning is more or less as follows: 'It is *mathematical* economics; it is being condemned by an authoritative scholar in *mathematical* sciences; *ergo* the new doctrines are worthless'.

Those arguing in this way fall in the so-called sophism *by confusion.*

Certainly, if Prof. Bertrand had exclusively raised objections on the mathematical aspects of both the theorem of *moral hope* and the new economic theories, he would have provided much food for thought. But he says absolutely nothing about mathematics, and his discussion deals instead with the principles on which those theories are founded. Such principles belong in the moral and economic sciences; when dealing with them, therefore, authority acquired in other sciences, such as, for instance, mathematics, carries no weight, however great it may be.

On the other hand, in view of Prof. Bertrand's exceptional merits, we cannot be satisfied with this reason alone, but we think it necessary to study the causes that led so learned and worthy a man to such conclusions.

First of all, let us quote an opinion that we believe Prof. Bertrand himself gave only through lack of information.

Indeed, when reading the illustrious mathematician's work, the doubt arises that he may have not always had in mind Prof. Walras's book, for otherwise one could not explain the strange misunderstanding into which he fell. He writes:[I]

> L'ingénieux auteur, dont je prendrai la liberté d'abréger les explications, suppose que le possesseur d'une quantité *a* d'une certaine denrée tire de cette possession une certaine utilité, une certaine satisfaction de ses désirs, que chaque parcelle acquise accroît successivement, de telle sorte

que, la quantité possédée passant de x à $x + dx$ l'avantage soit pour lui représenté par $\varphi(x)dx$. La possession de a équivaut alors à l'intégrale

$$\int_0^a \varphi(x)dx.$$

[The ingenious author, whose explanations I shall take the liberty of abridging, supposes that the possessor of a quantity a of a certain commodity derives from such possession a certain utility, a certain satisfaction of his desires, which each portion successively acquired increases, in such a way that when the possessed quantity passes from x to $x + dx$, the benefit to him may be represented by $\varphi(x)dx$. The possession of a is then equal to the integral $\int_0^a \varphi(x)dx$.]

So far, so good, and this is indeed the view of Prof. Walras, Jevons, etc. Then Prof. Bertrand continues with a statement, which we shall shortly discuss; he says: 'Le prix réglé par les conditions du marché n'a aucune relation nécessaire avec la fonction φ, qui varie d'un individu à un autre'. ['The price governed by the conditions of the market has no necessary connection with the function φ, which varies from one individual to another.']

Of this he gives no proof whatsoever, and continues:

> Si l'on nomme p le prix de chaque unité achetée ou vendue . . . il devra acheter ou vendre une certaine quantité de marchandise . . . et cesser ses achats ou ses ventes quand on aura $\varphi(x)$ = p. Si $x = a$ est la racine de cette équation, a est ce que M. Walras nomme la rareté de la marchandise pour la personne considérée. [If one calls p the price of each unit that is bought or sold . . ., he will have to buy or sell a certain quantity of good . . . and stop buying or selling when it is $\varphi(x) = p$. If $x = a$ is the root of this equation, a is what Mr Walras calls the *rareté* of the good for the person under consideration.]

Now, one just has to open Prof. Walras's book and skim through it even very superficially, to see that it is $\varphi(x)$ that he calls the *rareté* of the commodity, and most definitely not a, which is instead the quantity of commodity bartered at price p. If necessary, this can also be seen in what Prof. Walras openly says:[2] 'Et en appelant rareté l'intensité du dernier besoin satisfait par une quantité consommée . . .' ['And by calling *rareté* the intensity of the last need satisfied by a consumed quantity . . .'].

Prof. Bertrand has instead assumed, we do not understand how, that it was the quantity consumed (*quantité consommé*) $x = a$ that Prof. Walras called *rareté*!

But let us go back to the above-cited statement. It can perhaps be partly explained with these words:

> Cette définition, sans parler de l'inconvénient de disposer d'un sens d'un mot bien connu et usuel [and on this one could agree with the illustrious mathematician], parait avoir le défaut grave de perdre toute signification quand l'on applique aux commerçants, qu'il faudrait, au contraire, avoir surtout en vue dans les problèmes de ce genre. [This definition, to say nothing of the inconvenient of using the meaning of a well-known and quite common word, seemed to have the serious fault of losing any meaning when applied to traders, whom one should have in mind most of all in these kinds of problems.]

Prof. Bertrand has detected here, with great acumen, a flaw of the new theories. The latter very often suppose, more or less implicitly, that only consumption determines prices. But does the intervention of traders not modify those prices? Maybe not, but it is necessary to demonstrate it, since it is not at all obvious. On the other hand it seems to us that Prof. Bertrand strays further from the truth when he states that it is mainly by traders that prices are determined, and we cannot see how he could demonstrate this proposition. In fact, it seems clear to us that since traders only buy to re-sell, it is the consumers that must ultimately have the most important role in fixing prices; this is something we have already discussed (on p. 43) and shall have to discuss again. Meanwhile, we note here that the fact that this subject has not been properly clarified has in turn given rise to another mix-up.

Prof. Walras supposes that before going to the market every individual can write in a table, next to their supposed prices, the quantities of commodities he would buy at those prices. This table is the same as the *person's demand schedule* of Prof. Marshall.[3]

On this topic Prof. Bertrand remarks:[4]

> Un marchand de blé achête des millions d'hectolitres et sait ce qu'ils lui ont coûté; il vend au cours du jour quand il y trouve profit, quelquefois à perte quand il prévoit la baisse, pour éviter une perte plus grande, conserve en magasin quand il espére la hausse, et ne se règle nullement sur les avantages que peuvent lui procurer les diverses parties de la provision. [A wheat trader buys a few million hectolitres and knows what they cost him; he sells in the course of the day when he finds it profitable, sometimes at a loss when he foresees a price fall, in order to avoid heavier losses, he keeps in store when he hopes in a price rise, and does not take into any consideration the advantages that the different parts of the stock can afford him.]

All very true. But those who will eat the bread made with that wheat will however base their demands on the utility they can obtain from the various parts of the stock. And since the trader is totally dependent on these people, if he is wise he will have to adjust his prices precisely on the utility that the various parts of the stock have for the consumers.

We must confess that when we first read the above-mentioned remark by Prof. Bertrand, we were persuaded by it, and it was only by thinking about it time and again that we finally realized the capital importance of distinguishing between consumers and their suppliers, and were therefore able to understand how that proposition had to be modified. New theories are often rejected for the only reason that people have not been careful enough in seeking that element of truth they can hold. And we fear that many people who discuss Prof. Walras's book have not read it with the care it deserves.

After this digression, let us go back to Bernoulli's theorem. We believe it useful, for the sake of clarity, to divide it in two parts:

First: the *utility* of one lira for an individual is not the same if this man owns 100 lire or if he owns 200.

> L'avantage moral qu'un bien nous procure n'est pas proportionnel à ce bien et il dépend de mille circonstances souvent très difficiles à définir, mais dont la plus importante et la plus difficile est celle de la fortune.[5] [The moral advantage that a good affords us is not proportional to that good and it depends on a thousand circumstances that are often very difficult to define; but the most important and most difficult among them is chance.]

If we replace the words *avantage moral* with the word *utility* used in an economic sense, which is not the same as its common meaning, we have the expression of the principle that informs the new economic theories.

Laplace continues: 'En effet il est visible qu'un franc a beaucoup plus de prix pour celui qui en a cent que pour un millionnaire'. ['It is indeed clear that one franc is worth much more to the man who has a hundred francs than to a millionnaire.']

This is the principle of the decrease of the final degrees of utility with the increase of quantity. And we have already pointed out that it is generally true, apart from some exceptional cases; with this restriction, therefore, we believe that the first part of the theorem should be entirely accepted.

Second: Daniel Bernoulli also decided to measure that decrease of the final degrees of utility. Let us hear more from Laplace.

> On ne peut donner de principe général, pour apprécier cette valeur relative. En voici cependant un proposé par Daniel Bernoulli et qui peut servir dans beaucoup de cas. 'La valeur relative d'une somme infiniment petite, est égale à sa valeur absolue divisée par le bien total de la personne interéssée.' [It is impossible to give a general principle to evaluate this relative value. Meanwhile, here is one proposed by Daniel Bernoulli, which can be useful in many cases. 'The relative value of an infinitely small amount is equal to its absolute value divided by the total good of the person involved.']

This second part of the theorem cannot be accepted. It is impossible to demonstrate that if the *utility* of one lira for the man who has 100 lire is 1, it will be precisely $\frac{1}{2}$ when that individual has 200 lire. And why not $\frac{1}{3}$, $\frac{1}{4}$ or any other fraction?

Here we find ourselves in a case that is perfectly similar to that of Malthus's well-known theory.

Malthus was right in saying that mankind, like any other animal species, has a natural tendency to increase in numbers more than the increase in sustenance allows. The mistake, which was not Malthus's own but his opponents', was in thinking that it was possible to measure that tendency precisely, by using the two progressions about which so much, and so foolishly, one has argued.

The theorem of *moral hope* has been used to explain a paradox in the calculus of probability.

Tom and Dick play heads or tails with a coin, with the following conditions: First: the game will end when tails comes up. Second: Dick gives Tom two lire if tails comes up on the first toss, four lire if it comes up on the second, eight lire if it comes up on the third, etc. Third: Dick and Tom are even if tails does not come up in the first m tosses, that is, let us say, in the first 100 tosses.

The calculus of probability shows that in order for the game to be fair, it is necessary that before the start, Tom gives Dick m lire, which in the given case is 100 lire. But no reasonable man would accept such an agreement. From where does this discrepancy originate?

Bernoulli's principle offered *one* solution to the problem. It was immediately recognized that if from a mathematical point of view two games are identical – in the first of which one hopes to win 100 lire by betting one lira, with a probability of $\frac{1}{100}$, whilst in the second one hopes to win 101 lire by betting 100 lire, with a probability of $\frac{100}{101}$; in actual terms there is an enormous difference between them, and no one would play the second game. The only conclusion that can be drawn from it is that many more considerations, beside mathematical probability, concur in the determination of human actions. As Laplace[6] most rightly states:

> Mais l'avantage moral que peut procurer une somme espérée, dépend d'une infinité de circonstances propres à chaque individu, et qu'il est impossible d'évaluer. La seule considération que l'on puisse employer est que plus on est riche moins une somme très-petite peut être avantageuse, toutes choses égales d'ailleurs. [But the moral benefit that a hoped-for amount can afford depends on an infinity of circumstances pertaining to each individual, which it is impossible to evaluate. The only consideration one can use is that, all other things being equal, the richer one is, the less beneficial a very small amount can be.]

Bernoulli's principle makes these considerations more precise, but it is a false kind of precision.

The paradox we have discussed was explained by Poisson[7] in a different way. He finds a limit to the amount to be paid to Tom, in the possibility for Dick to fulfil his commitment. Thus, if Dick owns 100 millions lire one finds that Tom can only give Dick 26 lire, before the start of the game.

Prof. Bertrand[8] denies the existence of a paradox. He says that provided that the number of tosses can be very large, theory will end up agreeing with reality. He therefore postulates a machine capable of tossing a coin 100,000 times per second, and continues on this path.

It seems to us that in this way the question is entirely shifted. When such machines exist, when men become accustomed to games where 100,000 tosses are performed in one second, then perhaps the paradox will no longer exist. But who ever mentioned anything about this? The question being asked is completely different. When we say that no reasonable man would risk 100 lire at that game, we are talking about a man like those that exist at present, and about a game as it can be played now, and we ask why in these conditions (and not in others!) mathematics gives one answer, and common sense another.

In order to invalidate Poisson's solution, which for our part we are far from accepting, Prof. Bertrand even puts forward the hypothesis that one could gamble grains of sand or molecules of hydrogen. But in this case, how can he be so sure that a *reasonable* man would not risk even hundreds of them? For our part we are only too willing to play that game with Prof. Bertrand, even giving him those hundreds of grains of sand, or molecules of hydrogen, and we think that no one could accuse us of not being reasonable, if with such little outlay, which could well be said to be close to zero, we could gain the pleasure of spending a little time with that distinguished scientist.

But ultimately Prof. Bertrand's words could be interpreted as meaning that the paradox finds its explanation in the impossibility of performing a number of tosses large enough for mathematical probability to be taken into account *in reality*.

We do not want to deny that this, or Poisson's, consideration may have considerable weight for educated people; but we think that the feeling, shared by cultured and uncultured alike, that a game of that kind would be rejected, primarily derives from Bernoulli's principle, or from a similar one, since everyone considers the hope of winning too remote and uncertain.

We had to recall all this because it was necessary in order to understand how Prof. Bertrand can absolutely reject Bernoulli's principle.

He states that

> l'espérance mathématique [mathematical hope] has been replaced by l'espérance morale, dans le calcul de laquelle une fortune dépend non du nombre d'écus dont elle se compose mais des satisfactions qu'elle procure. Le problème ainsi posé Bernoulli a l'**audace** de le résoudre . . .

> Jamais compte n'a été ni ne sera réglé de la sorte.[9] [moral hope, in the calculation of which a fortune does not depend on the number of crowns of which it consists, but on the satisfactions it procures. Bernoulli has the **audacity** of solving the problem so formulated . . . No account was or will be ever ruled by chance.]

But who ever proposed the theory of *utility* to settle accounts? Accounts are ruled by law and justice, and *utility* in an economic sense has nothing to do with it.

It is truly extraordinary that Prof. Bertrand finds the following words by Buffon blameworthy: 'l'homme sensé n'en considère (de l'argent) ni la masse ni le nombre, il n'y voit que les avantages qu'il peut en tirer' ['a sensible man does not consider either the quantity or the amount (of money); all he sees in it are the benefits it can afford him'].

Prof. Bertrand's answer to these words is as follows:

> Si l'homme sensé dont parle Buffon n'est pas un cynique égoïste, il pourra sans thésauriser, faire bon usage des millions qu'on lui suppose. On pourra les doubler, les décupler, et les doubler encore sans ralentir la progression constante du bien qu'il peut faire. N'a-t'il pas une famille à enrichir, des misères à soulager etc. [If the sensible man mentioned by Buffon is not a selfish cynic, he will be able, without accumulating, to make good use of the millions that we suppose he owns. It will be possible to double them, to decuple them, and to double them again without slowing down the constant progression of the good he can do. Is there not a family to make rich, some paupers to assist, etc.]

All this is perfectly fine, but off the point. Mr Buffon's words give a very good account of the economic principle that goes under the name of *variety of human needs*. But how does this principle contradict the other, according to which all that man sees in money is the means to acquire the commodities he consumes, or, more generally, the economic goods he enjoys, and the pleasures he attains? Nor is there any contradiction with the other principle, according to which human needs, though countless, are not all of the same intensity, so that the greater the available amount is, the less intense the unfulfilled needs are. And this is the foundation of Bernoulli's principle.

Prof. Bertrand speaks about the *extension* of human needs, and Bernoulli's principle deals with their *intensity*. They are two essentially different things. The extension is infinite, to be sure; and so what? What can one infer from this against the *intensity* being ever-decreasing?

In our society that intensity is certainly not constant. We agree with Prof. Bertrand that a millionaire will know what to do even with a single lira added to those he already has, but the *need* for that lira is not as intense for him as it is for a starving man. Perhaps in a society of saints the desire of the millionaire to have an extra lira to give to the poor is as intense as the desire of the hungry to have a lira of bread. But for that society of saints it will be necessary to study a new political economy, entirely different from the one that applies to the men in our societies.

As for the first part of Bernoulli's theorem, this should suffice; let us now discuss the second part.

Ultimately, Bernoulli's calculation ends up assuming a hyperbola for the curve describing the final degree of utility of money.

Prof. Marshall wisely observes that one should not consider the entire wealth of an individual, but only his income; and this is what immediately appears from our reasoning about the final degrees of utility so far.

Let q_a be the amount available to an individual in the time unit. We are looking for the final degree of utility of this money. In these cases it is always necessary to distinguish whether we are dealing with money made of a substance that can be used for other purposes, and therefore has a degree of utility of its own, or with a money that is merely an instrumental good. Bernoulli's theorem obviously regards the latter case, since it does not in the least deal with the *utility* of gold as a commodity, and can be applied to a country with metallic money as well as to a country with paper money.

The equations we shall have to use are those we have already recalled

$$q_a = p_b r_b + p_c r_c + \dots \qquad (5)$$

where q_a must be supposed to be known. And the other

$$(\alpha) \quad \frac{1}{p_b} \varphi_b (r_b) = \frac{1}{p_c} \varphi_c (r_c) = \dots .$$

The common value of these quotients is equal to the final degree of utility of the money

$$\varphi_a (q_a),$$

which does not exist on its own but is only determined by these equations.

Let the number of commodities $B, C, D \dots$ be $n - 1$; The equations (α) will be $n - 2$, and with (5) we shall have $n - 1$ equations with which we shall be able to determine r_b, $r_c \dots$ when $p_b, p_c \dots$ are known, or vice versa.

It should be noticed that in the general case, previously discussed, q_a was not known independently of $r_b, r_c \dots$ and φ_a was known. We shall discuss the consequences of this change in the following paragraph; now we shall continue with our analysis of Bernoulli's theory.

If we were to follow it, we should have

$$\varphi_a (q_a) = \frac{H}{q_a}. \qquad (39)$$

In order to have the total utility, it would not be possible to integrate starting from

$q_u = 0$, because the function becomes infinite. We have already mentioned this difficulty (on pp. 16–17), and the way to avoid it. In the present case we assume that a certain value

$$q_u = g$$

is the minimum necessary to support life, and therefore, by integrating from that limit to any value of q_u, for the total utility one has[10]

$$H \log \frac{q_u}{g}.$$

The hyperbola to which equation (39) refers has the generic properties of the curves that illustrate the final degrees of utility, that is, it decreases when the consumed quantity increases; but who is to say that instead of the hyperbola *PQ* the final degree of utility of money is not illustrated by another curve like *AB* (see Figure 4.1)?

On this matter we are in the dark. Nevertheless, since in order to use mathematical formulae it is necessary to give substance to ideas and choose one of those curves, one can also make use of *PQ*, provided this is only for research, and never for demonstration purposes.

Indeed, a part of the conclusions to which we shall come will depend on the properties that the curve *PQ* shares with all the other curves, including *AB*; if this part could be isolated, one might consider it proven. Another part of our conclusions, however, will depend on the particular shape of the curve *PQ*; this part will contain no evidence in support of its being true or not.

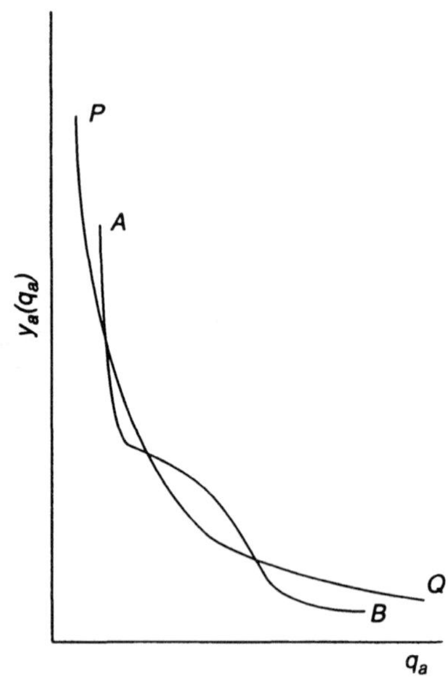

Figure 4.1

Having taken this course of action, it seems to us that it is perhaps possible to find a different curve, one that may be more accessible than *PQ* to the probing of economics.

Let us start by observing that from a logical point of view we begin with the consideration of the final degrees of utility of the goods that are directly consumed, and go back and determine the final degrees of utility of instrumental goods, and finally of money.

For an absolutely essential commodity,[11] the curve of the final degree of utility is likely to be asymptotic to the *y*-axis, in relation to which those degrees are measured, or it may intersect it at a great distance from the origin. These two cases can be fused into one, since little error will come from substituting one curve for the other in the proximity of the axis, all the more so in view of the fact that we can leave aside exceptional cases like that of a whole population starving to death.

In other words, it is acceptable for us not to worry about what happens to the curve of the final degrees of utility between *P* and the *y*-axis.

To remain with the case of an absolutely essential commodity, this curve will have to descend very rapidly towards the *x*-axis, since the more urgent needs are also those that are satisfied with lesser quantities of commodity (see Figure 4.2).

For man, thirst is an even more urgent need than hunger, but a small quantity of water suffices to satisfy it, and every increment to that quantity, provided it is still exclusively for drinking purposes, has zero utility. The same can be said about bread. Every day man needs a certain quantity of it; if he has less – in the case, as we are supposing, that he cannot replace it with other foodstuff – every further reduction makes him suffer hunger and causes him extreme distress. On the other hand, he derives little pleasure, if any, from an increment above the quantity he needs to have his fill. Hence it follows that for water, bread and other similarly essential commodities, there must be a point like *Q*, not too far from the origin and very close to the abscissa axis, such

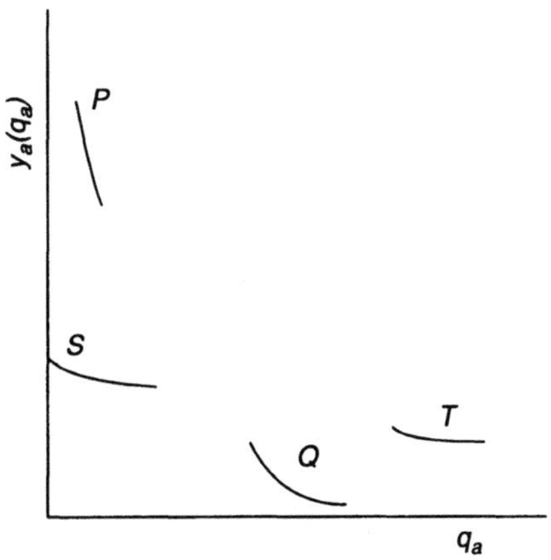

Figure 4.2

that to its left the curve rises rapidly, whereas to its right it soon becomes virtually indistinguishable from the abscissa axis.

What becomes then of the curve between P and Q, we do not know, except, of course, for the property that the ordinates always decrease when the abscissae increase.

For those commodities whose consumption is more for the sake of pleasure than for urgent need, the curve of the final degrees of utility must be flatter on the abscissa axis and be similar in shape to $S.T$.

It is easy to see how Bernoulli's equilateral hyperbola cannot give us those graphs of the final degrees of utility. On the other hand we can make use of a hyperbola of a different kind and of a higher-than-second degree.

For instance, Figure 4.3 shows a hyperbola whose equation with reference to the oblique axes OA, OB is

$$y_1 = \frac{1}{x^2}.$$

If we take the axis O_1C as the axis of the final moments of utility, and the axis O_1B as the axis of the quantities, the hyperbola referring to the two rectangular axes O_1C, O_1B can give us the shape of the final degrees of utility.

It seems likely that the degree of the hyperbolic curve must vary when the commodities vary, and in this case it is easier to consider an exponential curve.

The curve of this kind that immediately comes to mind, in order to obtain the shape shown in Figure 4.4, is the curve so often used in the calculus of probability

$$y = ae^{-ax^2}.$$

This curve has an inflection point at G, at a distance from the origin equal to

$$\frac{1}{\sqrt{2a}}.$$

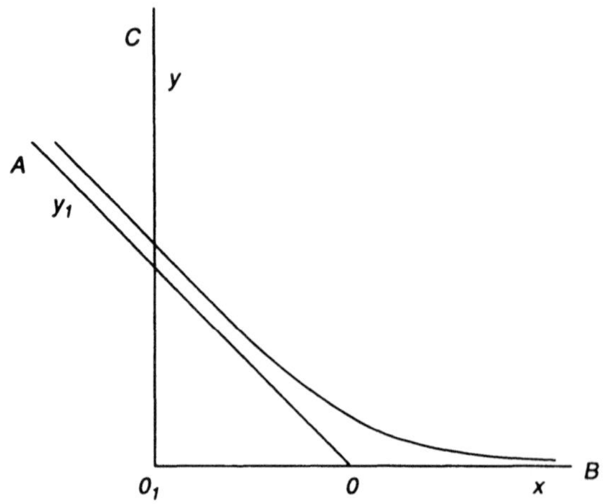

Figure 4.3

It is easy to see that only the part of the curve to the right of G can be useful to us. Therefore we shall take the axis O_1B as the axis of the quantities r, and O_1C as the axis of the final degrees of utility, $\varphi(r)$, and in general we shall assume

$$\varphi(r) = ae^{-\alpha x^2}, \quad x = r + \sqrt{\frac{1}{2\alpha}}.$$

In Figure 4.5 we have drawn three such curves, corresponding to different values of the constants. Curve *I* can illustrate the final degrees of utility for an essential commodity, curve *II* will refer to a commodity whose use is much less necessary, and curve *III* will apply to a luxury commodity.

Curves can be drawn for the commodities of all the possible intermediate qualities; in fact, it will be useful to consider them.

In order to form a very broad idea, at least, of the phenomenon, we can gradually vary the curves of the final degrees of utility and the prices, by assuming

$$a = He^{-ku}, \quad \alpha = N^2e^{-2nu}, \quad p = Pe^{mu}$$

and to the various values of the parameter u, that is, to the values

	$0,$	$\Delta u,$	$2\Delta u$	...
will correspond the commodities	$B,$	$C,$	D	...
and therefore the values of p equal to	$p_b,$	$p_c,$	p_d	...
and the values of r equal to	$r_b,$	$r_c,$	r_d	...
and the values of x equal to	$x_b,$	$x_c,$	x_d	...

and similarly for the other quantities.

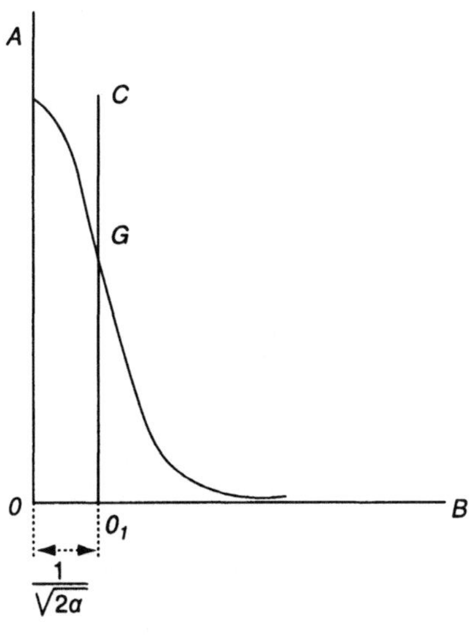

Figure 4.4

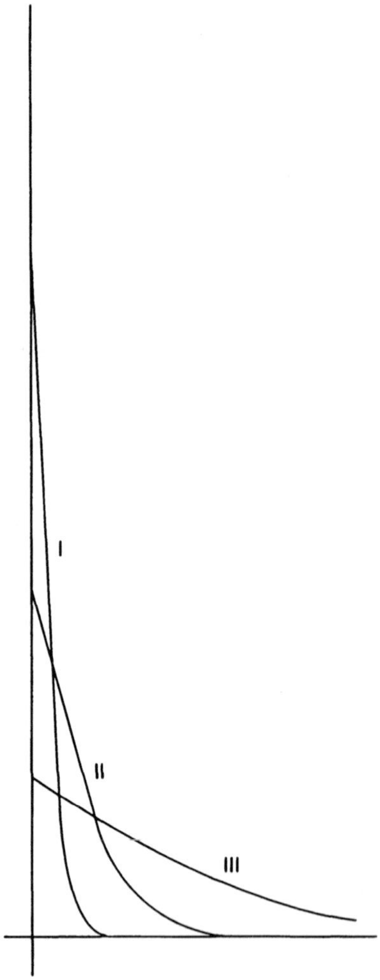

Figure 4.5

According to these hypotheses, the above recalled equation (5) becomes

$$q_a = p_b\left(x_b - \sqrt{\frac{1}{2a_b}}\right) + p_c\left(x_c - \sqrt{\frac{1}{2a_c}}\right) + \ldots = \sum_{u=0}^{u=\sigma} p\left(x - \sqrt{\frac{1}{2a}}\right). \tag{40}$$

The sum will have to stop when the quantity r is no longer positive. Therefore, out of all the possible values of u, it is useful to make σ equal to the value immediately below the quantity obtained from the equation

$$x - \sqrt{\frac{1}{2a}} = 0.$$

As usual, with m we shall indicate the final degree of utility of money, that is, we assume

$$\varphi_u(q_u) = m,$$

and then

$$m = e^{\mu}.$$

Equations (a) are all included in the equation

$$m = \frac{1}{p}\,\varphi(r),$$

where u is given the values 0, Δu, $2\Delta u$, $3\Delta u$. . . .

From this equation one obtains

$$ax^2 = \log\frac{a}{p} - \mu$$

that is

$$x = \frac{1}{\sqrt{a}}\sqrt{G - hu - \mu} = \frac{1}{\sqrt{a}}\sqrt{\beta^2 - hu}$$

where, for the sake of conciseness, we have assumed

$$G = \log\frac{H}{P}, \quad h = k + \omega, \quad \beta^2 = G - \mu.$$

With this value for x we shall find the value u_1 of u that satisfies the equation

$$\frac{1}{\sqrt{a}}\sqrt{\beta^2 - hu_1} = \frac{1}{\sqrt{2a}},$$

from which we obtain

$$u_1 = \frac{\beta^2}{h} - \frac{1}{2h}$$

and the limit for the sum that gives q will be u_0, with 0 an integer, such that the value u_1 is contained between $0\Delta u$ and $(0 + 1)\Delta u$; whereas the lower limit u_0 is equal to zero.

When the number 0 is large, the sum can be calculated with the well-known formula

$$\Sigma\, X = \frac{1}{\Delta u}\int_{u_0}^{u_0} x\,du + \frac{\Delta u}{2}(x_0 + x_0) + \frac{\Delta u}{12}(x'_0 - x'_0) + \dots.$$

In our case

$$X = p\left(x - \sqrt{\frac{1}{2a}}\right) = \frac{P}{N}e^{mu}\left(\sqrt{\beta^2 - hu} - \sqrt{\frac{1}{2}}\right)$$

and therefore it is

$$q\Delta u = \frac{1}{n}\sqrt{\frac{h}{n}}\frac{P}{N}e^{\frac{n}{h}\beta^2}\int_{\tau_0}^{\tau_1} e^{-y^2}\,dy - \left(\frac{1}{n} - \frac{\Delta u}{2}\right)X_0$$
$$+ \left(\frac{\Delta u}{2} - (u_1 - u_0)\right)X_0 + \left(\frac{(\Delta u)^2}{12} - \frac{(u_1 - u_0)^2}{2}\right)X'_0 - \frac{(\Delta u)^2}{12}X'_0 \quad (41)$$

where it is

$$\tau_0 = \sqrt{\frac{n}{2h}}, \quad \tau_1 = \beta\sqrt{\frac{n}{h}},$$

$$X'_0 = nx_0 - \frac{P}{N}e^{mu_0}\frac{h}{2\sqrt{\beta^2 - hu_0}}, \qquad X'_0 = nX_0 - \frac{P}{N}\frac{h}{2\beta}.$$

We can observe that with the curves we have assumed for the final degrees of utility, the law *of the variety of human needs* is satisfied, since the number of our curves can be infinitely extended.

When m is very small and μ is therefore negative and large, it is possible to take into account only the first term of formula (41), since in comparison with it the others are very small.

The integral appearing in that term is found to be very close to the constant quantity

$$A = \int_{\tau_0}^{\infty} e^{-y^2}\,dy$$

and therefore one obtains

$$mq^{\frac{h}{n}} = \left[\frac{1}{n\Delta u}\sqrt{\frac{h}{n}}\frac{A}{N}\right]^{\frac{h}{n}} H\left(\frac{1}{P}\right)^{1-\frac{h}{n}} \quad (42)$$

and if one had

$$\frac{h}{n} = 1$$

one would obtain precisely Bernoulli's hyperbola.

Let us go back to formula (41), and in order to have some idea of the curves it represents let us give a numerical example.

Let us assume

$$a = 0.06e^{-2.1u}, \quad a = 100e^{-0.7}$$

and therefore

$$H = 100, \quad k = 0.7, \quad N^2 = 0.06, \quad P = 1, \quad n = 1.05.$$

Figure 11 shows indeed three of these curves that represent the final degrees of utility, that is,

the curves	I ,	II ,	III
correspond to the values of u equal to	0 ,	1 ,	2.

If we now suppose $\Delta u = 0.1$, there will be nine intermediate curves between curve I and curve II, and nine more between II and III.

Let us also suppose

$$p = e^{u}$$

and therefore

$$P = 1, \quad \omega = 1, \quad n = 2.05, \quad h = 1.7, \quad G = \log\frac{H}{P} = 4.6051702.$$

With these values we shall calculate the Table 4.1.

μ	$m = e^{\mu}$	q
4.1052	60.65	0
3.0	20.08	15
2.8	16.44	22
2.6	13.46	31
2.4	11.02	44
2.2	9.02	60
2.0	7.39	81
1.8	6.05	107
1.6	4.95	141
1.4	4.05	184
1.2	3.32	241
1.0	2.72	313

We have only taken into account the whole part of q, since there was no point in looking for more precise values when the data are only hypothetical, as they are here.

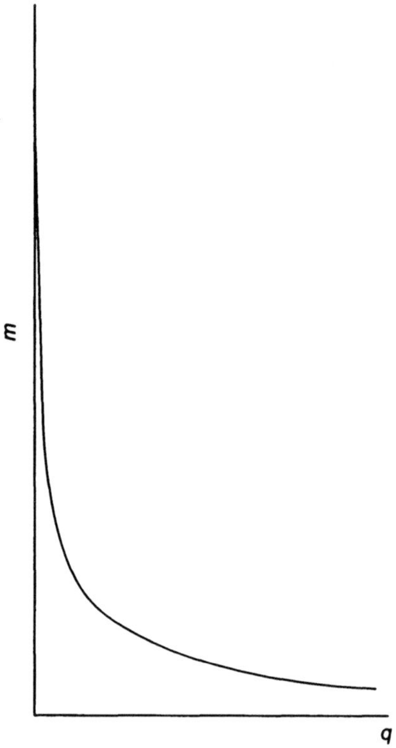

Figure 4.6

Figure 4.6 shows the curve of the values of q and m.

When m is very small, the curve approximates those for which equation (42) applies and becomes:

$$mq^{0.82927} = 340.$$

Prof. Marshall does use Bernoulli's hyperbola, but he mentions other hypotheses; among which the most likely seems to him to be Cramer's,[V,12] that makes the *utility* of money equal to the square root of the quantity of it, seems to him the most likely.

We do not believe that this or other hypotheses will come close to the truth. All we achieve, with them, are empirical propositions. The only rational way is to look for the final degrees of utility of the economic goods consumed or used by man, and from these *degrees* infer the degrees of instrumental goods, among which money is paramount.

Having said that, we still concede that for a long time to come Political Economy will have to follow empirical paths in its search for the solution to concrete questions; in the meantime, however, we must endeavour to perfect the rational science of economics, so that later we may substitute it, little by little, for the empirical.

Final degree of utility of money

We must now return to this topic, which we have already mentioned before; we shall not be able to exhaust it as yet, but there is a part of it that pertains to the study of individual economics and must therefore be covered here; as for the remainder, we shall deal with it later.

For many economists, as we saw with Cairnes, the concept of the *value* of gold approximates the final degree of utility of gold, and ends up becoming identical to it. Other economists consider a certain entity they call the *purchasing power of gold*, and often seem to take it as a measure of the *value* of this metal.

It is easy to understand what the purchasing power of gold is with regard to a certain merchandise. It is the unit divided by the price of that merchandise. But we must confess that we do not know what a generic purchasing power that might be applied to all merchandises is, nor have we so far seen precise definitions of it. Such definitions, when one tries to obtain them, are more or less close to the concept of *utility*, which alone is clear and well defined.[13]

It is strange to see how many economists, who are unaware of it or are rejecting it, have believed that they could manage by using clever combinations of prices, aimed at obtaining different types of averages.

It is easy to understand where the illusion originates. If **all** the prices increase at the same time in the same proportion, the phenomenon may appear likely to be due to a variation of some properties of the money used to measure those prices, rather than to a variation of the properties of *all* the economic goods. Actually, it is the final degree of utility of money that would have changed, but in this case nothing prevents us from describing how the phenomenon came to be, by saying that the *purchasing power* of money has changed.

This interpretation was later extended to other cases. And since averages are used, often somewhat shoddily, to be honest, in order to discern within a phenomenon the effects of some main causes from the effects of accessory causes, it was thought that they might provide some valuable help also in this case.

Much work has been done on this subject, and understandably so. To quote the insightful words of our own Messedaglia,[VI, 14]

> that is an important enquiry . . ., which studies the variations this real value[15] of money has undergone in various ages – that is to say, the history of monetary prices as far as it can especially depend not so much on causes of an industrial and commercial nature related to the production and trade of goods, but on other causes that directly affect money

itself, by modifying in various degrees its own purchasing power; such as, for instance, its comparative shortage or abundance, and the generally related shortage or abundance of precious metals.

Prof. Walras was the first to shed light on this difficult subject. We wish we could cite his words here, but limitations of space prevent us from doing so. Furthermore, this would not be very useful, since it will always be better for the reader to directly access the words of the learned Professor of Lausanne. We shall only relate what is necessary to pave our way for some remarks we believe we should add to his theory.[16]

Prof. Walras starts by examining Cournot's method. The essence of this method is expounded below; as for the details, the reader will find them in *Recherches sur les principes mathématiques de la théorie des richesses.*

Let us consider, as usual, the commodities $A, \; B, \; C \; \ldots$
whose prices are $1, \; p_b, \; p_c \; \ldots$

and let us mark on a line XY the points $A, B, C \ldots$, so that, $\overline{AB} = \log p_b$, $\overline{AC} = \log p_c$ . . . (see Figure 4.7).

Figure 4.7

We shall have

$$\overline{AC} - \overline{AB} = \log \frac{p_c}{p_b}$$

but

$$\frac{p_c}{p_b}$$

is the price of commodity C measured no longer using commodity A, but using commodity B. In general, therefore, the difference between the distances of two of the points marked on the line XY from a third point gives us the logarithm of the price of the commodity represented by one of those points.

The problem of the variation of prices is therefore transformed into the problem of identifying the *cause* of the movement of the points that represent those prices.

Let $A', B', C', D' \ldots$ be the new positions of the points $A, B, C \ldots$. If $\overline{BC}$ is equal or almost equal to $\overline{B'C'}$, and likewise also $\overline{CD}$ is almost equal to $\overline{C'D'}$ etc. it is said that it was most likely only point A that moved, rather than *all* the points $B, C, D \ldots$.

This is assumed as evident, but we would not be able to demonstrate it.

Here we come upon one of the mistakes that are usually made in using the calculus of probability, which consists in not making sure that the probabilities of the various cases under scrutiny are equal.

It is certain that if the probabilities of moving were a priori equal for all the points *A*, *B*, *C* . . ., the observation that the distances between points *B*, *C*, *D* . . . remain unchanged, whilst only the distances between those points and point *A* change would give a high probability to the hypothesis that it is point *A* that moved, rather than points *B*, *C*, *D*. . . . But this way of reasoning no longer works when a cause is known to exist that may favour the movement of points *B*, *C*, *D* . . . and not the movement of point *A*. And Cournot himself admits this, when he states:[17]

> If all the points of the system with the exception of one had not moved from their position, we should admit it to be likely that this single point had moved, unless the other system components were all interconnected so as not to be allowed to move independently from each other.

It does not take much; all that is required is that there exist causes that may affect the set of points *B*, *C*, *D*. . . .

But this is precisely what it is being argued about in the real case! All prices are supposed to have dropped, and we are looking for a reason. Some say, it is because gold has become rarer; no, others say, it is because the more society progresses, the more efficient human work becomes.

What light can Cournot's method shed on this question, if we have to have answered the question before using it?

Prof. Walras's observations refer to another part of the argument; we shall see them presently. In the meantime, what we have just said should suffice to invalidate Cournot's method.

Even if we disregard Prof. Bertrand's objections on the calculus of probability of *causes*, the analysis of which would take us a long time,[18] and also entirely accept the principles followed by Laplace, Poisson, Quetelet, etc., which are most in favour of Cournot's method, it is easy to perceive how fallacious the latter is.

For any point **C**, let τ_c be the a priori probability that a cause[19] exists that moves it, and σ_c the probability, also a priori, that if this cause exists the point will move from left to right.

Let us suppose that the event we observe is that points *B*, *C* . . . have maintained the distances between themselves, while moving away from point *A*, on the right. There can be only two *causes* of such an event: either *A* has moved from right to left, while points *B*, *C* . . . stayed still, or the latter points have moved from left to right, while *A* was still.

The probability of the first case is

$$\Pi_1 = \tau_a(1 - \sigma_a)(1 - \tau_b)(1 - \tau_c) \ldots$$

and the probability of the second

$$\Pi_2 = (1 - \tau_a)\, \tau_b \sigma_b \tau_c \sigma_c \ldots$$

thus, according to the principles of the probability of causes, having observed the points moving as described above, the probability that this is due to only point *A* moving is

$$\frac{\Pi_1}{\Pi_1 + \Pi_2};$$

and the probability that it is instead due to *B*, *C* . . . moving is

$$\frac{\Pi_2}{\Pi_1 + \Pi_2}.$$

If we do not know anything a priori about the probabilities of the causes, or about the probabilities of the motion being in one direction rather than the other, we must assume them all equal to ½. In this case, if θ is the number of points *A*, *B*, *C* . . . we shall have

$$\Pi_1 = \left(\frac{1}{2}\right)^{\theta + 1}, \quad \Pi_2 = \left(\frac{1}{2}\right)^{2\theta - 1}$$

$$\frac{\Pi_1}{\Pi_1 + \Pi_2} = \frac{2^{\theta - 2}}{2^{\theta - 2} + 1}, \quad \frac{\Pi_2}{\Pi_1 + \Pi_2} = \frac{1}{2^{\theta - 2} + 1}.$$

If for θ we take a number that is not even too big, such as for instance 6, for the probability of point *A* moving, and for the probability of points *B*, *C* . . . moving one would respectively obtain

$$\frac{16}{17}, \frac{1}{17}.$$

It would therefore be very likely that it was point *A* that moved, and Cournot's method would work.

But in real life matters do not stand in this way. The probability of industrial improvements, which tend to bring prices down, is certainly higher than $\frac{1}{2}$. Furthermore, this single cause, if existing, is enough to make a great number of points move in the same direction. The same must be said about lower transport costs for commodities and other similar reasons.

Let us therefore suppose that τ_a is, a priori, the probability of a cause that will certainly make point **A** move from right to left. Let τ_1 be the probability that a cause exists, which will certainly make a number θ_1 of points **B, C, D** . . . move from left to right; let τ_2 be the probability that another cause exists, which will make an additional θ_2 points move in the same direction, and so on. We shall have

$$\Pi_1 = \tau_u (1 - \tau_1)(1 - \tau_2) \ldots$$

$$\Pi_2 = (1 - \tau_u)\, \tau_1 \tau_2 \tau_3 \ldots$$

Before we observe the event under scrutiny, let it be

$$\tau_u = \frac{2}{3}, \quad \tau_1 = \frac{2}{3}, \quad \tau_2 = \frac{2}{3}, \quad \tau_3 = \frac{2}{3} \ldots$$

the result will be

$$\Pi_1 = \frac{2}{3^{\varepsilon + 1}}, \quad \Pi_2 = \frac{2^{\varepsilon}}{3^{\varepsilon + 1}};$$

where ε is the number of classes into which the number 0 of commodities has been divided, the first of which includes a number of commodities 0_1, the second a number 0_2, etc.

With these values, for the probability of A moving, and for the probability of the other points moving we find, respectively,

$$\frac{1}{1 + 2^{\varepsilon - 1}}, \quad \frac{2^{\varepsilon - 1}}{1 + 2^{\varepsilon - 1}}.$$

For $\varepsilon = 4$, for instance, these probabilities would be

$$\frac{1}{9}, \quad \frac{8}{9}.$$

If we accept the hypotheses that have been put forward, it is therefore possible to see that if the probability of a rise in the price of gold were a priori $\frac{2}{3}$, but $\frac{2}{3}$ were also the probability that easier transports have brought down the price of a number of commodities, and the probability that industrial improvements have caused the prices of other commodities to decrease, and likewise for two more classes of merchandise, then the probability that the price drop depends only on the increase in the value of gold would only be $\frac{1}{9}$, whereas the probability that the price drop is due to causes affecting other commodities would be $\frac{8}{9}$.

Cournot's method would instead have us believe that the price drop is very likely due to the increase in the value of gold!

We only intended to give a hypothetical example, and not to attempt actually to calculate the probability of a variation in the value of gold. In fact, we believe that our current level of knowledge makes it absolutely impossible to calculate such a probability in this way, and we therefore see anything that one might try to do in that direction as useless.

The calculus of probability can only be used to show us a few errors of reasoning, such as the one we have just discussed. And we dwelt on this error because it is frequently repeated. Many believe they can get close to the truth by looking for the *index numbers* of a large number of commodities; in fact, it is not single commodities they should consider, but aggregates, on which the same cause can be supposed to act in the same way to make their prices vary.

Prof. Walras rightly remarks that we must look into the variations of the final degrees of utility, and that it is in this sense that we can accept the terms of Cournot's problem; that is, if one has

$$p_c = \frac{\varphi_c(r_c)}{\varphi_a(q_a)},$$

when p_c becomes p'_c we can investigate if this variation is caused by a variation of φ_c, or by a variation of φ_a.

On the other hand, he believes that Cournot's solution has an empirical value that may be of some importance 'si les marchandises en présence sont en grand nombre et en quantités considérables sur le marché' [if the merchandises involved are in large number and in considerable quantities].

We have just seen that this is not enough. It is not only on the number of commodities that one should focus, but rather on their distribution in classes according to their dependence on the above-mentioned causes. But how to determine this distribution is as difficult a problem as the one it should help to solve. Add that not all the movements are in the same direction, and the uncertainty of the conclusions will be further increased. One can therefore see that Cournot's method has no merit whatsoever and must be abandoned.

Jevons assumes the geometric average of prices as the measure of the variation of the *value* of gold. All that section of his study that focuses on how to eliminate periodical variations in order to take into account only those variations that have a more stable effect and could be said to be centuries-old is worthy of great praise and holds valuable teachings that can greatly benefit the economist, whatever method he may choose to adopt. But we are forced to pass over all these considerations, which would be superfluous here, and it is understood that our discussion will only refer to centuries-old variations.

Let $\quad p_b, \quad p_c, \quad p_d \quad \ldots$
be certain prices that after a certain time become $\quad p'_b, \quad p'_c, \quad p'_d \quad \ldots$.

According to Jevons,

$$M = m\sqrt{\frac{p'_b}{p_b}\frac{p'_c}{p_c}\frac{p'_d}{p_d}\cdots}$$

gives us the average variation of the prices, and

$$\frac{1}{M} = m\sqrt{\frac{p_b}{p'_b}\cdot\frac{p_c}{p'_c}\cdot\frac{p_d}{p'_d}\cdots}$$

gives us the variation of the *value* of gold; m represents the number of commodities B, C, D. . . . We shall here report Prof. Walras's analysis of these formulae using our notations.

Let us suppose, as usual, that for the commodities	A,	B,	C . . .
when their prices are	1,	p_b,	p_c . . .
the used quantities are	q_a,	r_b,	r_c . . .
and when their prices are	1,	p'_b,	p'_c . . .
the quantities are	q'_a,	r'_b,	r'_c . . . .

We shall therefore have

$$\varphi_a(q_a) = \frac{1}{p_b}\varphi_b(r_b) = \frac{1}{p_c}\varphi_c(r_c) = \ldots$$

$$\varphi_a(q'_a) = \frac{1}{p'_b}\varphi_b(r'_b) = \frac{1}{p'_c}\varphi_c(r'_c) = \ldots .$$

And from these equations we shall obtain

$$\frac{1}{M} = \frac{\varphi_a(q'_a)}{\varphi_a(q_a)} \sqrt[m]{\frac{\varphi_b(r_b)}{\varphi_b(r'_b)} \cdot \frac{\varphi_c(r_c)}{\varphi_c(r'_c)} \ldots}$$

and therefore

$$\frac{\varphi_a(q'_a)}{\varphi_a(q_a)} = \frac{\sqrt[m]{\frac{p_b}{p'_b} \cdot \frac{p_c}{p'_c} \ldots}}{\sqrt[m]{\frac{\varphi_b(r_b)}{\varphi_b(r'_b)} \cdot \frac{\varphi_c(r_c)}{\varphi_c(r'_c)} \ldots}}. \qquad (43_a)$$

Consequently, it appears that 1 divided by the geometric average of the quotients of the prices does not give the quotient between the new and the old final degree of utility of gold, but one must take into account the quantity

$$\sqrt{\frac{\varphi_b(r_b)}{\varphi_b(r'_b)} \cdot \frac{\varphi_c(r_c)}{\varphi_c(r'_c)} \ldots},$$

which cannot be assumed equal to 1, as would be necessary for Jevons's formula to give us the quotient of the final degree of utility of gold.

Other averages would give different expressions, and one would have

$$\frac{\varphi_a(q'_a)}{\varphi_a(q_a)}\left(\frac{p'_b}{p_b} + \frac{p'_c}{p_c} + \ldots\right) = \frac{\varphi_b(r'_b)}{\varphi_b(r_b)} + \frac{\varphi_c(r'_c)}{\varphi_c(r_c)} + \ldots \qquad (43_\beta)$$

$$\frac{\varphi_a(q'_a)}{\varphi_a(q_a)}\frac{1}{\dfrac{p_b}{p'_b}+\dfrac{p_c}{p'_c}+\ldots}=\frac{1}{\dfrac{\varphi_b(r_b)}{\varphi_b(r'_b)}+\dfrac{\varphi_c(r_c)}{\varphi_c(r'_c)}+\ldots}. \tag{43$_\gamma$}$$

Prof. Walras uses a formula he calls the *multiple standard* [*étalon multiple*], which is simply the formula

$$q_a = r_b p_b + r_c p_c + \ldots,$$

from which one obtains

$$\frac{\varphi_a(q'_a)}{\varphi_a(q_a)}\frac{r'_b p'_b + r'_c p'_c + \ldots}{r_b p_b + r_c p_c + \ldots}=\frac{r'_b\varphi_b(r'_b)+r'_c\varphi_c(r'_c)+\ldots}{r_b\varphi_b(r_b)+r_c\varphi_c(r_c)+\ldots}. \tag{43$_\delta$}$$

And this is as far as Prof. Walras goes.[20] This is acceptable when dealing with one individual, but Prof. Walras seems to extend these equations to society as a whole. For instance, he says he can calculate *social wealth* with the formula

$$r_b p_b + r_c p_c + \ldots,$$

which would not make sense if r_b, r_c ... were not the quantities consumed by the whole society. Furthermore, he discusses the *rareté* (final degree of utility) of gold as if it existed independently, and not in relation to each individual, for which reason it clearly appears to us that what he means is some averaged *rareté*.

We have seen that the equation

$$\varphi_a(r_a)=\frac{1}{p_b}\varphi_b(r_b)=\frac{1}{p_c}\varphi_c(r_c)=\ldots$$

only applies in the case of one individual, whereas in general it changes shape when dealing with an aggregate. And the possibility we mentioned of being able to preserve that formula by considering saving is only theoretical and cannot be said to exist in reality.

This subject is of too great an importance in the new science of economics for us not to try to assess most clearly how things stand.

Let us go back to what we were saying in the section in chapter 3 entitled 'Averaged final degrees of utility for more than one person'. The economic goods *A*, *B*, *C*, ... are all real direct goods, and have therefore their own final degree of utility,

that is	$\varphi_a(r_a)$,	$\varphi_b(r_b)$,	$\varphi_c(r_c)$	....
Their prices are	1,	p_b,	p_c. ...	....

I. The equations that must be satisfied are the n equations marked (31), the θ equations marked (33), and the $(n-1)\theta$ equations

$$\begin{cases}\varphi_{1a}(r_{1a})=\dfrac{1}{p_b}\varphi_{1b}(r_{1b})=\dfrac{1}{p_c}\varphi_{1c}(r_{1c})=\ldots\\[2ex] \varphi_{2a}(r_{2a})=\dfrac{1}{p_b}\varphi_{2b}(r_{2b})=\dfrac{1}{p_c}\varphi_{2c}(r_{2c})=\ldots\\[2ex] \ldots\end{cases} \tag{44}$$

from these the $(n-1)(0-1)$ equations marked (32) are obtained; there remain $n-1$ equations, that are those on the same page, with which p_b, p_c are determined: that is

$$p_b = \frac{\varphi_{1b}(r_{1b})}{\varphi_{1a}(r_{1a})}, \quad p_c = \frac{\varphi_{1c}(r_{1c})}{\varphi_{1a}(r_{1a})} \quad \ldots \tag{45}$$

In the paragraph just mentioned we saw that the number of these equations exceeds by one the number of the unknowns; in this way, it still occurs.

Equations (31), (33), and (44) are a total of $n0 + n$. Once we have eliminated the $n0$ quantities $r_{1a}, r_{1b}, \ldots r_{2a}, r_{2b} \ldots$ we shall be left with n equations, whilst the unknowns $p_b, p_c \ldots$ we have to determine are only $n-1$.

II. All this still applies when A is an exclusively instrumental good. This condition entails that φ_a no longer exists independently; 0 equations out of the (44) disappear. Furthermore, if we do not want to take saving into account, we must suppose that no money is either spent or put aside, and it must therefore be

$$r_{1a} = 0, \quad r_{2a} = 0, \quad \ldots \quad r_a = 0;$$

thus, 0 quantities that were to be eliminated disappear. The first of equations (31) also disappears, because all the quantities in it are zero. But equations (33), where the quantities $r_{1a}, r_{2a} \ldots$ are made equal to zero, and (44), from which $\varphi_{1a}, \varphi_{2a} \ldots$ have been taken out, show that it is only possible to determine the quotients

$$\frac{p_c}{p_b}, \quad \frac{p_d}{p_b}$$

and not p_b as well.

To sum up in one sentence all that has been said: $0 + 1$ equations disappear, but 0 quantities that were to be eliminated plus one unknown vanish as well, and therefore we are in the very same conditions as before.

III. Finally, there is the consideration that for the sake of brevity we called *of saving*, which changes, as we have already shown, the solution to the problem.

Whether or not A is an economic good with its own degree of utility, the above-mentioned circumstance operates by changing equations (12) and (33).

Indeed we suppose that income no longer perfectly balances expenditure, but there is a surplus or a shortfall.

We can leave this difference indeterminate. In this way, the 0 equations (33) are no more, and instead of having one equation too many, we have $0-1$ equations too few.

We have made use of this to demonstrate that also for an aggregate of people it is theoretically possible to have the final degree of utility of a commodity depending on the quantity of that good only. But it is obvious that since the various individuals certainly do not aim at achieving this goal, when making use of their savings, and since at any rate they mostly lack the power as well as the will to do so, in reality it would be extremely odd to have that form of the final degree of utility.

We can instead suppose that the θ quantities

$$r_{1a}, \quad r_{2a} \ldots$$

are known, which takes us back to considering an aggregate of people having a fixed income; and, if some $r_{1a}, r_{2a} \ldots$ were positive, it would instead be a fixed expenditure they ought to have.

With this, the θ equations (33) apply once more.

(*α*) If A is a direct economic good, we go back to the very case expounded in paragraph I.
(*β*) If A is only an instrumental good, what was said in paragraph II changes.

$p_b, p_c \ldots$ can be determined separately, and not only the quotients of $n-2$ of them, divided by the other one. The fact that $\varphi_{1a}, \varphi_{2a} \ldots$ no longer exist still removes θ equations from the (44). Therefore, far from having one equation too many, we are θ – 1 equations short, if we wish to determine $p_b, p_c \ldots$ as a functions of

$$r_a, \quad r_b, \quad r_c \ldots$$

This means that $p_b, p_c \ldots$ do not depend only on the sum total r_a, but also on the partial sums $q_{1a}, q_{1b}, \ldots$

This could easily have been foreseen a priori. Total supply and demand in a society do not depend only on total wealth, but also on the way wealth is distributed. One can therefore see that when calculating the final degree of utility of money for the society, it will be necessary to take at least such distribution into account. But what else should be taken into account, and how, only mathematics can tell us.

We notice that case (*β*) is precisely the case we considered in our study of Bernoulli's theorem.

For the science of economics there is an essential difference between questions I and II, and question III.

In paragraphs I and II we examine the conditions of equilibrium of production and consumption, and do not consider money, which is only used as a vehicle to obtain the barters under scrutiny. Saving can be included among the economic goods covered by those formulae, provided it is considered as having its own final degree of utility.

In paragraph III we accept a fact for which no explanation is given, namely that individuals must receive, or pay, fixed amounts. In reality these circumstances occur for an aggregate of people who possess government or other bonds that give a fixed yield, and their conversion is not taken into account; likewise, if we are dealing with people who must pay a fixed yearly expenditure, and cannot convert it to a one-off payment of a certain amount.

The laws for the phenomena covered in paragraph III would not apply to those in possession of bonds whose yield is variable, nor to those that can repay the capital instead of having to continue to pay a fixed sum of interest.

Both for the former and the latter persons the quantities

$$r_{1a}, \quad r_{2a} \ldots$$

cannot be supposed to be known and invariable, but depend on the other quantities, and such dependence must be taken into account.

It behoves us to look now for the expressions of the final degree of utility of money not for one individual, but for an aggregate of people.

Errata-corrigenda

Many a misprint has occurred, which we shall show in an errata-corrigenda at the end of this study.[XIII]

5 Considerations on the fundamental principles of Pure Political Economy, V

(*Giornale degli Economisti*, October 1893)

Most general form of the final degrees of utility

Before delving any further in our research on the average [final] degrees of utility, it would be beneficial, in our opinion, to consider them in their most general form, as already indicated (June 1892 issue, p. 23; Chapter 2); for only in this way can some of their qualities be fully illustrated.

If one were writing a synthetic treatise, one's starting point should be the subject matter we are about to cover; then one would have to move from the general case down into the particular cases. In this way the exposition would proceed in a more orderly fashion and would be more elegant. But for those who are not yet *au fait* with the topic, it is beneficial, instead, to proceed from the particular to the general, which is what we have done. By now, the reader who has followed us so far will have grown accustomed to dealing with final degrees of utility, and will be ready for the increasing degree of abstraction that is unfortunately part and parcel of a higher degree of generality.

We have already seen that Prof. Edgeworth considers the final degrees of utility as functions of all the commodities consumed by the individual.

However, he introduces a restriction.

To be precise, he supposes that they are the partial derivatives of a single function, which is the same as admitting that a function exists which represents the total utility of the commodities.

In this case the total utility of the consumption of a certain number of commodities is independent of the order in which they have been consumed. This would be inadmissible, if one wished to consider the utility of consumption directly. It is indeed evident that the pleasure afforded by a meal is not the same if one eats it in the order to which one is used, or if one started instead with the coffee and finished with the soup. But we have already suggested (January 1893 issue, p. 75; Chapter 4) that we do not think that the economic utility of a commodity should be confused with the utility of uninterrupted consumption. If one keeps them distinct, as we believe they should be, it hardly matters in what order the various foods one is eating are bought, because one is not compelled to follow the same order in consuming them. Therefore we think that for an individual there are no serious difficulties a priori in accepting the restriction used by Prof. Edgeworth, and that on the contrary it occurs easily.

* The case where total utility exists corresponds perfectly to the cases considered by the science of mechanics,[1] where there exists a *function of the forces*.

Almost all authors who have written about the mathematical theories of Political Economy assume as evident a priori the existence of a function representing total utility. But this existence is not demonstrated, at least in the most general cases.

Let us suppose therefore that for a man who owns

the quantities	ρ_a,	ρ_b,	$\rho_c \ldots$
of the economic goods	A,	B,	C ...

the utility (positive or negative) of an increase $d\rho_a$ (positive or negative) of ρ_a is φ_a, which can be a function of all the variables ρ_a, ρ_b, ρ_c. ... Let the functions φ_b, $\varphi_c \ldots$ have similar meaning.

The functions φ_a, φ_b, $\varphi_c \ldots$ are the only quantities that actually exist. And it is from them that we must set out in order to acquire the concept of *total utility*, and not vice versa.

Prof. Edgeworth starts by considering only two economic goods, and we believe that his example is worth following, because in the case of two economic goods, and then also of three but no more, our reasoning can take a concrete form, which is easily understood also by those who are not very familiar with mathematical abstractions.

Let us indicate (in Figure 5.1) the quantities of economic good A with the abscissae, and the quantities of economic good B with the ordinates. The state of an individual who owns a quantity $\overline{OP}$ of A, and a quantity $\overline{OQ}$ of B is represented by point M.

When *total utility* exists, two paths MTN and MSN followed in moving from M to N, lead to the same total utility at N, which generally does not happen if *total utility* does not exist.

When the curve one follows to move from point M to point N is set, the two variables cease to be independent. One depends on the other by means of the equation of the chosen curve.

Among the infinite number of lines passing through a point M, Prof. Edgeworth singles out two. One, called *line of indifference*, is characterized by the fact that utility does not vary on it. To an individual it makes therefore no difference to be in one rather than another of the states represented by any point on the line. The other line, called *line of preference*, is the line along which the individual prefers to move, and we shall presently see how it is defined.

As we have often recalled above, Prof. Edgeworth supposes that total utility always exists; however, these lines still exist in the most general case.

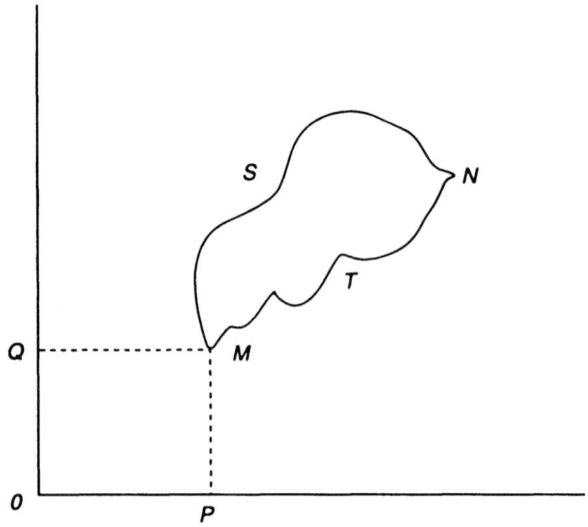

Figure 5.1

Let us suppose that starting from M, one must move a very small distance dt (Prof. Edgeworth talks of taking *a small step*); we shall have

$$dt^2 = dp_u^2 + dp_h^2;$$

and the variation of utility will be

$$dU = \varphi_u dp_u + \varphi_h dp_h.$$

If this variation is made equal to zero, we obtain the equation of the *line of indifference*

$$0 = \varphi_u dp_u + \varphi_h dp_h.$$

If we look for the way to make this variation maximum, we shall obtain the equation of the *line of preference*. By indicating with δ the differentiation symbol when we consider the two variables dp_u and dp_h, if we suppose that dt is constant, we have

$$0 = 2dp_u\delta dp_u + 2dp_h\delta dp_h,$$

and then for the maximum (or for the minimum) of dU

$$0 = \varphi_u\delta dp_u + \varphi_h\delta dp_h;$$

and therefore

$$\varphi_u dp_h - \varphi_h dp_u = 0, \quad \frac{dp_u}{\varphi_u} = \frac{dp_h}{\varphi_h}.$$

This is the equation of the lines of preference. One can see that they are orthogonal to the lines of indifference.

They can also be obtained by observing that

$$dp_a = dt\cos\alpha, \quad dp_b = dt\sin\alpha;$$

where α is the angle formed by dt with the p_a axis. The variation of utility is

$$dU = dt(\varphi_a\cos\alpha + \varphi_b\sin\alpha).$$

The direction of the line of indifference is given by

$$\varphi_a\cos\alpha + \varphi_b\sin\alpha = 0,$$

that is

$$\tan\alpha = -\frac{\varphi_a}{\varphi_b};$$

and the maximum of $\varphi_a\cos\alpha + \varphi_b\sin\alpha$ will be obtained by giving α a value that differs by 90° from the previous one (see Figure 5.2).

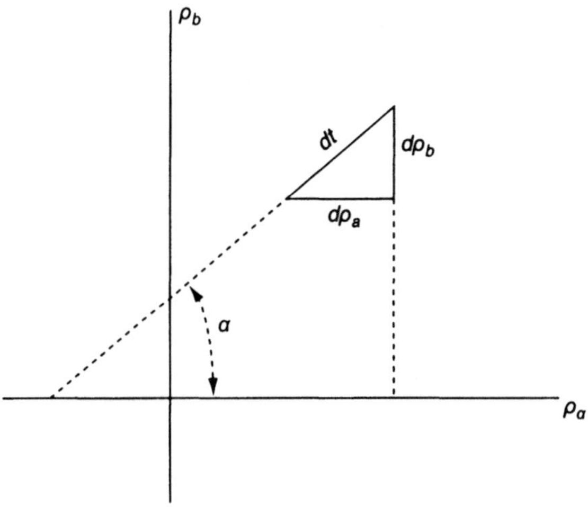

Figure 5.2

If there are three economic goods, it will be possible to represent their quantities with three rectangular coordinates.

Also in this case, if total utility exists, two different paths followed in going from point M to another point M' lead us to the same utility in M'; this does not happen if total utility does not exist.

Instead of a line of indifference, we have a surface of indifference having the following equation

$$0 = \varphi_a dp_a + \varphi_b dp_b + \varphi_c dp_c;$$

the lines of preference are still the orthogonal trajectories of the surfaces of indifference, and have the equation

$$\frac{dp_a}{\varphi_a} = \frac{dp_b}{\varphi_b} = \frac{dp_c}{\varphi_c}.$$

When total utility exists, as we have now supposed, one obtains

$$\varphi_a = \frac{\partial U}{\partial p_a}, \quad \varphi_b = \frac{\partial U}{\partial p_b}, \quad \varphi_c = \frac{\partial U}{\partial p_c}.$$

If there are only two economic goods, the equation

$$U = z$$

represents a surface. The lines of indifference are the projections of the contour lines of that surface on the plane $p_a\, p_b$ (which is supposed to be horizontal); and the lines of preference are the projections of the line of maximum slope.

This observation affords us a very elegant way of expounding the theory of the transformation of economic goods when there are only two of them, by making use of geometry.

Let the rectangular coordinates of a point on the horizontal plane represent the quantities of economic goods owned by an individual. Let us draw the perpendicular to the plane in that point, and mark on it a distance equal to the total utility that the individual derives from the ownership of those quantities of economic goods. By repeating the same construction for all points on the plane, we shall obtain a surface that we shall call surface of utility, whose various points represent the conditions of the individual. He will try as much as he can to make the point representing his conditions climb as high as possible; in other words, he will try to achieve as much utility as possible. He will do his best to prevent that point from falling. It will make no difference to him if the point moves, provided it does not go up or down. But the so-called contour lines are precisely the lines by following which one does not go up or down, and they will therefore be lines of indifference. The line of maximum slope are those along which one climbs fastest, and they will therefore be lines of *preference*. If one wishes to have an even more tangible image, let us consider a man at the foot of a mountain, to whom a lira is paid for every meter he climbs. To this man, to move along a contour line or to stay still is the same thing. And he will prefer to climb, if possible, along a line of maximum slope.

The price of *B* in *A* is

$$-\frac{dp_a}{dp_b}.$$

The condition that the various small portions of commodity successively transformed do not vary defines a straight line whose equation is

$$(p'_a - p_a) + p_b(p'_b - p_b) = 0;$$

where p'_a and p'_b are, as always, quantities of goods A and B.

If a point is moving on the line that represents price, until when will it keep moving? Obviously, it will keep moving until there is a line, among the various lines of indifference the point encounters while moving, to which the straight line followed is tangent; for when the point gets to where the straight line very briefly fuses with the line of indifference, going further, going back, or staying still will all be the same to the individual.

Let us draw a plane that is perpendicular to the plane of p_a p_b, and passes through the straight line followed by the point. This plane will intersect the surface of *utility* along a certain curve – it will follow a certain path on the side of the mountain. The point will keep moving on that curve until the curve becomes a tangent to a contour line. The individual in question will continue to climb along the path until that same path overlaps a contour line for a very short section.

But what will happen to the path beyond that point? If it keeps always overlapping a contour line, to keep moving or to stop will make no difference to the individual. If after having shared a very short section with a contour line the path goes down instead of going up, the individual will stop for good. We shall have a stable equilibrium. If after having coincided for that short section with the contour line, the path keeps going up, the individual will still be able to stop, but the equilibrium will be unstable, and he will easily go further and resume climbing.

When there are more than two economic goods we cannot have such a clear illustration of utility. For more than two economic goods a similar method to the one above could be applied, provided hyperspace were taken into account; but as regards the abstraction, there is not much difference from the exclusively analytical considerations.

In what follows we shall always suppose that total utility exists, unless otherwise indicated.

The locus of indifference is given by the equation

$$0 = \varphi_a dp_a + \varphi_b dp_b + \varphi_c dp_c + \ldots; \qquad (46)$$

and since the second member is precisely dU, it follows that the equation of this locus is

$$U = \mu,$$

with μ being an arbitrary constant.

For two economic goods it is a curve; for three economic goods it is a surface; for m economic goods it is a geometric *variety* with m dimensions.

The locus of preference is a line given by the equations

$$\frac{dp_a}{\varphi_a} = \frac{dp_b}{\varphi_b} = \frac{dp_c}{\varphi_c} = \ldots . \tag{47}$$

Finally, one has the equations with partial derivatives

$$\frac{\partial U}{\partial p_a} = \varphi_a, \quad \frac{\partial U}{\partial p_b} = \varphi_b, \ldots \tag{48}$$

The prices p_b, p_c . . . calculated in A can be constant or variable, but one will always have

$$p_b = -\frac{\partial q_a}{\partial q_b}, \quad p_c = -\frac{\partial q_a}{\partial q_c} \ldots \tag{49}$$

with q_a, q_b, q_c . . . being the quantities of economic goods owned in the subsequent bartering, which therefore become equal to p_a, p_b, p_c . . . when bartering ceases.

If the prices are known, the above equations establish a relationship between q_a and the other quantities q_b, q_c . . ., that remain the only independent variables, and one has

$$dq_a = \frac{\partial q_a}{\partial q_b} dq_b + \frac{\partial q_a}{\partial q_c} dq_c + \ldots;$$

that is

$$dq_a + p_b dq_b + p_c dq_c + \ldots = 0. \tag{50}$$

The transformations will continue until dq_a, dq_b . . . are on a locus of indifference (46), or, in other words, until it is

$$dq_a = dp_a, \quad dq_b = dp_b \ldots .$$

Then, by eliminating dp_a between (50) and (46), one obtains

$$(\varphi_b - p_b\varphi_a)dp_b + (\varphi_c - p_c\varphi_a)dp_c + \ldots = 0.$$

Since dp_b, dp_c . . . are independent here, it must be

$$\varphi_b - p_b\varphi_a = 0, \quad \varphi_c - p_c\varphi_a = 0 \ldots .$$

We therefore find the following equations, which we already knew,

$$\varphi_a = \frac{1}{p_b}\varphi_b = \frac{1}{p_c}\varphi_c = \ldots; \tag{6}$$

and their true interpretation is now most clearly revealed to us.

They are only the equations of the locus, where, due to stable or unstable equilibrium, the transformations of economic goods cease. Therefore it comes as no surprise at all that they are not enough, on their own, to determine the phenomenon of the transformation of goods in its entirety. When, for instance, we only know the prices p_b, p_c . . ., through the above-mentioned equations we come to know the values of φ_a, φ_b, . . ., that is, of the partial derivatives of U, but only in the locus defined by equations (6) and (50); and, as one can easily understand, in order to acquire full knowledge of those derivatives, it is necessary to consider them also out of that locus. In this way the economic phenomenon is put in full light, but it is necessary to make use of some rather complex mathematical notions. We have thought it useful to start by considering only the final degrees of utility without using the more general considerations of total utility and the differential equations related to it, but in our opinion it would be more advantageous to use the latter immediately, if one were wishing to expound the new theories in a synthetic way.

Some examples of total utility

Let us consider two economic goods. Let us suppose

$$\varphi_a = a - \alpha p_a, \quad \varphi_b = b - \beta p_b.$$

The final degrees of utility are represented by straight lines (see Figure 5.3). Total utility must be zero when p_a and p_b are zero. Therefore one has

$$U = a p_a - \frac{\alpha}{2} p_a^2 + b p_b - \frac{\beta}{2} p_b^2$$

which is the equation of a paraboloid. The only part of the surface we must take into account is the part between the planes

$$p_a = 0, \quad p_a = \frac{a}{\alpha}, \quad p_b = 0, \quad p_b = \frac{b}{\beta}$$

because the degrees of utility cannot be negative.

The projections of the lines of *indifference* on plane $p_a p_b$ are ellipses whose equation is

$$\frac{\alpha}{2} x^2 + \frac{\beta}{2} y^2 = \mu,$$

and one has

$$x = \frac{a}{\alpha} - p_a, \quad y = \frac{b}{\beta} - p_b$$

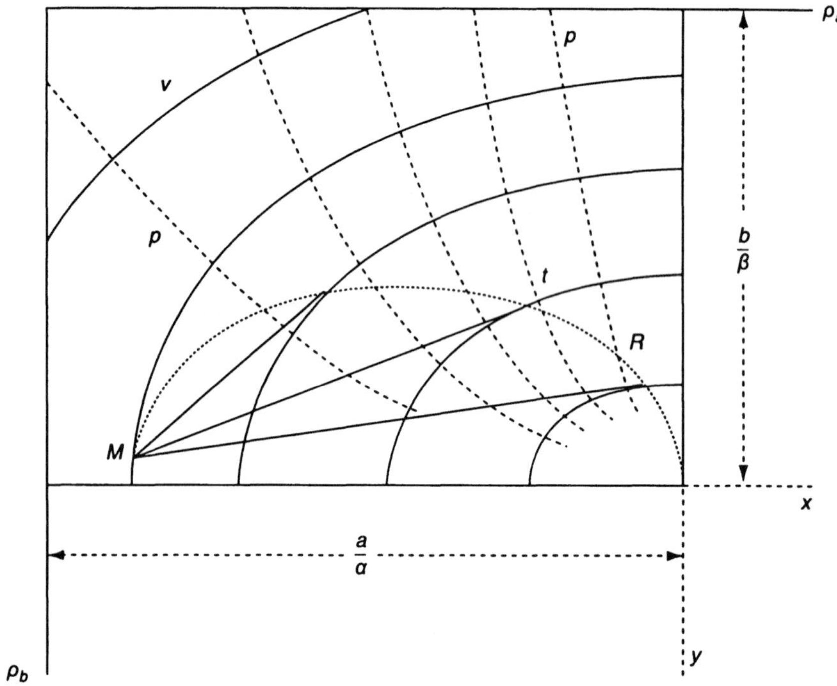

Figure 5.3

$$\mu = c - U, \quad c = \frac{a^2}{2\alpha} + \frac{b^2}{2\beta};$$

U varies from zero to its maximum value, which is c; therefore μ varies from c to zero.

The projections of the lines of maximum slope, or lines of *preference*, are the curves

$$y^{\alpha} = hx^{\beta}$$

where h is an arbitrary constant.[2]

Let the quantities of economic goods owned by an individual be represented by the coordinates of point M; if from M we draw a straight line Mt, this represents the barters of good B for A with a constant price (see Figure 5.4). And this price is equal to the trigonometric tangent of angle ω, that is to the slope of Mt on the p_b axis. Mt represents barters of B for A, since it is obvious that the quantity of B decreases while the quantity of A increases. The line Mt' would instead represent barters of A for B.

If the price p_b is equal to the slope on the p_b axis of the tangent at M to the line of indifference that passes through that point, no barter of a finite quantity is possible with a constant ratio, that is with a constant price. If the price p_b is greater or lesser than the slope, the possible barters are represented by

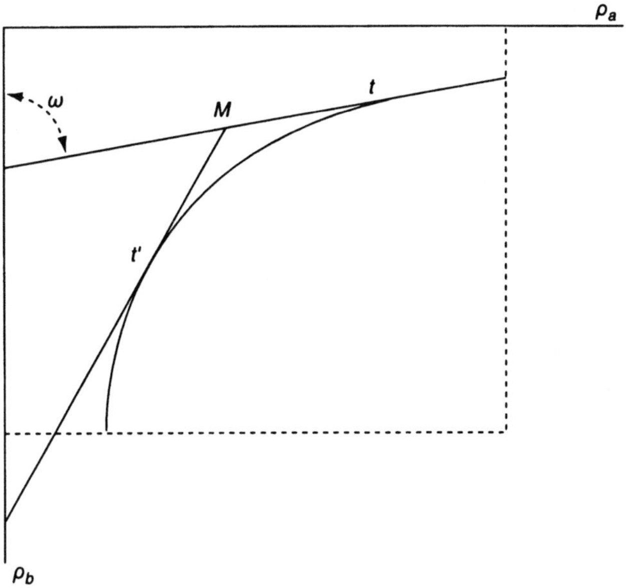

Figure 5.4

straight lines indicating barters of B for A or of A for B, according to the direction one follows on the lines.

If the two tangents that can be drawn from M to the ellipse are entirely included in the projection of the part of the surfaces of utility that we are considering, as would happen for point M that has the two tangents Mt, Mt', then both barters of B for A and barters of A for B are possible. And to the individual who has the quantities of goods represented by the coordinates of M, bartering some B for A, with a price given by the slope of Mt, or bartering some A for B with a price given by Mt' makes no difference.

It should be pointed out that since it is possible, for a very small section, to substitute straight lines for the curves representing any final degrees of utility, it follows that what we have just expounded can also be used, with the necessary modifications, in the study of the phenomenon when the final degrees of utility are represented by curves.

Let us go back to the case where those degrees are represented by straight lines, and look for the locus of the points of tangency t, that is the points where bartering ceases if successive exchanges are carried out at a constant price, and starting from an initial state represented by point M, whose coordinates are ρ'_a and ρ'_b. We shall have

$$p_b = \frac{\rho_a - \rho'_a}{\rho_b - \rho'_b};$$

and by replacing this value in the equation

$$a - a p_u = \frac{1}{p_h}(b - \beta p_h),$$

we shall obtain the equation for that locus, which we shall be able to express in the following form

$$\alpha\xi^2 + \beta\zeta^2 = \frac{1}{4}\alpha\left(\frac{a}{\alpha} - \rho'_u\right)^2 + \frac{1}{4}\beta\left(\frac{b}{\beta} - \rho'_h\right)^2,$$

where the coordinates ξ and ζ refer to rectangular axes that are parallel to the axes ρ_u and ρ_h, and whose origin has the coordinates

$$\frac{1}{2}\left(\frac{a}{\alpha} + \rho'_u\right), \quad \frac{1}{2}\left(\frac{b}{\beta} + \rho'_h\right),$$

which are therefore also the coordinates of the centre of the ellipse.

Let us see two more forms of the final degrees of utility. Let us suppose

$$\varphi_u = \frac{a}{\alpha + \rho_u}, \quad \varphi_h = \frac{b}{\beta + \rho_h}.$$

The final degrees of utility are represented by hyperbolae, and ρ_u and ρ_h can extend from zero to infinity (see Figure 5.5). For total utility we have

$$U + c = a\log(\alpha + \rho_u) + b\log(\beta + \rho_h),$$

$$c = a\log\alpha + b\log\beta.$$

Total utility can increase beyond all limits. The equation for the projections of the lines of indifference is

$$(\alpha + \rho_u)^a(\beta + \rho_h)^b = \mu;$$

and for the projections of the lines of preference is

$$\frac{1}{a}(\alpha + \rho_u)^2 - \frac{1}{b}(\beta + \rho_h)^2 = h.$$

These lines of preference are therefore hyperbolae, and μ and h are arbitrary constants.[3] The locus of the points of tangency t is a hyperbola

$$(\rho'_u - \xi)\frac{a}{\alpha + \xi} + (\rho'_h - \eta)\frac{b}{\beta + \eta} = 0$$

where ρ'_u and ρ'_h are the coordinates of point M; ξ and η are the coordinates of the point of tangency t, with reference to the axes $\rho_u\ \rho_h$.

Let us finally suppose

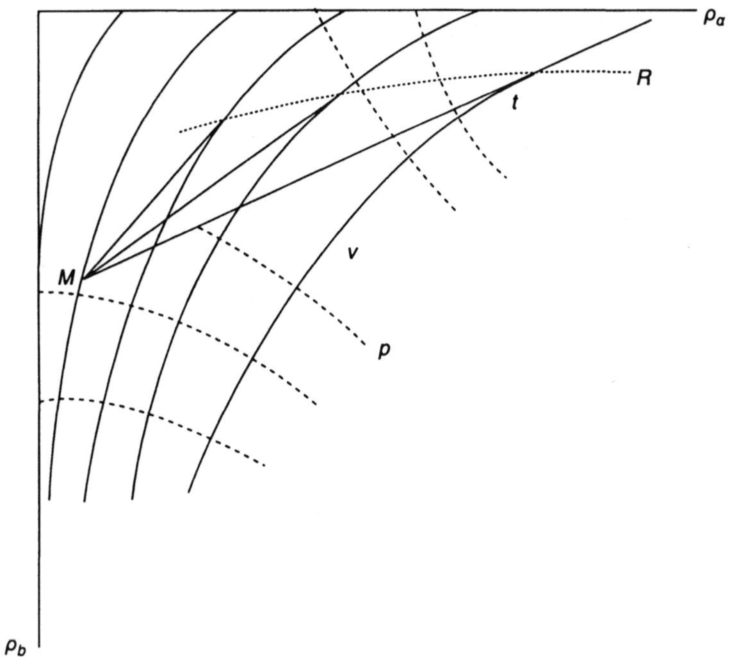

Figure 5.5

$$\varphi_a = \frac{a}{a + \rho_a}, \quad \varphi_b = b - \beta\rho_b.$$

The final degree of utility of *A* will be a hyperbola; the final degree of utility of *B* will be a straight line. ρ_a can extend from 0 to infinity; ρ_b from 0 to $\frac{b}{\beta}$ only. Total utility will be

$$U + a\log a = a\log(a + \rho_a) + b\rho_b - \frac{1}{2}\beta\rho_b^2.$$

The equation for the projections of the lines of indifference is

$$a\log(a + \rho_a) + b\rho_b - \frac{1}{2}\beta\rho_b^2 = \mu,$$

where μ is an arbitrary constant that varies from $a\log a$ to infinity. Only the strip of the plane ρ_a, ρ_b included between $\rho_b = 0$ and $\rho_b = \frac{b}{\beta}$ must be considered. The equation for the projections of the lines of preference will be

$$\rho_a^2 + 2a\rho_a + \frac{2b}{\beta}\log(b - \beta\rho_b) = h,$$

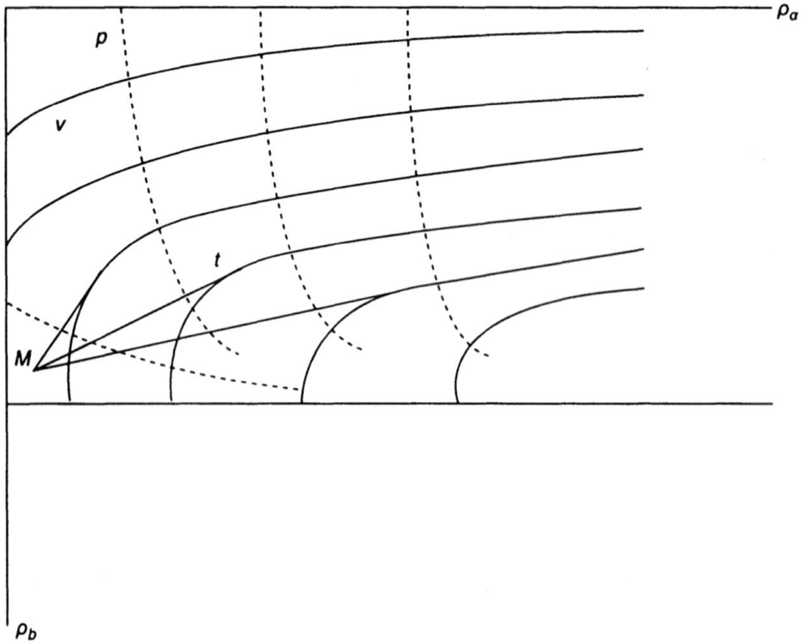

Figure 5.6

where h is an arbitrary constant (see Figure 5.6[4]).

Let us see an example of three economic goods. Let us suppose

$$\varphi_a = a - \alpha p_a, \quad \varphi_b = b - \beta p_b, \quad \varphi_c = c - \gamma p_c.$$

Total utility is

$$U = a p_a - \frac{\alpha}{2} p_a^2 + b p_b - \frac{\beta}{2} p_b^2 + c p_c - \frac{\gamma}{2} p_c^2.$$

The locus of indifference is given by this very equation, where U is made equal to an arbitrary constant. Therefore it is an ellipsoid.

The lines of preference have the following differential equations

$$\frac{dp_a}{a - \alpha p_a} = \frac{dp_b}{b - \beta p_b} = \frac{dp_c}{c - \gamma p_c};$$

by integrating them, one obtains

$$(a - \alpha p_a)^{\frac{1}{\alpha}} = h_1 (b - \beta p_b)^{\frac{1}{\beta}} = h_2 (c - \gamma p_c)^{\frac{1}{\gamma}},$$

where h_1 and h_2 are arbitrary constants.

If subsequent barters take place with constant prices, that is if

$$p_a - p'_a + p_b(p_b - p'_b) + p_c(p_c - p'_c) = 0,$$

the location where the barters cease will be the point of tangency of this plane with a surface of indifference.

Final degrees of utility corresponding to particular laws of supply and demand

We have already discussed this question, but we shall re-examine it now in the light of the more general principles that we have just expounded.

In our opinion the new Political Economy is facing no problem of greater consequence than this. It may have been good advice at the beginning of the study of the new doctrines not to increase their difficulty with these somewhat difficult investigations. But Jevons was already warning us about the benefits that a deeper knowledge of the final degrees of utility could yield, and if we wish science to progress it is not possible to do without it.

Finally, its opponents are partly right when they say that all that complex mathematical apparatus is quite superfluous, in order to provide somewhat more accurate demonstrations of already known truths. It would be so, if it did not have to lead us to higher and as yet unknown truths. We shall never reach these truths, if we content ourselves with knowing only that final degrees of utility generally decrease when the quantity of the commodity increases. It really is too little, and it behoves us to push forward our investigations, with the particular aim of paving the way for the actual possibility, in the future, of measuring those degrees of utility.

While at present we still do not know the numerical laws of supply and demand, we shall be able to find them when a greater abundance and an increased accuracy of the statistical data will allow us to find relationships between prices and consumed quantities. As we have already remarked, the only real phenomena we know are single sales, and it is from them that we must start off in order to find the properties and the measurements of the final degrees of utility.

Let us go back to consider two economic goods, and let us briefly dwell on the concrete case of Figure 5.3. The coordinates of point M represent, as we have seen, the quantities of goods owned before bartering. The ellipse R is the locus of the points of tangency t where bartering ceases. Formula (6) only applies on this ellipse. Therefore, if we did not know the law of the final degrees of utility, but only knew the law of supply and demand, we could only calculate the values of the final degrees of utility on that ellipse, but not outside it. We would be, to use an earlier comparison, like a man who is compelled to follow a path on a mountain without being able to step out of it on either side. He will certainly be able to experience that part of the mountain along the path, but will not know what there is either side of it.

The shape of that path depends on the way one makes the price vary. We have so far supposed that various tangents were drawn from point M to the contour lines. We can instead admit some other law; for instance, we can suppose that the tangents drawn to these curves are parallel. In this case the price will be constant. For Figure 5.3 the locus of the points of tangency will be a straight line.

If we wish to know the partial derivatives across the whole surface of utility, it is evident that we shall have to gradually change path so as to cover that entire surface, obviously for the part that is being considered. This will be achieved by moving point M, where the various tangents meet, or by changing the direction to which they were made parallel in the second case.

Let us give analytical form to these considerations.

If we are dealing with the tangents meeting at M, if the coordinates of that point are ρ'_u and ρ'_h, it will be

$$(\rho_u - \rho'_u) + p_h(\rho_h - \rho'_h) = 0, \quad \varphi_u = \frac{1}{p_h}\varphi_h; \qquad (\alpha)$$

ρ_u and ρ_h are the coordinates of point t, that is the owned quantities of goods when bartering ceases.

If ρ'_u and ρ'_h are constant, the first of the equations (α) establishes a relationship between ρ_u and ρ_h, which therefore cease to be independent variables, and so φ_u and φ_h lose the general form of the partial derivatives of U, and become the expressions into which those derivatives change when the above-mentioned relationship is established between ρ_u and ρ_h. Consequently, we cannot know the general form of those partial derivatives, if we do not find a way to turn ρ_u and ρ_h back into independent variables. And the way will be to make one, or both, of the coordinates ρ'_u and ρ'_h vary as a function of a parameter. Therefore it is necessary to know not just one of the laws of supply and demand, but all the laws that are obtained by making the quantity of at least one of the owned goods vary. If we know them, we shall have

$$p_h = f(\rho'_u, \rho'_h, \rho_h). \qquad (\beta)$$

Let us suppose that ρ'_u may vary, ρ_u and ρ_h are independent variables, and we have

$$\varphi_u = \frac{\partial U}{\partial \rho_u}, \quad \varphi_h = \frac{\partial U}{\partial \rho_h};$$

and the second of the (α) gives

$$\frac{\partial U}{\partial \rho_u} = \frac{1}{p_h}\frac{\partial U}{\partial \rho_h};$$

this is a partial derivatives equation, by integrating which we shall find U.

This method of reasoning is general and applies to any number of goods.

In order to free the dependent variable, let us introduce a new variable, which can be the quantity of money owned by the individual under consideration. We must therefore obtain the laws of supply and demand that apply when the individual owns various quantities of money; when we have these laws, equation (6) will give us the following partial derivatives equations:

$$\frac{\partial U}{\partial \rho_a} = \frac{1}{p_b}\frac{\partial U}{\partial \rho_b} = \frac{1}{p_c}\frac{\partial U}{\partial \rho_c} = \ldots; \qquad (51)$$

by integrating them we shall find total utility U.

The way the final degrees of utility depend on the laws of supply and demand is now very clear, and in our opinion the explanation we have just given must be preferred to those we gave in the August 1892 issue (see chapter 3, pp. 51–58). We may also try different ways to reach the truth on other occasions, and we shall let the reader decide which way he judges to be the best.

At first we decided to attempt to study this phenomenon without considering the most general forms of the final degrees of utility, in order to show that it was necessity, and not our desire to increase mathematical abstractions, that led us to the course we are now following.

Furthermore, the current topic relates to another of no little moment.

A serious dispute is taking place in the new science. On the one side, Prof. Walras is strenuously defending the necessity not to confuse utility curves with price curves, that is, the necessity to consider the final degree of utility of numeraire (or of currency) as variable. On the other side, many among the best authors, though not exactly denying Prof. Walras's principle, still maintain that they can disregard it in practice with impunity.

Not only has Prof. Walras demonstrated on many occasions how such behaviour may lead to serious mistakes, but it is also worth noticing how close he came to guessing that also in other matters that principle is essential to science. Let the matter we are going to discuss be proof of it; this is a matter he did not consider, and on which it is impossible to shed any light, unless one takes into account the variations of the final degrees of utility of the goods that are bartered.

To begin with, we see that we must not talk about *one* law of supply or demand, but of *various* laws, according to the quantity of goods owned before bartering. For a company, adding up the various demands, produces one single law, but this depends on social wealth and on the way this wealth is distributed, so that through another way we come to see how important it is to consider the relationship of these *averaged demands*, or of the *averaged final degrees*, with the single demands and the single *final degrees*.

But we could draw many other consequences from the formulae we have just noted.

Let us consider equation (6), where we shall revert to making all the variables ρ_a, ρ_b, ρ_c

... independent, by making the locus to which those equations refer walk over the whole surface of utility; that is by introducing a parameter t, which allows equation (50) to be satisfied independently from a relationship between the $p_a, p_b, p_c \dots$.
Let us assume

$$dt = dp_a + p_b dp_b + p_c dp_c + \dots;$$

according to how it will best suit us, we shall now be able to either suppose that $p_a, p_b \dots$ are independent, or make $t, p_b, p_c \dots$ independent; in this latter case p_a will depend on them. We shall need different symbols of differentiation, which we shall determine as in Table 5.1.

With these symbols, we shall have

$$dt = dp_a + p_b dp_b + p_c dp_c + \dots$$
$$0 = \delta p_a + p_b \delta p_b + p_c \delta p_c + \dots \quad (52)$$
$$\delta U = \frac{\partial U}{\partial p_a}\delta p_a + \frac{\partial U}{\partial p_b}\delta p_b + \dots.$$

Equation (52) may be not integrable, in which case there is no total utility that can be coupled with the laws of supply and demand that we have assumed. If equation (52) is integrable, we shall have

$$G(t) = f(p_a, p_b \dots)$$

where G is an arbitrary constant.

Since

$$\frac{\partial U}{\partial p_b} = p_b \frac{\partial U}{\partial p_a}, \quad \frac{\partial U}{\partial p_c} = p_c \frac{\partial U}{\partial p_a} \dots,$$

we have

$$\delta U = \frac{\partial U}{\partial p_a}(\delta p_a + p_b \delta p_b + \dots) = 0;$$

and therefore, if F is an arbitrary constant

$$U = F(t),$$

Table 5.1

Independent Variables	quantities that stay constant when differentiating	symbols of differentiation	
		partial	*total*
$p_a, p_b, p_c \dots$		∂	d
$p_b, p_c \dots$	t	∂	δ

so that, by including the arbitrary function G in the symbol F, we have

$$U = F(f(p_a, p_b, \ldots)),$$

and

$$\frac{\partial U}{\partial p_a} = \frac{\partial f}{\partial p_a} F', \quad \frac{\partial U}{\partial p_b} = \frac{\partial f}{\partial p_b} F' \ldots \tag{53}$$

if we have

$$p_b = \frac{\chi_b(p_b)}{\chi_a(p_a)}, \quad p_c = \frac{\chi_c(p_c)}{\chi_a(p_a)} \ldots,$$

the conditions for the integrability of equation (52) are satisfied, and we have

$$f = \int \chi_a dp_a + \int \chi_b dp_b + \ldots,$$

and

$$\frac{\partial U}{\partial p_a} = \chi_a F'(f), \quad \frac{\partial U}{\partial p_b} = \chi_b F'(f) \ldots$$

Thus in the first example we examined we had

$$p_b = \frac{b - \beta p_b}{a - \alpha p_a}$$

therefore

$$\frac{\partial U}{\partial p_a} = (a - \alpha p_a) F'(a p_a - \frac{\alpha}{2} p_a^2 + b p_b - \frac{\beta}{2} p_b^2)$$

$$\frac{\partial U}{\partial p_b} = (b - \beta p_b) F'(a p_a - \frac{\alpha}{2} p_a^2 + b p_b - \frac{\beta}{2} p_b^2).$$

Let us stop for a while in order to express in common parlance some of the propositions we have obtained by using mathematics.

The only phenomena Political Economy has to consider are the most general laws of supply and demand.

When considered in their most general form possible, these laws establish a certain relationship between the prices and the quantities of the various goods owned by the individual. In other words, if the quantity of money owned by an individual is known, and the prices of bread, wine, clothes, etc. are also known, the quantities of those goods he will purchase are determined.

When there are more than two economic goods, not all the laws of supply and demand can be coupled with the condition that total utility must exist.

For the reasons we have previously mentioned, we believe that when one considers the economic phenomena alone, one must assume that total utility exists. If we therefore suppose that the general conditions are satisfied, we shall be able to add that there are laws of supply and demand that cannot be coupled with final degrees of utility which for each good depend only on the quantity owned. On the other hand, these final degrees can only depend according to a certain law of the various quantities of goods.

There are other laws of supply and demand that can be coupled with the condition that the final degree of utility of each good depends only on the quantity of that good. But beside this the final degrees of utility can have infinite other forms that depend on all the quantities of the various goods according to a certain law.

So far, those relationships between the final degrees of utility and the laws of supply and demand had not been discovered, and we do not know how they could be demonstrated without resorting to mathematics.

We believe we should point out here yet again that in our opinion it is almost certain that in reality the final degree of utility of a good does not depend on the owned quantity of that good alone, but also on all the other quantities of goods. In order for this not to be true, it would be necessary to suppose that our enjoyments are independent from each other. They may well happen to be so to a certain extent, but to a certain extent they are certainly not. In order to enjoy some aesthetic pleasures most men want first to be well fed. Drinking without eating, or eating without drinking, may be not enjoyable. Finally, the various goods we use are partially complementary and must not be considered totally independent.

It could also be that this mutual dependence of enjoyments has only a negligible effect on the economic phenomenon, and that it is possible, at least approximately, to assume the final degree of utility of each economic good as equal to a function of the quantity of that good alone. But this cannot be granted a priori; it is necessary to refer to experience and find out whether it confirms or rejects this hypothesis. And until this can be done, it is not acceptable arbitrarily to restrict the possible form of those degrees of utility.

Even though infinite forms of final degrees of utility and of total utility may correspond to the same law that ties together prices and quantities, neither the indifference loci nor the lines of preference change in shape.

If we only have two economic goods equation (52) can always be integrated. Let μ be one of its integrability factors; we shall have

$$f(p_a, p_b) = \int (\mu dp_a + \mu p_b dp_b).$$

The projections of the lines of indifference will have the equations

$$f(p_a, p_b) = m;$$

where m is an arbitrary constant.

Total utility will be an arbitrary function of f. The final degrees of utility will be

$$\frac{\partial U}{\partial p_a} = \mu F(f), \quad \frac{\partial U}{\partial p_b} = \mu p_b F(f);$$

where F is an arbitrary function.

This case is not identical to the case we have already examined in the August 1892 issue, because then we were considering φ_a and φ_b as functions of any kind, and we were studying the phenomenon only at the point at which bartering ceases.

Now we have instead introduced the condition that φ_a and φ_b are the partial derivatives of a certain function, and we are studying the economic phenomenon on the whole surface of utility.

When there are three goods, in order for total utility to exist we must have

$$\frac{\partial p_b}{\partial p_c} = \frac{\partial p_c}{\partial p_b}.$$

In common parlance we shall say that in order for total utility to exist, it is necessary that the increase of a very small quantity of C makes the price of B vary by precisely the same amount by which the price of C varies for a very small increase of B equal to the increase of C we have already considered.

To express it in an even more tangible way, let the three goods be: money, bread and wine. As a very small quantity let us consider 100 grams. It is necessary that the increase in consumption of 100 grams of wine makes the price of bread vary by precisely the same amount the price of wine varies for an increase in consumption of 100 grams of bread.

Similar conditions exist when one considers more than three economic goods.

If good A was ideal money only, φ_a would no longer be known, and in fact one would have to determine that final degree of utility of the ideal money.

We must establish the laws according to which the prices vary in subsequent bartering. Let us suppose that the values of $dp_b, dp_c \ldots$ are positive, and that only the value of dp_a is negative and equal to $d\mu$. This means that with the quantity of money $d\mu$ one purchases the quantities $dp_b, dp_c \ldots$ and we have

$$d\mu = p_b dp_b + p_c dp_c + \ldots;$$

by integrating we shall obtain the value of μ that corresponds to the values of p_b, $p_c \ldots$ Let $\mu', p'_b, p'_c \ldots$ be the values of these quantities before the purchases and let us suppose that the way in which $p_b, p_c \ldots$ vary in the successive purchases depends only on

$$p_b, p_c \ldots;$$

we shall obtain

$$\mu - \mu' = \int_{\rho'_b}^{\rho_b} p_b d\rho_b + \int_{\rho'_c}^{\rho_c} p_c d\rho_c + \ldots .$$

If, for instance, the prices fell when the quantities increase, since it is

$$p_b = p'_b - 2h_b\rho_b, \quad p_c = p'_c - 2h_c\rho_c \ldots$$

we would obtain

$$\mu - \mu' = p'_b(\rho_b - \rho'_b) + p'_c(\rho_c - \rho'_c) + \ldots$$
$$-h_b(\rho_b^2 - \rho'^2_b) - h_c(\rho_c^2 - \rho'^2_c). \ldots$$

If, on the other hand, prices are constant, this formula, as we already know, is reduced to the first line.

In the August 1892 issue we have already given an example of how to determine this final degree of utility of ideal money. But in that case we were making two hypotheses, namely: first, that the degree of utility of a commodity depended only on the quantity of that commodity; second, that all subsequent bartering took place with the same price. This latter hypothesis, as we shall presently see, is not necessary in order to obtain the formulae written in that issue, but the former is so. It behoves us to consider the general case, since certainly that first hypothesis cannot be considered as absolutely true in reality.

Far from blaming those who first studied the new science for accepting those hypotheses, we believe on the contrary that they did the right thing, because the human mind must always proceed from the simple to the compound. Thus, in astronomy it all started by considering the sun and a single planet, overlooking the attractions of all the other planets, and only with the progress of science was it possible to take into account the perturbations of the elliptical orbits. It would indeed be a mistake, and a very serious one at that, to believe that the theories of pure economy can be exported straight away into the real world; as it would have been a mistake for an astronomer to say: 'Through mathematics I have demonstrated that planetary orbits must be elliptical, therefore I do not care about the observations that demonstrate that they are not so'. It is necessary, in Pure Economics, to avoid the danger of falling into sophisms of this kind. We are not at the crossroads of having either to accept all its theorems blindly, or to refuse to have faith in mathematics. The dilemma does not hold, because there is a third hypothesis, which is, namely, that the premises are not true, or only partly true.

With this one answers an objection that is often heard against the new theories. They say: 'Mathematics is not, after all, so safe a method of deduction, since we can see that there are economists who by using it come to opposite conclusions'. But what is so surprising in this, if those economists move from different premises? One could oppose the same objection to any kind of reasoning. So, since from different premises one can rightly draw different conclusions, shall we say that to reason rightly or wrongly makes no difference?

On our part, we accept the use of mathematics in Political Economy and deem it advantageous, but by no means can we agree with all the consequences that some scholars may like to draw from it, starting from premises that do not convince us. And in many cases it is to mathematics itself that we resort in order for the mistake to be revealed. This is the way we followed for the ratio of the utility of customs protection, that was said to have been demonstrated by Cournot, and for another similar one by Messrs Auspitz and Lieben.

When someone arises and states that the new Political Economy mathematically demonstrates that intervention by the 'State' in the economic matters of a country is beneficial, we answer that in such a proposition words are completely taken out of their natural meaning, and we ask to see the face of those beautiful equations that lead to so extraordinary, and to us very new, consequences. Someone with a good imagination can shape his ideal 'State', and picture its rulers as διοτρεφεις [Zeus's progeny], as good old Homer defined them; but if someone asks of experience what they actually are like, he sees them as old Hesiod already saw them, and knows that

> Τής δὲ Δίχης ῤόθος ἑλχομένης ᾗ χ' ἄνδρες ἄγωσι δωροφάγοι, σχολιῇς δὲ δίχηῇς χρίνωσι θέμιστας.[5]

And to those who do not like Greek we shall say in common parlance that there exist no mathematics capable of covering up the indecent behaviour of rulers who made use of the powers granted to them by the law on issuing banks, in order to extort money from them for their friends, for their supporters, for the bribing of voters, and even for merry-making; by asking more from those who were already at fault, and by exploiting their knowledge of that fault in order to avoid refusals.[I] And do not try to tell us that these are unusual occurrences. Now, in Argentina, in Greece, in Spain, in Russia, a few or many years ago, in France, at the time of the *assignats*,[II] in England, at the time of Pitt,[III] one can see the faults and shameful actions of those who, while appointed by the law to ensure that money is not counterfeited, counterfeit it themselves, as our friend and teacher G. de Molinari says. And therefore, those peoples who do not take away the power of evil doing from the hands of such a corrupt lot, do not act in a more sensible way than one who entrusted his herds to the wolves.

The reader should refrain from thinking that these words are off the subject, since it behoves us to reassure him that while we may sometimes lead him into the most abstract regions of mathematical reasoning, we never lose sight of the earth and as far as we are able we wish to build on solid ground.

Let us suppose, as we have previously done

$$\mu - \mu' = \int_{p'_b}^{p_b} p_b dp_b + \int_{p'_c}^{p} p_c dp_c + \ldots,$$

that is, by assuming

$$v_a = \mu - \mu', r_b = p_b - p'_b, r_c = p_c - p'_c \ldots$$

we shall have

$$v_a = \int_0^{r_b} p_b dr_b + \int_{0,}^{r_c} p_c dr_c + \ldots \quad (\alpha)$$

$$m = \frac{1}{p_b} \varphi_b = \frac{1}{p_c} \varphi_c = \ldots.$$

By following the same path we followed in our writings of the August 1892 issue, we shall have

$$\frac{\partial \varphi_b}{\partial r_b} \frac{\partial r_b}{\partial p_b} + \frac{\partial \varphi_b}{\partial r_c} \frac{\partial r_c}{\partial p_b} + \ldots = \frac{1}{p_b} \varphi_b + p_b \frac{\partial m}{\partial p_b}$$

$$\frac{\partial \varphi_c}{\partial r_b} \frac{\partial r_b}{\partial p_b} + \frac{\partial \varphi_c}{\partial r_c} \frac{\partial r_c}{\partial p_b} + \ldots = p_c \frac{\partial m}{\partial p_b}$$

$$\ldots.$$

From these equations we obtain the values of

$$\frac{\partial r_b}{\partial p_b}, \frac{\partial r_c}{\partial p_b} \ldots;$$

therefore, let the Jacobian determinant be

$$R = \begin{vmatrix} \frac{\partial \varphi_b}{\partial r_b} & \frac{\partial \varphi_b}{\partial r_c} & \ldots \\ \frac{\partial \varphi_c}{\partial r_b} & \frac{\partial \varphi_c}{\partial r_c} & \ldots \\ \frac{\partial \varphi_d}{\partial r_b} & \frac{\partial \varphi_d}{\partial r_c} & \ldots \\ \ldots & & \end{vmatrix}.$$

And since φ_b, φ_c . . . are the partial derivatives of U, one can see that this determinant is the *Hessian* of function U.

Let us call H''_i the minor determinant corresponding to the element of the ith row and n^{th} column. We shall have

$$R\frac{\partial r_b}{\partial p_b} = \frac{\varphi_b}{p_b}H^1{}_1 + \frac{\partial m}{\partial p_b}(p_bH^1{}_1 + p_cH^1{}_2 + \ldots)$$

$$R\frac{\partial r_c}{\partial p_b} = \frac{\varphi_b}{p_b}H^2{}_1 + \frac{\partial m}{\partial p_b}(p_bH^2{}_1 + p_cH^2{}_2 + \ldots)$$

$$\ldots\ldots$$

Let us differentiate equation (α), and let us observe that since the quantity of ideal money is supposed to remain constant, one must have

$$\frac{dv_a}{\partial p_b} = 0;$$

therefore

$$0 = r_b + p_b\frac{\partial r_b}{\partial p_b} + p_c\frac{\partial r_c}{\partial p_b} + \ldots\ldots$$

By substituting the values for the partial derivatives of r_b, r_c . . . that we have, and by supposing

$$N^{(\prime)} = p_bH^{(\prime)}{}_1 + p_cH^{(\prime)}{}_2 + \ldots,$$

$$N_{(\prime)} = p_bH^1{}_{(\prime)} + p_cH^2{}_{(\prime)} + \ldots,$$

$$M = p_bN_1 + p_cN_2 + \ldots = -\begin{vmatrix} 0 & p_b & p_c & \ldots \\ p_b & \frac{\partial\varphi_b}{\partial r_b} & \frac{\partial\varphi_b}{\partial r_c} & \ldots \\ p_c & \frac{\partial\varphi_c}{\partial r_b} & \frac{\partial\varphi_c}{\partial r_c} & \ldots \\ \ldots & & & \end{vmatrix}$$

we shall have

$$M\frac{\partial m}{\partial p_b} = -Rr_b - \frac{\varphi_b}{p_b}N_1. \tag{54}$$

Then we shall obtain

$$\frac{\partial r_b}{\partial p_b} = \frac{-r_b + \frac{\varphi_b}{p_b}\left(\frac{H^1{}_1M}{RN^1} - \frac{N_1}{R}\right)}{M}N^1. \tag{55}$$

When	φ_b	φ_c	φ_d	...
are only functions of	r_b	r_c	r_d	...
we have				

$$R = \varphi'_b \varphi'_c \varphi'_d \ldots, \quad H^1{}_1 = \varphi'_c \varphi'_d \ldots,$$

$$N_1 = N^1 = p_b H^1{}_1$$

$$M = p^2{}_b \varphi'_c \varphi'_d \ldots + p^2{}_c \varphi'_b \varphi'_d \ldots$$

By substituting these in formula (54), we have

$$\frac{\partial r_b}{\partial p_b} = \frac{-r_b p_b + \frac{\varphi_b}{p_b}\left(T - \frac{p_b^2}{\varphi'_b}\right)}{T\varphi'_b}; \tag{56}$$

where

$$T = \frac{p_b^2}{\varphi'_b} + \frac{p_c^2}{\varphi'_c} + \ldots.$$

We obtain therefore the same formula we found on page 49 of the August 1892 issue (see Chapter 3, p. 49), except that the indices *a, b, c* must be replaced by *b, c, d*. . . .

When the final degrees of utility depend on the quantities of all the commodities, one can see that it is necessary to add other terms to those of formula (56). On the other hand all these new terms will have as a factor one at least of the partial derivatives of the final degree of an economic good, calculated with respect to the quantities of the other goods. Therefore, if the variation in the final degree of utility of a commodity, when the quantities of the other commodities vary, is very small compared with the variation of that final degree when the quantity of the commodity to which it belongs varies, it will be possible to consider formula (56) to be approximately true.

We can see now that instead of using the few properties of the final degrees of utility that are known to us in order to demonstrate which laws supply and demand will have to follow, it will be better to go the opposite way and make use of the knowledge of those laws that we shall be able to acquire from experience in order to find out the properties of the final degrees of utility. The properties we know so far do not allow us to demonstrate the law of demand with absolute certainty; but from the fact, that can be directly observed, that demand decreases when price increases, we instead draw the consequence that as far as this phenomenon is concerned, each of the final degrees of utility can approximately be considered to be dependent only on the quantity of the commodity to which it belongs.

Let the final degrees of utility be once again a function of all the quantities of commodities, and let us solve the equations in order to find the quantities as a function of the final degrees, in other words, let us suppose

$$r_a = \psi_a(\varphi_a, \varphi_b \ldots)$$
$$r_b = \psi_b(\varphi_a, \varphi_b \ldots)$$
$$\ldots$$

by substituting the values

$$\varphi_b = p_b\varphi_a, \quad \varphi_c = p_c\varphi_a \ldots$$

it will be

$$r_a = \psi_a (\varphi_a, p_b, p_c \ldots)$$
$$r_b = \psi_b (\varphi_a, p_b, p_c \ldots)$$
$$\ldots .$$

If prices are constant, it will also be

$$0 = r_a + p_b r_b + p_c r_c + \ldots$$

and by supposing

$$X = r_a + p_c r_c + p_d r_d + \ldots = \psi_a + p_c\psi_c + p_d\psi_d + \ldots$$

we shall have

$$p_b r_b + X = 0. \tag{57}$$

By eliminating φ_a between this equation and the other equation

$$p_b\varphi_a = \varphi_b (r_b, \psi_c, \psi_d \ldots),$$

we shall obtain an equation between r_b and p_b that will give us the law of supply and demand. But it will be easier to study these laws by directly considering the two equations we have just written, without eliminating φ_a, and seeking instead which values of r_b and p_b correspond to the values that are subsequently fixed for φ_a.

Prof. Walras believes that in general, after increasing with price, supply must then decrease and probably end up being asymptotic to the price axis, and assume a shape similar to the shape of the curve here illustrated (see Figure 5.7[6]).

It is beneficial to examine what relationship there is between the shape of this curve and the curve of the final degrees of utility.

For the moment we shall limit our investigations to the case of formula (56). In order

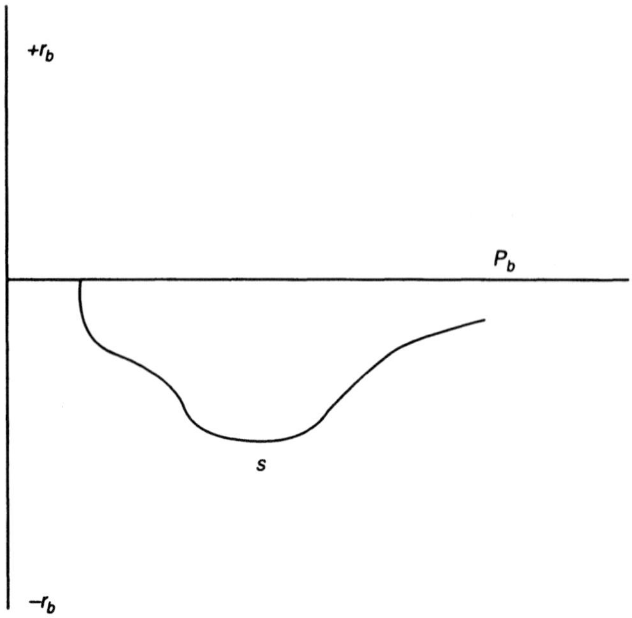

Figure 5.7

to have in that formula indices equal to those which have almost always been used in this study,

the letters	b,	c,	d,	e
will be replaced with the letters	b,	a,	c,	d,
and therefore the prices	p_b,	p_c,	p_d,	p_e
become	p_b,	1,	p_c,	p_d.

Formula (56) does not change, but we have

$$T = \frac{1}{\varphi'_a} + \frac{p_b^2}{\varphi'_b} + \frac{p_c^2}{\varphi'_c} + \ldots .$$

Let us suppose

$$r_a = a_0 + a_1\varphi_a + a_2\varphi_a^2 + \ldots$$

$$r_c = c_0 + c_1\varphi_c + c_2\varphi_c^2 + \ldots$$

$$r_d = d_0 + d_1\varphi_d + d_2\varphi_d^2 + \ldots$$

$$\ldots .$$

By replacing φ_c, φ_d with the values obtained from the usual equilibrium equations, we shall have

$$r_a = a_0 + a_1\varphi_a + a_2\varphi_a^2 + \ldots$$
$$r_c = c_0 + c_1p_c\varphi_a + c_2p_c^2\varphi_a^2 + \ldots \qquad (\alpha)$$
$$r_d = d_0 + d_1p_d\varphi_a + d_2p_d^2\varphi_a^2 + \ldots$$
$$\ldots\ldots$$

These equations express the quantities of commodity that are necessary, after transforming them into *A*, in order to have certain final degrees of utility. From the properties that are supposed to exist for those degrees, it follows that the quantities must decrease when the final degrees increase, that is the derivatives of those expressions are always negative, within the limits within which they are considered. Then, if one supposes that all the commodities *A, C, D* . . . are on demand, while *B* is on offer, which is always possible, by putting under the label *B* all the commodities on offer, one will see that there must be a value of φ_a that sends to zero all the quantities

$$r_a, r_c, r_d \ldots$$

together; in other words, that the expressions (α) made equal to zero have one common root. They must also have one only, even each of them considered separately, because the curves representing the final degrees of utility cannot intersect the coordinate axes, or any straight line parallel to them, at more than one point.

Let us suppose that subsequent bartering takes place with constant prices. The usual equation

$$r_a + p_br_b + p_cr_c + \ldots = 0$$

will give equation (57), which can be written

$$p_br_b + h_0 + h_1\varphi_a + h_2\varphi_a^2 + \ldots = 0 \qquad (\beta)$$

where we have supposed

$$h_0 = a_0 + c_0p_c + d_0p_d + \ldots$$
$$h_1 = a_1 + c_1p_c^2 + d_1p_d^2 \ldots$$
$$h_2 = a_2 + c_2p_c^3 + d_2p_d^3 \ldots.$$

We shall return later to the case where the derivative of r_b becomes zero because the denominator of the formulae (56) becomes infinite; let us now consider the case where the numerator is zero. We shall have

$$-r_bp_b + \varphi_a\left(T - \frac{p_b^2}{\varphi'_b}\right) = 0.$$

It is easy to see that

$$T - \frac{p_b^2}{\varphi'_b} = h_1 + 2h_2\varphi_a + 3h_3\varphi_a^2 + \ldots$$

wherefore

$$-r_b p_b + h_1\varphi_a + 2h_2\varphi_a^2 + 3h_3\varphi_a^3 + \ldots = 0.$$

By adding this equation to (β), in order to determine the values of φ_a of that correspond to the points where the supply curve has its tangents parallel to the price axis, we shall have

$$0 = h_0 + 2h_1\varphi_a + 3h_2\varphi_a + 3h_2\varphi_a^2 + \ldots. \qquad (\gamma)$$

It is evident that the second member of the equation is the derivative with respect to φ_a of

$$\varphi_a X = (r_a + p_c r_c + p_d r_d + \ldots) = h_0\varphi_a + h_1\varphi_a^2 + h_2\varphi_a^3 + \ldots.$$

Because of the properties of the final degrees of utility we have just recalled, and because of the form we have now given to the latter, the equation

$$\varphi_a X = 0,$$

within the limits we are considering, it cannot but have two roots, namely one

$$\varphi_a = 0,$$

and the other given by the value of φ_a that sends to zero the expressions (α), and therefore their sum X.

It is known that between two roots of an algebraic equation, the derivative of the equation has **at least** one root, corresponding to a maximum or to a minimum. Therefore the equation (γ) has **at least** one real root, and there exist a point like s on the supply curve (Figure 5.7).

The equation (β), or its equal (57)

$$p_b r_b + X = 0$$

gives us

$$r_b = -\frac{X\varphi_a}{\varphi_b}.$$

With the exception of the case where the value of φ_a that makes $X = 0$ were also to make $\varphi_b = 0$, one can see that for that value one will have

$$r_b = 0;$$

in other words, this is the point where the individual starts selling. The case we have excluded would be that of an individual owning such quantities of both the goods he could sell and the goods he could buy, as to be satisfied with them. And it is manifest that no bartering is done by this individual.

Since it is excluded that φ_a and φ_b are both equal to zero at the same time, the value

$$\varphi_a = 0$$

will make also $r_b = 0$, and since

$$p_b = \frac{\varphi_a}{\varphi_b},$$

one can see that this latter zero value of r_b corresponds to an infinite value of p_b, that is to an asymptote, which is the price axis.

We have therefore demonstrated, for the forms of the final degrees of utility we have considered, that the supply curve has a shape like the curve illustrated in Figure 5.7, and Prof. Walras's hypothesis is justified.

But we must add something to it.

Between two roots of an equation is included at least one root of the derivative, but there could be more, provided they are an odd number. Equation (γ) can therefore have 1, 3, 5 . . . roots, and the supply curve can show an undulating profile (see Figure 5.8).

In order to clarify the matter, we give a numerical example in the footnote.[7]

Furthermore, the root of (γ), or the least of its roots, if there are more than one, can be very large, so that point s can end up very distant and the curve can take on a shape similar to that in Figure 5.9; a shape with which we shall now have to deal by introducing hyperbolic terms in the equations of the curves of the final degrees of utility.

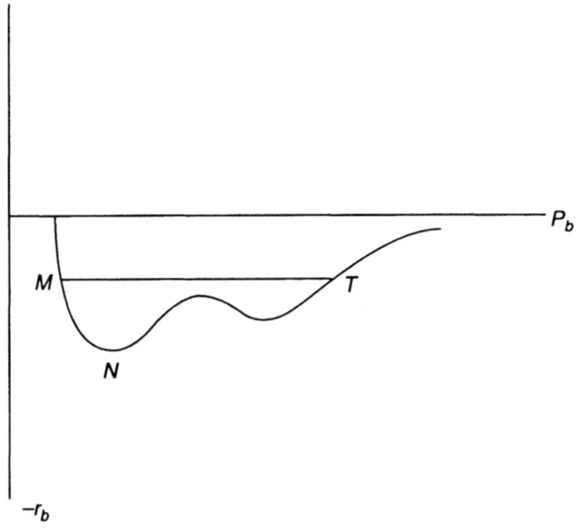

Figure 5.8

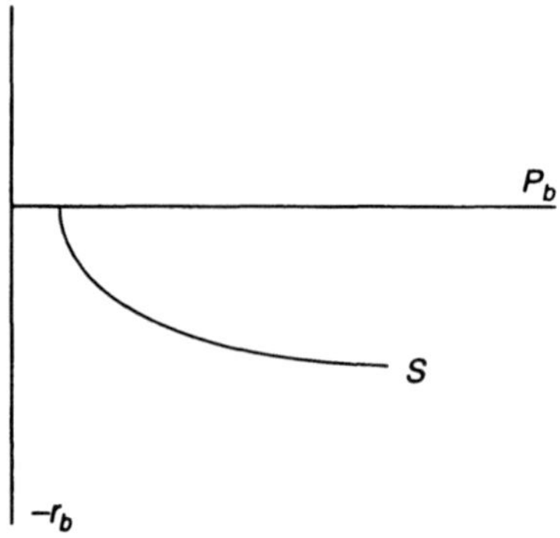

Figure 5.9

It should be noted that the owned quantity of commodity can be lesser than the maximum quantity. In this case the section *MNT* of the curve must be replaced in Figure 5.8 by the straight segment *MT*, whose distance from the price axis is equal to the owned quantity. Similar steps should be taken in the cases of the other figures.

Let us now suppose that in the expressions of $r_a, r_c, r_d \ldots$ there are negative powers of $\varphi_a, \varphi_c, \varphi_d \ldots$. In the formulae ($\alpha$) we shall therefore have to add some terms of the following kind

$$\frac{\alpha_1}{\varphi_a} + \frac{\alpha_2}{\varphi_a^2} + \ldots$$

$$\frac{\gamma_1}{p_c \varphi_a} + \frac{\gamma_2}{p_c^2 \varphi_a^2} + \ldots$$

$$\frac{\delta_1}{p_d \varphi_a} + \frac{\delta_2}{p_d^2 \varphi_a^2} + \ldots.$$

In formula (β) the following terms will have to be added

$$\frac{K_1}{\varphi_a} + \frac{K_2}{\varphi_a^2} + \ldots,$$

where

$$K_1 = \alpha_1 + \gamma_1 + \delta_1 + \ldots$$

$$K_2 = \alpha_2 + \frac{\gamma_2}{p_c} + \frac{\delta_2}{p_d} + \ldots$$

$$K_3 = \alpha_3 + \frac{\gamma_3}{p_c} + \frac{\delta_3}{p_d^2} + \ldots$$

. . . .

In formula (γ) this will produce the new terms

$$-\frac{K_2}{\varphi_u^2} - 2\frac{K_3}{\varphi_u^3} - 3\frac{K_4}{\varphi_u^4} - \dots.$$

The term in K_1 is missing, but since it also disappears when differentiating, we can still replace (γ) with the other equation

$$\frac{d}{\partial\varphi_u}(X\varphi_u) = 0.$$

Let us suppose that all $K_2, K_3 \dots$ are not zero.

The curve representing X has the r_u axis as an asymptote, and intersects the φ_u axis. Its derivative is always negative; it can also be zero, but it can never be positive.

The curve $X\varphi_u$ intersects the φ_u axis at the same point where the curve X intersects it; and it has as an asymptote the r_u axis. Its derivative

$$\frac{d}{d\varphi_u}(X\varphi_u) = X + \varphi_u\frac{dX}{d\varphi_u}$$

is negative when the curve intersects the axis and when it approaches its asymptote, and so in the limits within which it is considered, either does not change sign, or changes it an even number of times. Therefore equation (γ) has either no roots, or an even number of them. This is sufficient to exclude the shape in Figure 5.7.

The equation

$$X + p_b r_b = 0, \qquad (\varepsilon)$$

which can be written

$$X\varphi_u + r_b\varphi_b = 0,$$

shows that the value of φ_u that sends X to zero also gives the value zero for r_b, since we excluded that φ_u and φ_b could be zero at the same time.

For very small φ_u, X is very large, and so also is

$$X\varphi_u,$$

with the exception of the case, that will be later examined, where X were not to contain other negative powers of φ_u, with the exception of the first. The second equation shows that r_b will have to be very large. One could also suppose the case where instead of making r_b very large in order to satisfy that equation, one made it very small, and φ_b had terms with negative powers of r_b higher than the first. But this case must be excluded for the following considerations. Let θ be the highest negative power of r_b in φ_b; when r_b is very small, this term is by far greater than the others, and φ_b can be assumed equal to it, that is for very small values of r_b

$$\varphi_b = \beta_\theta r_b^{-\theta}$$

and our equation will become

$$X\varphi_u + \beta_\theta r_h^{-\theta+1} = 0.$$

Since the term $X\varphi_u$ is positive, in order to satisfy the equation it is necessary that the second term be negative. But the sign of

$$\beta_\theta r_h^{-\theta+1}$$

is opposite to the sign of

$$-\theta\beta_\theta r_h^{-\theta-1},$$

which therefore will have to be positive. This is the value of the derivative of φ_h when r_h is very small, and for the properties that the final degrees of utility are supposed to have, it should instead be negative. It is therefore necessary to exclude the hypothesis of r_h being very small, and we are left only with the hypothesis of a very large r_h with a very small φ_u.

Let n be the highest positive power of r_h in φ_h, and m the highest negative power of φ_u in X; for very small φ_u and very large r_h, the equation under consideration will change into another between these terms only, that is

$$K_m\varphi_u^{-m+1} + b_n r_h^{n+1} = 0.$$

Let us suppose that b_n is negative and n is odd. We shall obtain

$$r_h = -\left(-\frac{K_m}{b_n}\right)^{\frac{1}{n+1}} \varphi_u^{\frac{m-1}{n+1}}.$$

Likewise, equation (ε) becomes

$$K_m\varphi_u^{-m+1} + p_h r_h = 0;$$

and consequently, by replacing r_h with its value

$$p_h = K_m\left(-\frac{K_m}{b_n}\right)^{-\frac{1}{n+1}} \varphi_u^{-\frac{n(m-1)}{n+1}}.$$

The exponent of φ_u cannot be equal to zero unless m is equal to one; which has already been excluded. Otherwise it is always negative and so p_h is infinite with r_h for very small φ_u, that is the supply curve is always increasing.

Here is a numerical example. Let there be two commodities, and let us suppose

$$r_u = 40 - 2\varphi_u + \frac{40}{\varphi_u^2},$$

$$r_h = 60 - \varphi_h = 60 - p_h\varphi_u;$$

we shall have

$$p_b = \frac{30}{\varphi_u} + \sqrt{\left(\frac{30}{\varphi_u}\right)^2 + \frac{40}{\varphi_u} - 2 + \frac{40}{\varphi_u^{\,3}}}.$$

And it will be possible to draw Table 5.2.

Table 5.2

φ_u	=	20	15	10	5	2	1	0.1
r_u	=	0	10.18	20.4	31.6	46	78	439.8
p_b	=	3	4.187	6.32	12.51	30.748	61.27	661.1
$-r_b$	=	0	2.44	3.23	2.53	1.498	1.27	6.11

The two roots of the equation

$$\frac{d}{d\varphi_u}(\varphi_u X) = 0,$$

that is of

$$40 - 4\varphi_u - \frac{40}{\varphi_u^{\,2}} = 0,$$

are of one, about 10 and of the other, about 1.057. The former gives a maximum for r_b, the latter a minimum.

The supply curve has a shape like the one shown here (see Figure 5.10). Except that our drawing is not in the right proportion with the numbers of the table, because in that case in order to see the shape of the curve it would have been necessary to make it much larger.

It should be pointed out that if any αγεωμετρητος objected that infinite

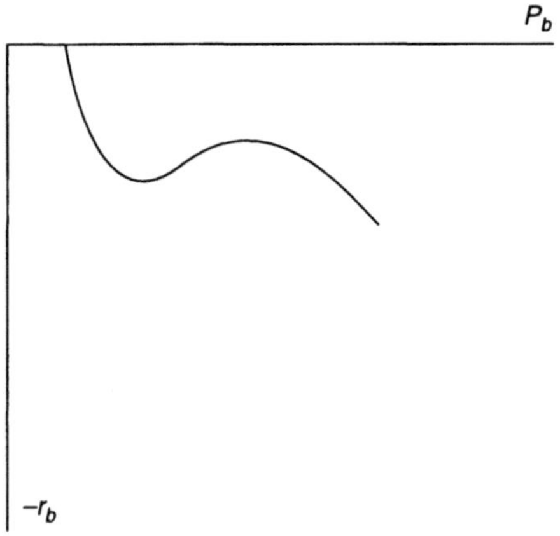

Figure 5.10

prices or quantities should not be taken into account, we would answer that this does not occur at all, and that it is possible to stop the hyperbolic curve at any point very close to the axis, without a change in the consequences we have now drawn. And on the other hand, this can also be inferred from the curves that intersect the axes, when one supposes that the point s of Figure 5.7 moves *very far* from the origin, both in the direction of the price axis, and in the direction of the quantity axis.

If in the expression of the final degrees of utility of r_a, r_c . . . the constant term and all the terms containing positive powers of φ_u go to zero, those curves no longer intersect the r_u axis, since they have it as an asymptote. Again, from equation (ε) one obtains

$$p_h r_h = -\frac{K_1}{\varphi_u} + \frac{K_2}{\varphi_u^2} - \ldots .$$

For very small values of φ_u what we have just said still applies.

For very large values of φ_u one has a very small r_u, and

$$p_h r_h = -\frac{K_1}{\varphi_u};$$

by replacing p_h with its value

$$\varphi_h r_h = -K_1.$$

Therefore the supply curve intersects the r_h axis, but it does not reach it except for an infinite value of φ_u. This might appear to be an oddity, and it is worth having a better look at what follows in an example.

Let us make

$$X = \frac{K_1}{\varphi_u} + \frac{K_2}{\varphi_u^2} + \ldots \quad , \quad \varphi_h = b - \beta r_h,$$

it will be

$$p_h r_h + \frac{K_1}{\varphi_u} + \frac{K_2}{\varphi_u^2} = 0;$$

and by eliminating φ_u with the equation

$$p_h \varphi_u = b - \beta r_h,$$

we shall have

$$r_h + \frac{K_1}{b - \beta r_h} + \frac{K_2}{(b - \beta r_h)^2} = 0.$$

Let us multiply the two members of this equation by

$$(b - \beta r_b)^2;$$

this introduces the extraneous solution

$$b - \beta r_b = 0,$$

which therefore we shall have to discard whenever it appears; we shall obtain

$$K_2 p_b = (b - \beta r_b)(\beta r_b^2 - b r_b - K_1).$$

If we discard the extraneous solution, we can see that in order to send p_b to zero, it is necessary that

$$\beta r_b^2 - b r_b - K_1 = 0.$$

This is the equation of a parabola of which we only need the arc corresponding to positive p_b and negative r_b (see Figure 5.11).

This parabola intersects the negative r_b axis at a point A given by

$$r_b = \frac{b}{2\beta} - \sqrt{\frac{b^2}{4\beta^2} + \frac{K_1}{\beta}},$$

but it does not reach this point except for

$$\varphi_a = \infty.$$

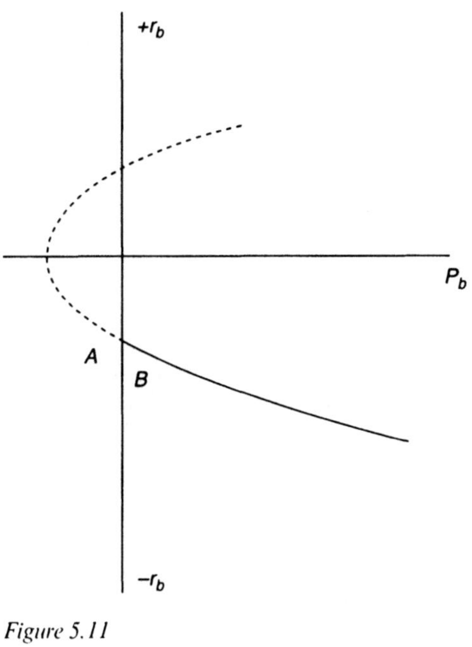

Figure 5.11

For a very large but finite value of φ_a, the supply curve does not start from A, but from a point B close to A.

Even though this form may appear odd, still the reader who would like to dwell upon it will see that it corresponds to real phenomena.

For instance, a worker does not sell a day nor a minute of his work under a certain price. At an even minimal price, greater than that limit, he starts selling his work, and the quantities he sells increase with the price. Then, with the price ever increasing, the sold quantity may well decrease, and the supply curve may have a shape similar to the curve in Figure 5.9.

When the economic goods are only two, or can be reduced to two by grouping some together, the properties of the supply and demand curves can be elegantly illustrated by using geometry.

Let us consider again Figures 5.3 and 5.4, and let us remember that price is given by the trigonometric tangent of ω.

The tangent at M to the line of indifference marks the price at which demand ceases to let supply start, or vice versa. If the angle ω increases, one can see in Figure 5.3 that the quantity of B that is sold increases up to the point of ellipsis R that is furthest from the x axis. Then that quantity decreases, and becomes zero when ω becomes 90 degrees; for that value the trigonometric tangent, that is the price, has infinite value. Therefore the supply curve is asymptotic to the price axis, since for that value of ω the sold quantity is zero.

But the lines of indifference could well be such that from M it is not possible to draw any tangent parallel to the p_a axis; furthermore, within the limits where the surface of utility is considered, the locus of the points of tangency might not have any point such that the ordinate of the curve decreases again after increasing. It is precisely these two cases that occur in Figure 5.5. The lines of indifference are curves that have as asymptotes parallel lines to the coordinate axes, and it is impossible to draw from M a tangent to such curves that is parallel to the p_a axis. Therefore, after increasing with the price, the supply will never be able to decrease. On the other hand, one can consider only a finite portion of the surface of utility, and these consequences will always be true.

It would not be difficult to extend this method to all the cases we have now examined through analysis, but we cannot expand this topic too much, since we have many more to study.

Something very important has been overlooked in what has been said so far, namely the variety of human needs. It is not right, while the prices are changing, to suppose that the number of bought commodities keeps constant. Nothing is more certain than the fact that the man with a greater amount to spend does not limit himself to purchase greater quantities of commodities, but also buys new types of commodities.

Therefore, the quantities we have named h_0, h_1, h_2 . . . K_1, K_2 . . . do not remain constant, but the variation of $p_b r_b$ adds or takes away terms from them.

The real curves of supplies must therefore have a shape not like only one of the curves we have found, but they must be composed of various parts of those curves. In other words, from a certain price to another there will be one section of those simple curves, then another will come among other prices, and so on.

If the sections are very small, the curve will be almost continuous. We shall come back to this topic to see in general what becomes of utility when one accepts this hypothesis of continuity. The study of these borderline cases is very useful, because it is much easier than the study of the cases they replace, and therefore it gives us the opportunity to have at least some idea of what otherwise we would not be able to know.

Vilfredo Pareto's notes

I

1 It was by considerations of this kind that we were moved to write the article[II] published in the January issue of this journal, on a theory by Cournot. We believe Cournot's conclusion to be untrue, although the reasoning that leads to it appears to be rigorous. *Latet anguis in erba* [the snake hides in the grass]. From where does the error originate? To this question we have attempted to find an answer.

2 *Principles of Economics*, p. 526. A number of mistakes, into which economists have fallen due to their neglecting to verify their theories with the facts provided by statistics, are shown by Cliffe Leslie, *Essays in political and moral philosophy*, N. XXV, p. 375, 1st edition.[VII]

3 Nothing on this topic could we add to what Mill stated so brilliantly in his *Logica*,[VIII] book VI, ch. VII, on the application of the direct experimental method to the social sciences. We also agree with his statement, book VI, ch. IX, on the 'concrete deductive' method being the only one that should be used in those sciences. In our opinion, Mill's only fault seems to be that he did not give due credit to the use of mathematics,[IX] nor can we accept what he says, elsewhere in the *Logica*, on the use of the theory of probability.[X] With all the respect due to an intellect of such sharpness and power, we take the liberty to observe that the true nature of that theory seems to have escaped him.

4 We point out here, once and for all, that, in making some remarks on the writings by the masters of the science of economics, we do not believe that we are failing to show them the respect which they deserve, nor that we are detracting from the value of their studies.

No human work is perfect and complete. *Quandoque bonus dormitat Homerus* [sometimes (even) the good Homer dozes off], and those who take notice of that sleep are perhaps incapable of writing even one single line that could be on a par with those of the divine poems that go under Homer's name. Consequently, we do not see ourselves as guilty of arrogance in discussing freely, when we seem to detect some fault in a work we deem worthy of admiration.

Since Political Economy is showing signs of becoming a positive science, it is fitting for it to follow the ways of such sciences. No mathematician has ever thought of being disrespectful to Euler,[XI] by observing that the reasoning that tries to determine, through the theory of probability, the sum of the indefinite series 1 – 1 + 1 – 1 + 1 . . . make no sense. Abel[XII] – who left such a profound mark on the science of mathematics that it will never be erased by time, as long as time shall be – uses divergent series; which, as any mathematics student of our times knows, is against the rules. Many of the greatest mathematicians gave imperfect demonstrations of true theorems. It is one's right, it is one's duty to point this out and rectify those demonstrations. And one could also add that those masters contributed more to the progress of mathematics by seeking new truths, than if they had wasted their time trying to perfect the demonstrations of the earlier truths which they had discovered.

5 *De l'échange de plusieurs marchandises entre elles* par Prof. Léon Walras, *Mémoires de la societé des ingénieurs civils*, Janvier 1891 [offprint, p. 8].

6 *Éléments d'Économie politique pure* [Lausanne: François Rouge; Paris: Guillaumin et Cie; Lausanne: Corbaz et Cie; Leipzig: Duncker & Humblot], 1889, p. 21.

7 'On the application of mathematics to Political Economy', reprinted from the *Journal of the Royal Statistical Society*, 1890, p. 18.

8 *Cours de M. Hermite*, Paris, A. Hermann [p. 115].

9 The excellent book by Messrs Auspitz and Lieben on the theory of prices[XXVIII] shows how the theories of mathematical economics can be used in a practical way in the study of prices.

10 'Di un errore del Cournot nel trattare l'economia politica colla matematica' – January issue of this journal.[XXXI] Only after publishing that article did we remember the article that in 1883 Prof. J. Bertrand[XXXII] had published on this topic in the *Bulletin des sciences mathématiques*, and it was with great pleasure that we saw that on some points we were in agreement with that illustrious mathematician.

11 In nearly all mechanics and astronomy treatises, the results of Reich's experiences are quoted as experimental evidence of the rotation of the earth. But Prof. Gilbert has shown (*Bulletin des sciences mathématiques*, 1882)[XXXVIII] that it is only *apparently* that those experiences agree with the theory. Indeed, in calculating the average, Reich arbitrarily discarded some experiences. Furthermore, the various experiences show very substantial differences from the average.

12 The symbol e is here the base of Neperian logarithms. Anyhow everything would be the same if one considered any other number greater than one.

13 Cf. what Arago says in his biography of Kepler:[XLI] 'L'important est de ne regarder toute idée théorique comme parfaitement établie qu'après qu'elle a été **sanctionnée par l'observation** et le calcul. Kepler s'est montré autant que possible fidèle à cette règle; il n'a jamais hésité à abandonner ses spéculations les plus chères, lorsque l'expérience venait à les ébranler.' [It is important to consider any theoretical idea as perfectly established only once it has been confirmed through observation and calculation. Kepler has demonstrated the greatest possible fidelity to this rule; he never hesitated to abandon hypotheses most dear to him, once they were invalidated by experience.]

See also all of the excellent book by **Herschel**, entitled *Discorso sullo studio della filosofia naturale*.[XLII] Herschel states (part II, ch. VI, § 188): 'Mathematical analysis undoubtedly provides great means either for representing the quantities obtained from experience in every circumstance, or later for determining, through comparison of the results with the facts, what those quantities should be in order to explain the observed phenomena, but no matter from what point of view one looks at this question, one must always go back to the experience every time there is anything to explain. **And this should be done even when the fundamental principles are deemed sufficiently true without direct experience.**'

But one only has to open any modern scientific book, to find similar ideas, and to add further quotations would be quite pedantic.

14 *Logica*, book VI, ch. VII.

15 Mill, loc. cit., book VI, ch. VIII.

16 *I principii di Economia pura* by Prof. Pantaleoni ([Barbera], Florence 1889) is worthy of notice for the lucidity with which it expounds these theories. Our reading of this book has prompted many of the considerations we are putting forward in this article, and has greatly clarified for us some ideas that other books had

left obscure. And we also have to thank that same friend of ours for the many suggestions that were very helpful to us in writing this work.

17 *Mathematical Psychics*, London, C. Kegan Paul & Co., 1881, p. 15.

18 Walras, *De l'échange de plusieurs marchandises entre elles*, Mémoires de la Societé des Ingénieurs civils (Paris, janvier, 1891).

19 The form $a+x$, y is only reported to keep it in harmony with the other notations. To be precise, Edgeworth, loc. cit., p. 34, says that 'x represents the sacrifice objectively measured, which can be the manual work that has been carried out, or commodities, or capitals that have been saved for some time, and y represents the objective reward for the individual in question.'

20 For those who are not very familiar with mathematical symbols, it will perhaps be better to recall that $\frac{\partial P}{\partial x}$ is the partial derivative of P, calculated assuming constant y. The total differential of P when the independent variables x and y vary, will be indicated with dP. As usual, $\frac{dP}{dx}$ will be the derivative of P, where y is considered a function of x. Similar notations apply with y.

21 *Principles*, 1891, p. 391. See the articles published by Prof. Edgeworth[XLV] and by Mr Berry[XLVI] in this journal, February, June and October 1891.

II

1 The French have both the world *monnaie* and the world *numeraire*. It is possible to take advantage of this and use the first term to indicate an actual form of money, such as that made out of precious metals, and keep the second term to indicate a form of money created for the sake of easier calculations. But since in Italian we only have the world *moneta*, here this word is used to indicate a common measure for prices, and not otherwise.

2 Since this work might end up in the hands of people who are not very familiar with mathematics, we apologise to those readers who know this science quite well and ask them to be patient, if we add here some notes which they might find redundant. Note, here, that

$$\frac{\partial P}{\partial r_a}$$

indicates the derivative of P calculated in relation to r_a, assuming that r_b, r_c . . . remain constant. It is therefore the ratio between the infinitesimal increment of P and the increment of r_a, assuming that the other quantities do not vary.

3 As dr_a and dr_b have opposite signs, p_b is positive, as indeed it should be.

4 Pantaleoni, *Principii di economia pura*, Barbera, Firenze, p. 59.

5 Pantaleoni, loc. cit., p. 191.

6 Wicksteed, *Alphabet of Economic Science*, London, Macmillan, 1888, p. 125. And before him, Jevons, loc. cit., p. 242: 'The theory represents in this way the fact that a person spreads out his expenditure in such a way as to equalise the utility of the final increments in each branch of expenditure'.

7 Before reading this paragraph, the reader who is not familiar with *Mathematical Psychics* by Prof. Edgeworth might want to see what we have to say on this topic further on.

8 In the following functions the *parameters* are u_b, u_c. . . .

9 The expression for dq_a we have given above is the total differential, i.e. the total variation undergone by q_a when r_b, r_c . . . increase by dr_b, dr_c. . . . What we are now

writing is the expression that represents a quantity having that total differential. Integral calculus teaches precisely how to extract the former quantity from the latter.

10 The quantities u_b, u_c . . . that have to be eliminated are $n - 1$; n equations are therefore needed. And this is precisely their number, $n - 1$ equations (3), plus one equation that gives the value of q_a.

11 In the March issue of this journal.[VI]

12 Cairnes, *Alcuni principi fondamentali di economia politica*, Italian translation (Florence, Barbera, [1877]), p. 439.

13 Cairnes, loc. cit., p. 437.

14 The more sciences expand, the more it becomes necessary to write specifically targeted treatises on them. For instance, Mr Boussinesq has now published a treatise on Infinitesimal Analysis for the benefit of those who study mechanics.[IX]

15 A small volume, such as *Principii di Economia Pura* by Pantaleoni, would suffice to give all the mathematical information an economist may need. And another, even smaller volume would do for mechanics. But at the moment they would have no readers, and it is therefore obvious that no publisher wishes to publish books that would remain unsold in their storehouses, for the sole benefit of moths and mice.

16 Bain, *L'Esprit et le corps*, Bibliothèque scientifique internationale, p. 239 ff.

17 Prof. Walras has first introduced this idea in science, with regard to the barter of commodities. *Élements d'Economie Pure*, p. 149.

III

1

As previously remarked, with the expressions	φ_a	φ_b	φ_c
we indicate, for the sake of brevity, the quantities	$\varphi_a(r_a)$	$\varphi_b(r_b)$	$\varphi_c(r_c)$
Their derivatives, calculated with respect to	r_a	r_b	r_c
are indicated with	φ'_a	φ'_b	φ'_c
and are identical to the partial derivatives	$\dfrac{\partial\varphi_a}{\partial r_a}$	$\dfrac{\partial\varphi_b}{\partial r_b}$	$\dfrac{\partial\varphi_c}{\partial r_c}$.

2 It should be kept in mind that p_a, p_b . . . are the independent variables. The expressions dr_a, dm . . . are total differentials, that is the variations of r_a, m . . . when the independent variables are increased by dp_a, dp_b. . . .

3 *Eléments*, p. 270.

4 By degree of utility of work we intend here the pleasure that the individual would derive from not working, that is the inconvenience, taken negatively, that he experiences when he works.

5 This restriction is imposed here to avoid being drawn now into the question of the averages of the final degrees of utility, which will be examined separately.

6 *Annales de l'Observatoire* I, p. 135.[VIII]

7 Someone who is not very familiar with mathematics may perhaps remark that the final degrees of utility are determined here without considering saving. In fact, the latter is indeed being taken into account, and it is necessary for r_a and r_b to be independent variables. And if they were not, we would not be able to equate the coefficients of the various powers of r_a and r_b *separately*. We would therefore not have any way to determine them, as we have instead done by considering r_a and r_b as independent variables.

8 Jevons, Italian translation in the *Biblioteca dell'economista*, p. 246.[IX]

9 loc. cit., p. 242.

10 *Mathematical Psychics*, pp. 83–93.

11 Laplace, [*Traité de*] *Mécanique Celeste* [Paris, Bachelier], vol. 5, pp. 301–302, édition 1825. '(Newton) observe encore que l'action de Jupiter sur Saturne dans la

conjonction de ces planètes, étant à l'action du Soleil Saturne dans le rapport de l'unité à 211, elle ne doit point être négligée. "De là vient, dit-il, que l'orbe de Saturne est dérangée si sensiblement dans chaque conjonction avec Jupiter, que les astronomes s'en aperçoivent"; cependant la théorie analytique des mouvements de ces deux planètes, qui représente exactement toutes les observations, nous montre que le dérangement de Saturne dans sa conjonction avec Jupiter, est presque insensible. . . . Cette remarque, déjà faite par Euler, fait voir qu'il ne faut adopter qu'avec une extrême réserve les aperçus les plus vraisemblables, tant qu'ils ne sont pas vérifiés par des preuves décisives.' [Moreover, Newton observes that the influence of Jupiter on Saturn in the conjunction of these planets, with Saturn being influenced by the Sun in this relationship by between unity and 211, must not be neglected. 'From this', he says, 'one deduces that the orbit of Saturn is much disturbed in every conjunction with Jupiter and that astronomers will notice it'. However, analytical theory of the movement of these two planets, which exactly represent all observations, indicate to us that the disturbance of Saturn in its conjunction with Jupiter is nearly imperceptible. . . . This observation, already made by Euler, shows that, until verified by decisive evidence, even the most plausible of theoretical indications are received with extreme precaution.]

Wurtz, [Charles Adolphe],[X] *La théorie atomique* [Paris, G. Bailliere et Cie], 1879, p. 16. 'Proust[XI] admettait que 100 p. de cuivre se combinent avec 17 1/2 à 18 p. d'oxygène pour former le premier oxyde ou semi-oxyde de cuivre, et avec 25 p. d'oxygène pour former le second oxyde, c'est-à-dire l'oxyde noir. Les chiffres exacts sont 12, 6 et 25, 2. **Si l'analyse des deux oxydes eût été plus correcte,** ***Proust aurait pu reconnaître la loi des proportions multiples***.' [Proust admitted that 100 particles of copper are combined with 17.5–18 particles of oxygen to form the first oxide or semi-oxide of copper, and with 25 particles of oxygen to form the second oxide, that is, black oxide. The exact values are 12.6 and 25.2. If the analysis of the two oxides had been more accurate, Proust could have discovered the law of multiple proportions.]

12 The history of all sciences clearly shows that the only study that benefits them is the study that has no other goal but looking for the truth. Among the numerous examples, we shall relate one of the least known.

Mr P. Tannery (*Bulletin des sciences mathématiques*, 1885, pp. 104–120),[XII] remarks that the most important problem for the history of ancient mathematics 'est de préciser les circonstances et de déterminer les causes de la décadence passée, en vue de connaître les précautions à prendre pour éviter une décadence future' [to specify the circumstances and determine the causes of decline in the past is to know the precautions to be taken in order to avoid a decline in the future]. And he fears that limiting one's purpose to the achievement of immediate benefits was the cause for the decadence of the study of science. 'Supposons maintenant que l'histoire démontre que, pour la Science, l'arrêt dans la marche en avant équivaut à un recul, qu'on ne peut vouloir se borner aux parties nécessaires pour les applications, sans arriver peu à peu à négliger de plus en plus la théorie et à n'en conserver finalement que des débris tout à fait insuffisants, que deviendrait dès lors la garantie de l'utilité?' [We now assume that history demonstrates that, for Science, the arrest of progress is equivalent to a regress; that one cannot possibly want to limit the parts necessary for the applications of science without managing, little by little, to neglect theory and to finally conserve only fragments of all its insufficiencies: what would the guarantee of usefulness then become?]

13 It is exactly with regard to this theory that Wurtz (*La Théorie atomique*, p. 73) states: 'Lorsque une idée théorique est juste, les exceptions qu'on constate d'abord s'evanouissent une à une, soit à la suite de nouvelles observations plus exactes que les anciennes, soit par une interpretation plus correcte des faits. Et il arrive quelquefois que ces exceptions donnent lieu à des développements intéressants de

la théorie et à une généralisation plus large.' [When a theoretical idea is right, the exceptions one immediately observes disappear one by one, both as a consequence of newer and more precise observations than the old ones, and because of a more correct interpretation of the facts. And sometimes it happens that these exceptions give rise to interesting developments of the theory and to wider generalization.]

14 The reader should be aware that we would never dare to compare such a perfect a science like Astronomy with such an imperfect science like Political Economy; but if those words could excuse Virgil[XVIII] for comparing bees and Cyclops, because of whom 'gemit impositis incudinibus Ætna' [Etna moans with set anvils)], they will also excuse our comparison, where after all the disproportion is smaller; for there is only one experimental method, even though its effects can vary very much.

15 Italy is one of the countries where the most advanced theories of the science of economy are studied the most. And even if we shall not mention such works as those by Loria[XXIII] and Pantaleoni, which are by now classic and well-known masterpieces, allow us to recall as praiseworthy the booklet, *La dottrina matematica di economia politica di Walras esposta dai prof. Errera Alberto, Zanon, Zambelli, Del Pozzo*, which first gave the Italians an account of the new theories.

16 *La statistique et ses ennemis*,[XXV] 1885, p. 7. 'N'est-ce pas une faiblesse assez ordinaire aux statisticiens les plus officiels que de chiffrer en francs et en centimes, ou en pounds, shillings et pence, des évaluations pour lesquelles le million serait encore une unité trop faible?' [Is the desire to express in francs and in cents, or in pounds, shillings and pence, valuations for which millions would still be too small a unit of measure, not a common enough weakness of official statistics?]

17 This particular case can be dealt with without having to use calculus of variations, but we are showing it here as an example of a more general class of problems, and therefore we are also using general methods.

18 *Mathematical Psychics*, pp. 34–35. 'No doubt these latter conditions are subjects to many exceptions, especially in regard to abstinence from capital, and in case of purchase not for consumption, but with a view to re-sale'.

19 *Iliad* VI, 488. No man, I say, exists that has escaped his fate.

IV

1 *Bulletin des sciences mathématiques*, 1883, I, pp. 302–303.

2 *Éléments*, p. 99. We must point out that we are quoting from the second edition (1889), whilst Prof. Bertrand was using the first. But on the definition of *rareté* there is no difference whatsoever between the two editions.

3 *Principles*, I, p. 153.

4 *Bulletin* [*des sciences mathématiques*, 1883,] I, p. 303.

5 Laplace, *Théorie Analytique des probabilités*, 1820, p. XV.

6 Loc. cit., p. 439–440.

7 *Recherches sur la probabilité des jugements*,[III] 1837, pp. 73–75.

8 *Calcul des probabilités*,[IV] pp. 65–67.

9 *Calcul des probabilités*, 1889, p. 66.

10 Marshall, *Principles*, I, p. 753.

11 We inform the reader that in this paragraph and in the next we are compelled to add purely economic considerations to the mathematical sections.

12 *Principles*, I, p. 754.

13 It is perhaps unnecessary to warn the reader that *utility* in the economic sense is not the same as utility in the ordinary sense.
From an economical point of view liquors have a high degree of utility for the drunkard, but from a moral and physiological point of view, far from being useful,

they are exceedingly harmful to him. Economic *utility* is only the property that some things have of satisfying man's needs. And it is quite surprising that there are people who believe that it is not possible to have an *economic* measure of this utility. Such measure has nothing to do with the psychological measure; it simply is an *index* used to assign to a thing its *economic* place, and in relation to the demand by a certain individual, or the supply by another.

14 'La Moneta', *Archivio di Statistica*, [1883/III–IV], pp. 27–28.

15 We do not believe this *real value* exists outside *utility* (in an economic sense).

16 Since we happened to meet a distinguished and authoritative economist who thought he could refute this theory by refuting, in its stead, an application of it by Prof. Walras, we believe we should openly state that even though we deem Prof. Walras' theory to be true and worthy of great admiration, we cannot however accept his applications of it. These are two essentially different matters.

The goal Prof. Walras sets himself is artificially to render *social wealth* valued in monetary terms almost constant, or as invariable as possible (except for its periodical variations), and as a means to this end he calls for the intervention of the State. Any method can be used to solve this problem posed in this way. The new theories are not necessary; one can use the old ones, or any others.

With regard to the method, the solution given by Prof. Walras seems to us considerably better than the alternative solutions one could now find; in fact, we cannot see in what other way such a difficult question could be answered. But this is not a good enough reason for us to accept that solution, because neither do we want the same goal, nor do we agree on the means that are to be used.

We do not want the same goal, because no one has taken the trouble to demonstrate that the little good that could be had by *artificially* reducing the non-periodical variations of *social wealth* would not be accompanied by much worse evils caused by such a perturbation of the laws of nature. We shall happily change our mind once this fear is shown to be unfounded. In the meantime, we shall stick to Spencer's[VII] remarks, which demonstrate that very often the measures aimed at saving society from one evil are the cause of worse troubles.

We do not agree on the means, because history shows that when governments have interfered with money, it was usually in order to falsify it. First among them, are those that today have the reputation of dealing with this matter in the most honest way. Suffice it to recall, on this subject, the use and the abuse of paper money by the English government at the beginning of this century.

It has become usual, nowadays, to excuse everything and everyone, and currency falsifiers have partaken in this indulgence, which is so broad as to embrace men of the ilk of Nero[VIII] and Tiberius.[IX] We are not arguing about this. Let us even admit, if one wishes, that nothing short of an honest motive inspired the actions of Philip the Fair[X] and of his worthy imitators, down to the government of Argentina and other well-known governments. But in our opinion it would be better for the common good if the honest and good people who are about to follow that course applied their skills to any other endeavour but the alteration of money. And there is nothing we could add, on this topic, to what Leroy-Beaulieu[XI] and Molinari rightly state. See what the latter writes on page 433 of *Notions fondamentales d'Economie politique* [Librairie Guillaumin et Cie], Paris, 1891.

17 Italian translation,[XII] p.79–80.

18 The careful reader of that illustrious mathematician's book on the calculus of probability will soon realize that the disagreement between Bertrand and Laplace is nothing but the centuries-old disagreement on the admission of *determinism*.

In the eyes of Laplace, Poisson, Quetelet, etc., everything in nature is determined. Chance therefore does not exist as such, and this word simply indicates our ignorance of certain causes. Therefore there are no absolute probabilities, but only probability with regard to one or more men. To the all-knowing, probability does not exist, all is certain. To the absolutely ignorant, if we can suppose that such a being may exist, everything has the probability of ½.

In the eyes of Prof. Bertrand, on the contrary, *chance* really exists. He does not say it explicitly, but lets it be understood at every moment: 'le hasard conduit tout sans surveillance ni délibération aucune, et précisément parce qu'il n'est aveugle il remplit le lit de tous les fleuves, arrose toutes les campagnes, et donne à chaque brin d'herbe sa ration nécessaire de gouttes d'eau' [chance runs everything without any surveillance or deliberation, and for the very reason that it is not blind, it fills the beds of all rivers, it waters all the fields, and gives every blade of grass its necessary ration of water droplets] (p. L).

This argument cannot be decided with mathematics; it pertains to philosophy.

19 In the calculus of probability, *cause* simply means an event whose occurrence gives a certain probability to another event.

20 The *social wealth* Prof. Walras would like to keep almost constant would be expressed by

$$m\sqrt{p_b p_c p_d \ldots}$$

or by another average, or, better still, in his opinion, by

$$r_b p_b + r_c p_c + \ldots$$

This he admits would perturb the conditions of the individuals. The consumers 'devraient consommer plus des marchandises qui auraient baissés et moins des marchandises qui auraient haussés de prix' [should consume more merchandises whose prices have fallen, and fewer merchandises whose prices have risen].
and furthermore: 'ce que certains producteurs perdraient par la baisse de prix de leurs produits, d'autres producteurs le gagneraient exactement par la hausse prix des leurs' [what certain producers would lose because of the fall in the price of their products is exactly what other producers would gain because of the rise in the price of theirs] (pp. 469–470).

It is precisely these changes that we see as dangerous; especially because they will provide politicians with new opportunities to rob their fellow citizens. But, as anyone can see, these considerations lie in part outside the field of Political Economy, and have nothing to do with the method that is being used.

We shall add that to show that mathematical deductions are not going to boost at all the authority of protectionist sophisms is not the least among our aims in writing these pages. Let our dear politicians look for other weapons, as these are not for them.

V

1 Dr Irving Fisher has learnedly and with very ingenious methods illustrated the similarities between the new economic theories and mechanics. See his work: *Mathematical Investigations in the Theory of Value and Prices*, Transactions of the Connecticut Academy, July 1892.

2 In Figure 5.3, we have supposed $\alpha = 5$, $\beta = 10$, $a = 150$, $b = 220$. In this figure and in Figures 5.5 and 5.6 the contour lines are indicated with the letter V, the line of maximum slope is indicated with the letter p. M is always the point whose coordinates are the quantities of goods owned before bartering; R is the curve that is the locus of the points of tangency.

3 In Figure 5.5 we have $\alpha = 3$, $\beta = 8$, $a = 1$, $b = 1$

4 In Figure 5.6 we have supposed $\alpha = 3$, $\beta = 5$, $a = 125$, $b = 90$.

5 The roar comes of justice being dragged by gift-devouring men, who pass perverse sentences. Hesiod, *Works and Days*, 220–221.

6 A similar figure can be found in *The geometrical theory of the determination of prices*, by Léon Walras, American Academy of Political and Social Science, Philadelphia, 1891.

7 If we are considering only two commodities, let us suppose

$$r_a = 24 - 22\varphi_a + 8\varphi_a^2 - 4\varphi_a^3;$$

and let this be the value of X, if we are considering more commodities. Let us also suppose $\varphi_b = 6 - r_b$.

We shall have

$$r_b = 3 - \sqrt{9 + r_a\varphi_a}$$

and shall be able to calculate Table 5.3.

Table 5.3

φ_a	r_a	$-r_b$	p_b
0.1	21.88	0.34	63
0.4	16.22	0.93	16.6
1.0	9.00	1.24	7.24
1.4	6.14	1.19	5.14
1.6	5.18	1.16	4.47
2.0	4.00	1.12	3.56
2.4	3.46	1.16	2.98
2.6	2.30	1.19	2.77
3.0	3.00	1.24	2.40
3.5	2.12	1.05	2.02
3.9	0.56	0.34	1.63
4.0	0	0	1.5

The maxima and minima are given by the equation

$$0 = 24 - 44\varphi_a + 24\varphi_a^2 - 4\varphi_a^3$$

that is

$$0 = 6 - 11\varphi_a + 6\varphi_a^2 - \varphi_a^3,$$

which has the three roots

$$\varphi_a = 1, \quad \varphi_a = 2, \quad \varphi_a = 3.$$

The value of p_b for very small r_a is obtained by observing that with this hypothesis one has

$$r_b = -\frac{r_a\varphi_a}{6},$$

$$p_b = -\frac{r_a}{r_b} = \frac{6}{\varphi_a} = \frac{6}{4}.$$

Figure 5.8 is not in the right proportion with the numbers of the table, because on a small scale the waves would not have been very visible.

Editors' notes

I

I Pareto refers to the demonstrations included in Isaac Newton's *Philosophiae Naturalis Principia Mathematica.*

II Pareto refers to his article 'Di un errore del Cournot nel trattare l'economia politica colla matematica', *Giornale degli Economisti*, January 1892, pp. 1–14, now in V. Pareto, *Oeuvres Complètes* (*OC*), vol. 26, Genève: Droz, 1982, pp. 5–18.

III Adolphe Thiers (1797–1877), French statesman and historian.

IV Pareto refers to the expository form adopted by Alfred Marshall in his *Principles of Economics.* Pareto had a look at the first edition (1890) of Marshall's book and studied the second edition (1891). Cfr. the letter to Pantaleoni of 3 October 1891 ['Thanks for Marshall's book. I had a look at, I think, the first edition. I will study the second one with great pleasure'], now in V. Pareto, *OC*, vol. 28.1, Genève: Droz, 1984, p. 67.

V Pareto proposes the distinction between the two methods – analytical and geometric – in his article 'Di un errore del Cournot nel trattare l'economia politica colla matematica', op. cit., pp. 12–14.

VI Pareto refers to the book written by the French politician and laissez-faire economist Yves Guyot (1843–1928), *La science économique*, Paris, Reinwald, 1887. Pareto reviewed it in 'Il signor Yves Guyot e il suo libro *La scienza economica*', in *L'Economista*, 26 August 1888, pp. 559–564, now in V. Pareto, *OC*, vol. 17, Genève: Droz, 1989, pp. 275–288.

VII Pareto refers to the book written by the leading exponent of the English historical school Thomas Edward Cliffe Leslie (1825–1882), *Essays in Political and Moral Philosophy*, published in 1879 by Hodges, Foster and Figgis, in Dublin.

VIII It is surely a *lapsus stili* (involuntary mistake) because the first Italian edition of J. S. Mill, *A System of Logic, Ratiocinative and Inductive, Being a Connected View of the Principles of Evidence and the Methods of Scientific Investigation*, London, Parker, 1843, was published in 1968 by the publisher Ubaldini, Roma. Pareto read Mill's book in 1874 in the French translation by L. Peisse, *Système de logique deductive et inductive. Exposé des principes de la preuve et des methodes de la recherche scientifique*, Paris, Librairie Philosophique de Ladrange, 1866, as it is mentioned in Pareto's letters to Emilia Peruzzi, 13 and 14 April 1874, V. Pareto, *OC*, vol. 27.1, pp. 342 and 348.

IX Pareto probably refers to Mill's conception that geometry and the science of numbers are deductive sciences and non experimental sciences, cfr.

Système de Logique, Book II, chapter IV, §4,7; chapter V, §1. The science of numbers has a fundamental role in the progress of a science from the experimental stage to the deductive stage: ibid., Book II, chapter IV, §§5,6,7.

X Cfr. *Système de Logique*, book III, chapter XVIII.

XI Leonhard Euler (1707–1783), Swiss mathematician.

XII Niels Enrik Abel (1802–1829), Norwegian mathematician.

XIII John Kells Ingram (1823–1907), professor of English Literature and Greek at the Trinity College, Dublin. He was a careful observer of the contemporary debate in economic theory, where he sympathized with the German Historical School. Ingram sought to develop a unified theory of economics along the lines of the French sociologist Auguste Comte's positivist philosophy. His writings on this topic include *A History of Political Economy* (1888).

XIV Here Pareto refers to the German-speaking Marginalist economists (Austrians and Germans), both the literary economists (Carl Menger, Eugen Bohm-Bawerk, Friedrich Wieser) and the mathematical economists (Rudolf Auspitz, Richard Lieben and Carl Wilhelm Friedrich Launhardt).

XV Jean-Baptiste Say (1767–1832), French economist. He was responsible for introducing much of the work of Adam Smith to continental Europe where he was considered the leading exponent of Classical school.

XVI Francesco Ferrara (1810–1900), Italian economist, politician and briefly Minister of Finance. He was the most important exponent of the Italian classical political economy.

XVII Jean Le Rond d'Alembert (1717–1783). French mathematician, physicist and philosopher, co-editor with Diderot of the *Encyclopédie*.

XVIII Pareto probably refers to Daniel Bernoulli (1700–1782), whose St Petersburg paradox he discusses in the *Considerazioni*. The original presentation of the problem and his solution were published in 1738 in Bernoulli's *Commentaries of the Imperial Academy of Science of Saint Petersburg*. Daniel Bernoulli is the son of Johann Bernoulli and nephew of Jakob Bernoulli. He was the ablest of the younger Bernoullis, a family of Dutch origin, who were driven from Holland by the Spanish persecutions, and finally settled at Basel in Switzerland.

XIX Joseph-Louis Lagrange (1736–1810), one the greatest mathematician of the eighteenth century. Born in Turin, the capital of the kingdom of Sardinia, he was baptized Giuseppe Lodovico Lagrangia.

XX Pierre-Simon Laplace (1749–1827), French mathematician and astronomer, one of the commanding figures of the mathematics and science of eighteenth century.

XXI Charles Hermite (1822–1901), French mathematician.

XXII *Teoria analitica delle probabilità* is the word-for-word translation of the Laplace's book titled *Théorie analytique des probabilité* (first edition, 1812).

XXIII Nicolas Léonard Sadi Carnot (1796–1832), French physicist, mathematician and engineer who developed the theory of heat engines in *Réflexions sur la Puissance Motrice du Feu* (*Reflections on the Motive Power of Fire*) (Paris, Bachelier, 1824) and laid the foundations of the second law of thermodynamics. He maintained that even under ideal conditions a heat engine cannot convert all the heat energy supplied to it into mechanical energy and that some of the heat energy must be rejected.

XXIV The First Law of thermodynamics states that energy cannot be created or destroyed. Rather, the amount of energy lost in a process cannot be greater than the amount of energy gained.

XXV Pareto refers to W. S. Jevons, *Theory of Political Economy*, London: Macmillan, 1871.

XXVI Pareto refers to Antoine Augustin Cournot, *Recherches sur les principes mathématiques de la théorie des richesses*, Paris: L. Hachette, 1838.

XXVII Pareto refers to Francis Ysidro Edgeworth, *Mathematical Psychics: An Essay on the Application of Mathematics to the Moral Sciences*, London: Kegan Paul & Co., 1881.

XXVIII Pareto refers to Rudolf Auspitz (1837–1906) and Richard Lieben (1842–1919), *Untersuchungen über die Theorie des Preises*, Leipzig: Duncker & Humblot, 1889.

XXIX Pareto refers to Alfred Marshall, *The Pure Theory of Foreign Trade*, privately printed, 1879.

XXX Louis Poinsot (1777–1859), French mathematician.

XXXI See *OC*, vol. 26, op. cit., p. 18.

XXXII Pareto refers to the reviews of L. Walras, *Théorie mathématique de la richesse sociale* and A. A. Cournot, *Recherches sur les principes mathématiques de la théorie des richesses*, op. cit., by the French mathematician Joseph Bertrand (1822–1900) and published in *Bulletin des sciences mathématiques et astronomiques*, 1883, pp. 293–303.

XXXIII Cfr. L. Walras, *Eléments d'Economie politique pure*, op. cit. pp. 3–21.

XXXIV Cfr. *Système de Logique*, op. cit. Book VI, Chapter IX.

XXXV Giovanni Battista Guglielmini (1764–1817), Italian physician.

XXXVI Johan Friedrich Benzenberg (1777–1846), German astronomer, geologist and physicist.

XXXVII Ferdinand Reich (1799–1882), German chemist.

XXXVIII Pareto refers to the article 'Les preuves mécaniques de la rotation de la terre' by the Belgian mathematician Philippe Gilbert (1832–1892) published in *Bulletin des sciences mathématiques et astronomiques*, 1882, pp. 189–223.

XXXIX Galileo Galilei (1564–1642). Italian physicist, astronomer and philosopher (born in Pisa) who is closely associated with the scientific revolution.

XL Jean Bernard Léon Foucault (1819–1868), French physicist.

XLI Francois Jean Dominique Arago (1786–1853) was a French mathematician, physicist, astronomer and politician. He wrote a biography of Johannes Kepler (1571–1630), German mathematician and astronomer, a key figure in the scientific revolution. This biography, from which Pareto quotes, is in *Notices biographiques*, Paris: Gide; Leipzig: Weigel, 1854–1859.

XLII Pareto refers to the Italian translation of the book written by the English astronomer John Frederick William Herschel (1792–1871), *A Preliminary Discourse on the Study of Natural Philosophy* (1831). It was translated in Italian by Gaetano Demarchi and published by Pomba in Turin.

XLIII Pareto refers to the critiques of the classical theory of value by William Thomas Thornton (1813–1880), *On Labour: Its Wrongful Claims and Rightful Dues, its Actual Present and Possible Future*, London, Macmillan, 1870. Pareto read Thornton's book in the Italian translation: Guglielmo Tommaso Thornton, *Del lavoro. Delle sue pretese e dei suoi diritti. Del suo presente e del suo futuro possibile*, edited by Sidney Sonnino and Carlo Fontanelli, Firenze, Barbera, 1875.

XLIV This type of market is perfect competition (Jevons's definition) or free competition (Walras's definition).

XLV Francis Ysidro Edgeworth, 'Osservazioni sulla teoria matematica dell'economia politica con riguardo speciale ai principi di economia politica di Alfredo Marshall', *Giornale degli Economisti*, March 1891, pp. 233–235.

XLVI Arthur Berry (1862–1929) was a Cambridge mathematician who, at the

Marshall's request, lectured on mathematical economics. The article quoted by Pareto is: Arthur Berry, 'Alcune brevi parole sulla teoria del baratto di A. Marshall', *Giornale degli Economisti*, June 1891, pp. 549–553. Edgeworth replied to Berry with the article 'Ancora a proposito della teoria del baratto', *Giornale degli Economisti*, September 1891, pp. 316–318.

XLVII Jean-Baptiste Labat (called simply Père Labat) (1663–1738), French clergyman, explorer and writer. He wrote a history of the West Indies, published in six volumes at Paris, in 1722, entitled *Nouveau Voyage aux isles de l'Amérique*.

XLVIII Astolfo is a character in *Orlando Furioso* by the great Italian poet Ludovico Ariosto (1474–1533). Here Pareto refers to Astolfo's journey to the moon to recover Orlando's lost wits.

XLIX Pareto refers to the parliamentary debate in Italy on the new strongly protectionist customs tariff that was approved on 14 July 1887 and came into force on 1 January 1888.

II

I Pareto refers to 'Gossen's Second Law' – that the exchange ratio of goods is equal to the ratio of marginal utilities of the traders – introduced by the German economist Hermann Heinrich Gossen (1810–1858) in *Entwicklung der Gesetze des menschlichen Verkehrs und der daraus fliessenden Regeln für menschliches Handeln* [Development of the laws of human intercourse and their resulting rules for human behavior], Braunschweig, F. Vieweg, 1854.

II Philip H. Wicksteed (1844–1927), English economist.

III If the demand function of the good b is $p_b r_b = A_b$, with A_b constant, then $\varepsilon_{rb} = -1$.

IV He refers to the duty on wheat (30 liras per ton) introduced by the new 1887 customs tariff in Italy (see note XLIX, above).

V In mechanics, *D'Alembert's principle* is the principle permitting the reduction of a problem in dynamics to a problem in statics. This is accomplished by introducing a fictitious force equal in magnitude to the product of the mass and acceleration of the body, and directed opposite to the acceleration. D'Alembert introduced the principle in his *Traité de dynamique* (1743). It is an alternative form of Newton's second law of motion, which states that the force F acting on a body is equal to the product of the mass m and acceleration a of the body, or $F = ma$. In d'Alembert's principle, the force F plus the negative of the mass m times acceleration a of the body is equal to zero: $F - ma = 0$. In other words, the body is in equilibrium under the action of the real force F and the fictitious force (also called inertial force) $-ma$.

VI Vilfredo Pareto, 'La teoria dei prezzi dei signori Auspitz e Lieben e le osservazioni del Professor Walras', *Giornale degli Economisti*, March 1892, pp. 201–239; now in V. Pareto, *OC*, vol. 26, pp. 19–57.

VII John Elliot Cairnes (1823–1875), English economist, disciple of John Stuart Mill.

VIII Gustave de Molinari (1819–1912), a Belgian-born economist associated with the French *économistes*, a group of laissez-faire liberals. It was the editor of the *Journal des Économistes*, the publication of the French Political Economy Society, from 1881 until 1909. Pareto said he considered himself a disciple of Molinari.

IX Pareto refers to *Cours d'analyse infinitésimale, à l'usage des personnes qui étudient cette science en vue des ses applications mécaniques et physiques*, Paris, Gauthier-Villars, 1887–1890, written by Joseph Boussinesq (1842–1929), French physicist and mathematician.

X Alexander Bain (1818–1903), Scottish philosopher and psychologist.

XI Maurice Block (1816–1901), French free-trade economist.

XII Pareto refers to Carl Menger (1840–1921), *Grundsätze der Volkswirtschaftslehre* [Principles of Economics], Wien, Braumnalter, 1871.

III

I The equation is obtained by substituting the equation $\frac{\partial m}{\partial p_u} = -\frac{r_u + \frac{\varphi_u}{\varphi'_u}}{T}$ in the expression, $\frac{\partial r_u}{\partial p_u} = p_u \frac{\partial m}{\partial p_u} \frac{1}{\varphi'_u} + \frac{1}{p_u} \frac{\varphi_u}{\varphi'_u}$, then by developing and reducing the expression obtained.

II If $\frac{\partial m}{\partial p_u} > 0$.

III If $\frac{\partial m}{\partial p_u} < 0$.

IV Pareto's reasoning can be interpreted as follows: being the independent variables the n quantities $r_u, r_b, r_c \ldots$, the condition that φ_u depends only by r_u is expressed by the $n - 1$ equations $\frac{\partial \varphi_u}{\partial r_b} = 0, \frac{\partial \varphi_u}{\partial r_c} = 0 \ldots$; being that the functions $\varphi_u, \varphi_b \ldots$ are n, there will be $n(n-1)$ similar equations.

V The equations have been derived differentiating with respect to r_u and r_b the expression $\varphi_u(r_u) = \frac{1}{p_b} \varphi_b(r_b)$.

VI Pareto refers to the studies on family budgets made by Frédéric Le Play (1806–1862), French mining engineer and leader of the Christian socialist movement in France, founder of the *Société d'économie sociale* and of the journal *La réforme sociale*.

VII Augustin Cauchy (1789–1857), French mathematician and early pioneer of modern analysis.

VIII He refers to the article 'Recherches Astronomiques, Introduction' in *Annales de l'Observatoire de Paris*, 1855, pp. 73–155, written by the French astronomer Urbain Le Verrier (1811–1877), whose mathematical predictions led to the discovery of Neptune.

IX He refers to the Italian translation of Jevons's *Theory of Political Economy*, op. cit.: *La teorica dell'economia politica*, in Biblioteca dell'Economista, Series III, vol. II, Turin, Unione Tipografico-Editrice, 1878, pp. 175–311, edited by Gerolamo Boccardo (1829–1904).

X Charles Adolphe Wurtz (1817–1884), French chemist.

XI Joseph Louis Proust (1754–1826), French chemist.

XII He refers to the article 'Le vrai problème de l'histoire des mathématiques anciennes', written by the French mathematician and historian of mathematics, Paul Tannery (1843–1904).

XIII Josef von Fraunhofer (1787–1826), German physicist.

XIV William Hyde Wollaston (1766–1828), English chemist and physicist.

XV From the equation (14) we can obtain the value of r_u as a function of the other r, which are independent variables. The value of r_a makes it possible to calculate $\varphi_a(r_a) = \psi(r_b\varphi_b(r_b) + r_c\varphi_c(r_c) + \ldots)$.

XVI They are the condition equations necessary in order to determine the unknows $\varphi'_a(r_a), \varphi'_b(r_b). \ldots$

XVII By *individual*, Pareto here means the representative individual of modern microeconomics.

XVIII The great Roman poet Publio Virgilio Marone [Publius Vergilius Maro] (70 BC–19 BC)

XIX John Couch Adams (1819–1892), British mathematician and astronomer.

XX Johann Gottfried Galle (1812–1910), German astronomer.

XXI George Biddell Airy (1801–1892), British astronomer.

XXII Jean-Felix Picard (1620–1682), French astronomer.

XXIII Achille Loria (1857–1943), one of the most distinguished Italian economists at the end of the nineteenth century.

XXIV Alfred de Foville (1842–1913), French economist and statistician.

XXV Pareto refers to A. De Foville, *La statistique et ses ennemis: discours prononcé le 22 juin 1885 au Jubilé de la Societé de Statistique de Londres*, Paris, Guillaumin et Cie Libraires, 1885.

IV

I Georges Louis Leclerc, Comte de Buffon (1707–1788), French naturalist.

II Adolphe Quételet (1796–1874), Belgian astronomer, mathematician, statistician and sociologist. He was influential in introducing statistical methods to the social sciences.

III He refers to *Recherches sur la probabilité des jugements en matière criminelle et matière civile: précédées des règles générales du calcul des probabilités*, Paris, Bachelier, 1837, written by the French mathematician, geometer and physicist Siméon Denis Poisson (1781–1840).

IV He refers to *Calcul des probabilitiés*, Paris, Gauthier-Villars, 1889, written by Joseph Bertrand.

V He refers to Gabriel Cramer (1704–1752), Swiss mathematician.

VI Angelo Messedaglia (1820–1901), Italian economist and statistician.

VII Herbert Spencer (1820–1903), British philosopher, sociologist, liberal political theorist and major figure in the intellectual life of the Victorian era.

VIII The Roman emperor Nero Claudius Caesar Augustus Germanicus (37 BC–AD 68)

IX Tiberius Claudius Nero (42 BC–AD 37), the second Roman Emperor.

X Philip IV the Fair (*Philippe IV le Bel*) (1268–1314), King of France from 1285 until his death.

XI Pierre Paul Leroy-Beaulieu (1843–1916), French economist.

XII He refers to the Italian translation of Cournot's book *Recherches sur les principes mathématiques de la théorie des richesses*, op. cit. *Ricerche intorno ai principi matematici della teorica della ricchezza di Agostino Cournot*, in Biblioteca dell'Economista, Series III, vol. II, Turin, Unione Tipografico-Editrice, 1878, pp. 69–171.

XIII This errata was not published.

V

I Pareto refers to the scandal and bankruptcy of *Banca Romana*, one of the Italian six note-issuing banks, in the late nineteenth century (1889–1892). *Banca Romana* had been undermined by bad administration. It had gone far beyond its legal prerogatives in issuing notes in excess of what was permitted by the government. It emerged that several members of parliament had been allowed by the bank to open false accounts, and that counterfeiting had been carried on by the president of the bank. Moreover, several members of the Government, including the Prime Minister Giovanni Giolitti, were said to have illegally received large sums from the bank.

II *Assignats* were banknotes issued in France during the French Revolution. As there was no control over the amount to be printed, the *assignats* lost most of their nominal value.

III Pareto refers to the inflationary economic policy implemented by the British Prime Minister William Pitt (1759–1806) during the Napoleonic wars.

Index

Printed in the United Kingdom by
Lightning Source UK Ltd., Milton Keynes
136941UK00002B/227/P

9 780415 399197